# THE STATE OF EUROPEAN CINEMA

A N     USE OF

# The State of European Cinema

## A New Dose of Reality

**Angus Finney**

CASSELL

**Cassell**
Wellington House, 125 Strand, London WC2R 0BB
127 West 24th Street, New York, NY 10011

First published 1996

**British Library Cataloguing-in-Publication Data**
A catalogue record for this book is available from the British Library.

ISBN 0-304-33300-X (hardback)
0-304-33302-6 (paperback)

Designed and typeset by Kenneth Burnley at Irby, Wirral, Cheshire.
Printed and bound in Great Britain by Biddles Limited,
Guildford and King's Lynn.

# Contents

For my father, Nicholas, with love;
and in memory of Oscar Moore

# Acknowledgements

THIS BOOK'S ORIGINS stem from an extensive report written for the European Film Academy and *Screen International* in 1993, titled, *A Dose of Reality: The State of European Cinema.* The report created something of a stir within the European film industry. It was one of the first publications to lay out many of the European film industry's structural and inherent weaknesses, and did so in a sharply critical manner. Since then, considerable changes have taken place, which this book sets out to document and analyse. The overall position of Europe's film industry, however, still remains worryingly unstable and uncertain in its future. The case studies, however, which make a considerable contribution to the second section of the book, offer some very positive examples of Europe's creative film-making and commercial practice at its best.

The majority of this book is based on interviews and training work with film-making professionals, all of whom have been extremely helpful in its production. Secondary sources, including reports, studies, trade and general publications, are sourced chapter by chapter. I would like to thank the following people who have given interviews and ideas to me either in public forums or one a one-to-one basis:

Peter Aalbaek Jensen, Jean-Jacques Annaud, David Aukin, Karin Bamborough, Wouter Barendrecht, Daniel Battsek, Jacques Bidou, Michael Boehme, Nadine Borreman, Danny Boyle, Paul Brett, Peter Broughan, Timothy Burrill, Sylvain Bursztein, Hans de Weers, Bjorn Carlstrom, Mads Egmont Christensen, Bo Christensen, Fiona Clarke-Hackston, Stephen Cleary, David Collins, Judy Counihan, Jacques Delmoly, John Dick, Michael Dwyer, Jake Eberts, Bernd Eichinger, Barry Ellis Jones, Bjorn Erichsen, Stephen Evans, James Flynn, Michael Foster, Julian Friedmann, Dieter Geissler, Geoff Gilmore, Renee Goddard, James Graham, Ed Guiney, Joakim Hansson, John Hodge, Per Holst, Dominique Janne, Robert Jones, Terry Jones, David Kavanagh, Klaus Keil, Dieter

Kosslick, Rainer Kolmel, Michael Kuhn, Colin Leventhal, Cameron McCracken, Andrew Macdonald, Heather Mansfield, Derek Malcolm, Hansi Mandoki, Vaclav Marhoul, Maarten Melchior, Phyllis Mollet, Oscar Moore, Bertrand Moullier, Carole Myer, Lynda Myles, Sigrid Narjes, John Newbigin, Wendy Palmer, Andy Paterson, Chris Paton, Peter Paulich, Simon Perry, Nik Powell, Zakiya Powell, David Puttnam, Simon Relph, Raymond Ravar, Brian Reilly, Ryclef Rienstra, David Rose, Christian Routh, Volker Schloendorf, Chris Sievernich, Bernie Stampfer, Rod Stoneman, Paul Styles, Michael Swartz, Istvan Szabo, Michael Thomas, Stewart Till, Alex Usborne, Colin Vaines, Sytze van der Laan, Daniel Walker, Harvey Weinstein, Vibeke Windelov, Katrina Wood, John Woodward, Stephen Woolley, Colin Young, Krzysztof Zanussi.

In addition, the key bodies and festivals that have supported either directly or indirectly my work for this book include the European Film Academy; the MediaXchange; the European Film College; the Nordic Film & TV Fund; United International Pictures (UIP); the former European Script Fund; the Media Business School; the Irish Film Board; the British Film Institute's Library; British Screen Finance; the New Producer's Alliance; the Producers Alliance for Cinema and Television; the Dutch Film Fund; the Cinemart at the International Film Festival Rotterdam; the Cannes Film Festival; the Maurits Binger Film Institute; the Goteborg Film Festival; Festival du Film Britannique de Dinard; the International Festival for Film Schools, Munich; and the Waterfront Partnership, London.

A special thanks to Raymond Ravar, and the MEDIA I EAVE producers course, which supported the in-depth case studies on Rob Roy, Tales of a Hard City and Farinelli.

Key individuals helped with additional research for the book. I am particularly grateful to Simon Knight, who spent many hours researching certain areas, and whose diligent work was specifically used in the chapters on training, new technology and corporate interests in Europe. I also thank certain *Screen International* staffers and correspondents, including Ralf Ludemann, Mike Goodridge, Martin Blaney, Patrick Frater and Benedict Carver, all of whom were very helpful. Lastly, thanks to my transcriber, Julie Farrelly; my two consultant editors, Marion Döring (Manager of the European Film Academy) and Oscar Moore (Editor-in-Chief, *Screen International*); and my editor and publisher, Jane Greenwood.

*Angus Finney*
September 1996

# Foreword

**A**S A SELF-APPOINTED OPTIMIST for the European film industry, I believe that the numerous problems facing our cinema can be overcome. Before you close this book in disbelief, I would point out, however, that some serious planning and support is required if Europe's cinema is to once again find its way.

Such a comprehensive and ambitious plan has worked before. The European aircraft industry, which was totally dominated by North American companies from the 1950s to the 1970s, launched the airbus consortium. Everyone said that nothing would change. The group was supported with resources and was well structured. It took more than fifteen years to turn around, but that company now has the second largest share of commercial passenger aeroplanes in the world. It currently enjoys a very substantial market share and is highly profitable; which all goes to show that it can be done.

The big questions facing Europe's film industry is how and in what form should it compete? Does Europe want to carve out a decent slice of the market share? If so, then there will have to be certain circumstances, conditions and criteria that will have to be met. For such an approach to work, Europe would have to concentrate its resources and significantly reduce the number of films that it makes each year to around the 200 films Hollywood is currently making. Such a plan would require at least a billion dollars to be put into action.

I have no idea where that money would come from, and I suspect that such a plan would be politically unacceptable within the European Union. Most worrying of all, such a change in approach would probably result in Europe losing what it can do best. We would stop making small films that reflect our enormous and rich cultural diversity.

There are, however, more realistic strategies that could be put into place, which are examined in this book. We should try to harmonize the

European national subsidy systems, so that a European film-maker can apply to any of the state funds rather than just his or her own. We should constantly strive to minimize bureaucracy and administration in our public funding systems. We should consider how to create some kind of star system for our European actors to win greater recognition with the public. And we need to take a long-term view, realizing that it will take at least ten to fifteen years for such approaches to make their mark.

The European Film Academy has also had some recent experience in the art of 'creative survival'. Fortunately, thanks to a combination of the German National Lottery and the European Commission it is still very much alive. With funding now secured for a further three years, the Academy is keen over the coming years to open up its doors to more members from the industry, eventually bringing it from hundreds to thousands, and to encourage younger film-makers to join its ranks and attend the training programmes.

We want to rebuild and highlight the FELIX awards, so that the film-makers, the industry, the press and the public at large recognize a European Film Award as a significant achievement. This will take time, but we shouldn't forget that it took Hollywood's Film Academy half a century to reach such heights. Above all, we will aim to stimulate and encourage Europe's talent of today and tomorrow. We want us all to feel proud of our achievements and hopeful of fulfilling our potential. *The State of European Cinema: A New Dose of Reality* is one significant step among many towards achieving our goals.

*Nik Powell*
Chairman, European Film Academy

# Back to the Future: the New State of Play

'The thought of the future torments us and the past is holding us back; that is why the present is slipping from our grasp.'

Gustave Flaubert (1821–80), *Letters*

'The industries of the democratic countries in the post-war period have every reason to stand shoulder to shoulder against the imposition of quota, the creation of cartels and the raising of any and all barriers to the free flow of motion picture commerce.'

Jack Alicoate, *Film Daily*, 1945

THE INTERNATIONAL FILM INDUSTRY is a volatile meeting place of art and commerce, often depending on contradictory elements to fuel its progress. The key driving forces include cultural imperatives, high-risk financial speculation, political manoeuvres and, last but not least, the magic dust of entertainment.

The total value of the audiovisual market in the European Union is set to expand from $45 billion today to $120 billion by the year 2010,[1] and will be one of the most important centres for new employment opportunities. The production of feature films will make up a significant element of the audiovisual market, as software production – alongside sports programming and news gathering – will play a leading role in the growth of fresh ancillary and new technologically-driven markets.

The current exponential projections of growth, however, have a tendency to gloss over how demanding the business of film will become. It is a high-tech, high-investment industry that relies predominantly on talent and skilled labour to fuel its successes. So how does Europe currently stand on this promising threshold as we enter the next century?

Unconvincingly.

Europe has a shaky grip on its cinema market, hovering at an overall average throughout the Union of just 15 per cent of the annual box-office admissions for both 1993 and 1994.[2] Over the past 12 years, European films have lost half of their own theatrical market – down from 30 per cent to 15 per cent – and two-thirds of the cinema-going audience.[3] In most European territories, Hollywood-produced films are attracting around 70 per cent of the audience, while in some countries – including Germany and the UK – the figure exceeds 80 per cent. Only 10 per cent of Europe's films are shown in a second territory beyond their national border, and very few of these films are distributed successfully through-out Europe. And a low and declining number of European films are distributed in the US, the largest single theatrical market in the world.[4]

## The summer of supposed strategy

The weaknesses of the European industry in terms of infrastructure and commercial success have been the focal point for analyses and reports from Brussels, Strasbourg, Paris, Madrid and even London.

The Commission's White Paper *Job competitiveness and growth* adopted by the European Council, opened the new season of debate in late 1993. It was followed by a report by the Think Tank on audiovisual policy in the European Union in March 1994; and a Green Paper entitled 'Strategy options to strengthen the European programme industry in the context of the Audiovisual Policy of the EU', published the following month.

The latter paper identified four fundamental requirements for the future of the European programme industry:

- it must be competitive in an open worldwide market
- it must be forward looking and be involved in the development of the information society
- it must illustrate the creative genius and personality of the people of Europe
- it must be capable of transforming its growth into new jobs in Europe.

Clearly Europe's film industry was facing an enormous cultural and political challenge. A considered effort had been made to identify the problems during this season of debate, but the results were neither sharply focused nor particularly dynamic. For example David Puttnam, the British film producer and active political lobbyist, was so frustrated by the experience of the Think Tank's muddled proccess, that he decided to pull together his own key arguments in a supplementary document entitled 'A submission to the European Commission Think Tank on Audiovisual Policy'. The decision to make a separate submission speaks for itself.

What Europe's policy-makers needed to find throughout 1994 was the political will to agree and implement a unified action plan that had a direct relevance to the industry's present and future needs. Whether that has actually come to fruition, and what has been left in limbo, is one of this book's key areas of enquiry.

The publication of the Green Paper was followed by the European Audiovisual Conference, a meeting of senior European professionals in June/July 1994. Elements of the debate appeared realistic and forward-thinking, and the urgency of Europe's situation was underlined. As DGX's Ms Colette Flesch pointed out in her presentation of the Green Paper, there are some who believe that Europe's film industry is 'doomed to chronic loss-making, a luxury which the Europeans will be able to afford only through continued public-sector assistance'. She went on to underline the sense of responsibility to the sector, explaining that the European Union 'has a duty to guarantee the development of the market and continue its effort to support the programme industry'.

Grand statements were made. Marcelina Oreja, the commissioner then responsible for Culture and Audiovisual in DGX, argued that 'with the advent of the information society, a major part of our cultural future is in the melting pot. The European Union must equip itself with a framework of clear, motivating objectives and develop a proper strategy on content.' Jacques Delors, former President of the European Commission, claimed that 'Europe has every reason to be proud of its cultural diversity, but that cannot be an excuse for not having a united Europe. We need both healthy competition and increased co-operation.'

The key action-plan that was kick-started in the summer of 1994 was the planning of the EC's MEDIA II programme, designed to get under way in January 1996. While the strategy of the new five-year programme will be discussed in detail in Chapter 6, the broad points agreed were that the programme's funds should be doubled from ECU200 million to 400 million ($245 million to $490 million) over the new five-year programme, and that it should be focused on three main areas: development; training; and distribution.

The scatter-gun approach of the EC's original MEDIA I's programme with 19 projects, which had proliferated at remarkable speed from 1991 to 1994, was out. Instead, efforts to consolidate through increased central-ization and an industrialized approach won the day. Unfortunately, the money was subsequently reduced by ECU90 million ($110 million) the following summer, mainly due to British resistance to the original budget.

In a move that mirrored many of the findings of the Think Tank Report and the Green Paper, the vast majority of MEDIA II's budget was put aside for support of distribution. This emphasis was demanded by the French lobby, which argued vociferously for more support for marketing and promotion of films across borders. Concrete details on how distribution should be supported were distinctly lacking, however. The only real stab in this direction had come from the Think Tank, which suggested the for-mation of a consortium of existing distributors to form pan-European entities, to be supported by publicly funded soft-loans over a ten-year period. Private companies would be encouraged to apply to join the con-sortium, including a limited North American presence.[5]

The overall lack of detail on distribution was to come back to haunt both the industry and the Commission by early 1996. Without a clear concept of how to apply funding support on a strategically practical basis, there was always a danger that monies would be scattered across the prints, advertising and marketing costs of films that, in many cases, the market-place had already rejected.

Typically, the Brussels machinery took a painstakingly long time turn-ing its listening operation into an action plan. As late as November 1995, the precise shape of MEDIA II was still unclear. By June 1996, consider-ably later than MEDIA II chief Jacques Delmoly had initially promised, training and development Intermediate Organisations had been estab-lished, but distribution was still under negotiation. When the former EVE, European Film Distribution Office (EFDO), Greco and CNC-backed French bid for the distribution IO was put forward in spring 1996, the Commission rejected it on technical grounds, arguing that its adminis-tration was too expensive for the programme to operate (see Chapter 8).

## The GATT negotiations

The discussions about pan-European audiovisual policies and support structures need to be seen in the context of the GATT (General Agreement on Tariffs and Trade) talks, which were concluded amid strenuous debate during late 1993. By that stage the GATT trade negotiations between the world's major industrial nations were being held up by two key problem areas, one of which was whether film and television should be included in the overall agreement at all.

The argument was basically on the one hand about Europe's freedom to retain control over a predominantly cultural activity; and on the other hand about opening up Europe to a completely deregulated, free market. Given Hollywood's rising market share of Europe's box office since the mid 1980s, and the growing preoccupation within both the EU and Europe's national states about how best to stem that tide, it was hardly surprising that the talks triggered off a major row. Emotions ran high.

> **'I'm not about to be buggered by the US industry.**
> **We shouldn't allow them to deal with us**
> **the way they dealt with the Redskins.'**
>
> French film-maker Claude Berri[6]

However, far from inspiring a united European front, GATT served to expose how fragmented Europe's nation states are in their film policies. Although commentators at the time thought that GATT brought the British closer to the French, that was far from the truth. The final months of the negotiation also highlighted the tendency for French politicos, culturecrats and industryites to assume that what is best for France is also best for the rest of Europe. Jacques Toubon, France's then minister for culture, pounced on the talks as a chance to slam UIP, the Paramount-MGM-Universal Pictures distribution operation. United International Pictures (UIP) had just submitted its application to the Commission to renew its exemption from Article 85 of the Treaty of Rome for a further five years. Jurassic Park's release across Europe became a focal point for ranting about alleged American imperialism and subversion of European culture.

Meanwhile the French continued to insist on quotas to protect EU programming shares, despite their increasing anachronism and redundancy.[7] As David Puttnam and others have been keen to point out, quotas are a term and practice that have fast become outdated across most of Europe, despite Toubon's intransigence. 'As for competition,' he stated, 'we must try to avoid this on the cultural level as on the economic level. We like American cinema, provided that they do not want to crush everything.'

In response, Jack Valenti, president of the Motion Picture Association of America (MPAA), pointed out during September 1993's Deauville

Festival of American Film, that both America and Europe need to 'focus on the future now; those who don't will be left behind'. He warned against protectionism and trade barriers, but argued that the real answer was for the European industry to make films that people want to see.

This was typically disingenuous, given that Valenti was to spend the next three months aggressively campaigning for complete deregulation of the EU's audiovisual industries in GATT. Indeed, as *Variety* pointed out,[8] the 'Yanks' tough tactics' backfired somewhat, on the grounds that the aggressive stance taken by Valenti and others woke Europe up to the effects of Hollywood's market domination and how much ground their market was losing to the Americans. Specifically, US sales of programming rose from a modest $330 million in 1984 to a huge $3.6 billion by 1992, leaving no doubt about Europe's value as a market for American software.[9]

However, the reality surrounding GATT is that many of those campaigning on both sides of the Atlantic had little real understanding of what the key issues were and how they were ultimately resolved. The General Agreement of Tariffs and Trade was founded in 1947 with the ambition of liberalizing world trade. The round of new talks which started in Uruguay in 1987 had to be agreed by a deadline of 15 December 1994. The audiovisual sector (alongside agriculture) was one of the main outstanding issues threatening this deadline. It was also an issue that was drawing a line between American and European film communities – with Steven Spielberg and Martin Scorsese getting behind the MPAA, while Wim Wenders, Gerard Depardieu and other European luminaries lobbied Leon Brittan, Europe's trade commissioner, for film and television to be left out of GATT altogether (known as the 'cutural exception' position).

## An agreement to disagree

The European position – as largely defined and articulated by the French – gradually consolidated into the view that audiovisual industries did not belong in the GATT agreement at all, because, as culturally-driven businesses crucial to the national identity, they were not comparable to other export/import industries.

As Jacques Delors explained just before the GATT deadline: 'Culture is and always has been a cornerstone of the European tradition. It's nothing new for Europe to subsidize art – popes, monarchs and rich benefactors have done so for centuries.'

The American lobby was arguing for a significantly deregulated European film and TV market, which would abolish quotas and any direct subsidies that were seen to discriminate against Hollywood. As far as it was concerned, quotas and subsidies contravened the free-trade principles enshrined in GATT. In the words of Mickey Cantor, American President Clinton's negotiator, the issue was one of 'freedom of speech', suggesting that the European market had to be clear of barriers and its customers allowed to vote with their feet and their purse.

But as Michael Chanan, an academic author and film-maker, pointed out in an article in the UK film quarterly *Vertigo*,[10] the issues at stake were rather more subtle than they appeared from the flurry of press sound-bites.

'The GATT crisis was the result of a move during the 1980s by the US to change the arena for international regulation of intellectual property,' Chanan argued. 'The move corresponds to the growing importance of the culture industry in the global market-place, now including not only entertainments but also information. It represents an attempt to shift the balance from protection based on authorship towards the interests of corporate bodies, from film and record producers to computer software companies.'

Chanan went on to argue that the deadlock over GATT was something more fundamental than just French chauvinism or American industrial intransigence. He cited the right-wing French prime minister Edouard Balladur's question to the press at the time of the talks: was Europe to be 'a big market which will progressively melt into a vast free-trade zone dominated by American software and Japanese hardware, or a community with a strong identity of its own and a major international presence?' The close relationship between economic strength, cultural autonomy and creative renaissance was really the issue. Chanan suggested that 'it is not an accident that in a system which sees cultural creation as nothing more than a form of commodity production, the problems of world trade should rebound on film and television.'

By the end of 1993, the US industry had been the biggest beneficiary of the growth in Europe's audiovisual markets, while the European Union's annual audiovisual trade deficit with the US amounted to more than $3.5 billion by the end of 1992.[11] If GATT had been a boxing match, the talks would have been over before the first bell.

## The GATT fudge

The GATT was finally signed after an agreement to disagree over film and television was reached. A last-minute French-inspired olive branch offered the US a portion of receipts from the levy on blank video cassettes, but the Americans rejected this in favour of agreeing nothing. Leon Brittan upheld the French position, and the audiovisual sector was left out of GATT altogether.

The ramifications of this were somewhat misinterpreted by the European lobby. The US made it clear after GATT that it reserved the right to respond legally and to challenge policies that its industry considered discriminatory. Secondly, although film and TV were left out of GATT, the agreement only sanctioned those protectionist measures that were already in place. Any new EU legislation would be looked at with considerable concern by the US, and was likely to be challenged. As one Australian film executive, concerned about the similar GATT audiovisual exclusion for the Asia/Pacific region, put it: 'I wish culture had been included in the GATT deal. That would have been a safeguard for the future because it would have told the Americans how far they can go. As it is, they can ring us every second day and say: "What about your quotas?"'

By autumn 1995, after a period of relative quiet on the quota front, France's new culture minister, Philippe Douste-Blazy, placed quotas back on France's audiovisual agenda. Despite a surprising public reversal by Valenti when speaking to French and US film delegates at a ARP-organized conference at Beaune in October (including the extraordinary line: 'We have no right to inject ourselves into the debate about quotas amongst the 15 member states of the European Union') Douste-Blazy was unimpressed. He warned that 'the Americans remain opposed to quotas, no matter what they profess. They are opposed to them because they work.'

The minister supplied no further evidence to back up this controversial statement. It is highly doubtful that quotas have ever, or will ever help the European film industry, a fact that most film figures had privately already accepted following the GATT talks. As David Puttnam pointed out, 'the more we can get away from relying on cultural defence, and concentrate our energies on industrial success, the better'.

## The guarantee fund debate

In mid-1995 the European Commission put forward new plans for a ECU200 million European guarantee and investment production fund. The proposal was for a fund to underwrite European film and television productions by granting banks and financial institutions partial guarantees on loans and credit made available to film and programme makers.

The proposal enjoyed a number of advantages. It would require only modest amounts of cash and was not seen as a subsidy handout, but rather a way to underwrite risk finance for 'projects that have major European and international market potential', according to the Commission. Politically it was even more useful. As a non-direct subsidy it would avoid attracting the US film lobby's wrath, and existing European legislation which helps channel money into important but high-risk areas such as telecommunications could be adapted to help set up such a guarantee fund. But the creation of a new category of EU spending would be much harder to facilitate and put into practice.

Initially muddled and incoherent, the concept nevertheless attracted an interesting range of submissions.[12] The three main proposals and their ideas – including a PolyGram-fronted paper; a French proposal from l'ARP (the French Producer's Association), and a Euro Media Guarantee/Club of European Producers concept – are outlined in short below.

The PolyGram-led proposal suggested that the European Investment Fund (EIF) should provide long-term guarantees, soft-loans and off-balance-sheet funding to European companies involved in film and TV productions. Proposals from l'ARP, the French association of author-director-producers, were wider ranging, suggesting that ECU1.5 billion over five years should be invested in production, theatrical distribution and television broadcasting. The third, Euro Media Guarantee (EMG), proposed:

- long-term loans to distributors who create a European network and to independent exhibitors for cinema renovation
- short-term loans to small- and medium-sized film and TV producers which should learn to share risk in a more sophisticated manner than they do at present
- an attempt to attract venture capital into the sector to invest in both individual productions and companies' equity capital. Risk sharing by Guarantee Funds should be limited to 50 per cent

- minimum guarantees of receipts, which would allow distributors to build up catalogues of rights, which in turn give economies of scale and market muscle.

With these kinds of incentives and support mechanisms, Europe's producers would be inclined to create more products with an international ambition, EMG argued.

## The Guarantee gap

The Guarantee Fund scheme was strongly backed by Spain and France, given that both countries already operate domestic guarantee funds for the audiovisual sector. But the proposal once again split members down the middle. Germany and the UK resented the redirected use of the ECU90 million ($110 million) that was cut from the MEDIA II budget, and each argued that the fund was neither necessary nor workable on a pan-European basis. The other ECU110 million ($135 million) was expected to come from non-EC sources, both public and private. It was envisaged that the creation of a ECU200 million ($245 million) fund would make it possible to guarantee a level of production finance of ECU1 billion through mechanisms such as loan guarantees to banks. Those behind the plan pointed to the European Investment Fund (EIF), a financial body which is owned by the EC, the European Investment Bank and 76 national banks, and has established a guarantee fund of ECU2 billion ($2.45 billion). It provides support for pan-European projects in areas like telecommunications, alongside backing for smaller and medium-sized companies.

A final proposal for a Guarantee Fund was put to the Council of Ministers on 20 November 1995. Subsequent discussions elicited strong German opposition to the plan, and a lack of enthusiasm from the British and the Dutch. By the summer of 1996, however, interest in the plan resurfaced, but the precise funding mechanisms were the subject of considerable debate. Two key questions remained: Which banks and institutions would put up the ECU110 million needed to form the fund; and who would administer the 'risk management' side of the fund – examining the discounting contracts between producers and distributors, for example?

## Open arms across the Atlantic

One of the points woefully neglected by the European Commission and its handling of MEDIA I was (and still remains) the need to build stronger links of co-operation with the North American industry. Nevertheless, since GATT has been signed, considerable efforts have now been extended on building and stimulating film, television and other forms of media co-operation between the European and US film industries. Indeed, given that the audiovisual sector was specifically excluded from GATT, there was a clear imperative for the Americans and Europeans to establish new channels of dialogue and explore constructive, practical ways forward. Otherwise, with no formal treaty and no subsequent talks, both sides might simply have retreated to lick their wounds.

Over the past two years matters have moved forward at a cautious but reasonably encouraging rate. A steering committee in the form of a 'Roundtable' – made up of key MPAA members and European film-makers – held a series of meetings during 1994 and 1995. These have helped shore up the initial 'dialogue' approach, and place the talks on a potentially more concrete level. Leading figures on the European side include members from the Club of European Producers, who, as well as working to improve overall communication between the US and European industries, are also exploring areas such as training exchanges and potential investment and distribution opportunities.

The latter two areas were difficult to move forward, but training became the most promising area of the discussions, and was viewed enthusiastically by the US representatives as an area ripe for co-operation. On the European front, training and education occupied a front seat at the Brussels conference, making it a positive sector to explore on political grounds. Ideas included the systematic input of US experience in business management, through a combination of master classes; industry lectures; US-European tie-ins on the film-school front; scholarship and exchange systems and Hollywood studio 'placement' systems for young European film-makers.

Such plans turned into a reality in October 1995, when the Americans agreed to invest $2 million over a five-year period in European-based training schemes. Of this, $1 million was to be overseen by the European Film College in Ebeltoft, while the other portion was to be dealt with via two members of the European Parliament. (Both schemes are discussed in Chapter 3).

## US companies working with European talent

American film companies have long shown an interest in working with European film-making talent, both in front of and behind the camera.

However, individual talent is one thing, but defining areas where the American and European film industries can work on a much larger, corporate and strategic scale is more difficult. Part of the problem is that Americans, in their relationship with Europe, have tended to fall in and out of love with the idea of closer corporate relationships – a tendency recently dubbed as 'the old boom or bust cycle' by *Variety*.

Following the popular success of European films in the US (notably in the English language), including The Crying Game and Four Weddings and a Funeral, US studio executives and larger independent companies have grown excited about the prospect of finding their next big hit from European shores. Most of these initiatives have proved very cautious – with plush production offices and well-heeled executives, but few films put into production.

Inevitably, given the fate of sub-titled films in the US, these deals have been nearly all with British (and in some cases Irish) companies and talent. Indeed, according to *Screen Finance* newsletter's research in 1994, since 1988 34 UK productions have been financed wholly or in part by major American studios, spending more than $560 million during those six years.[13] No other European country has enjoyed such substantial investment in its production facilities. However, it can also be pointed out that the UK pays heavily for its 'shared language' with American, given Hollywood's corresponding domination of the UK box office.

While the UK has started to forge better links with its European partners – helped considerably by British Screen's keenness to encourage producers to work in Europe and not rely so heavily on US interest – non-English speaking talent and foreign-language films are still finding it difficult to build the kind of US links detailed above.

The key reason is that out of America's 26,000 screens, only 250 regularly play foreign-language cinema. Known dismissively as 'niche' or a specialized product, foreign-language film doesn't attract enough audiences in North America to justify a higher profile or wider distribution than at present. The collapse of the foreign-language market, despite exceptional recent performances by Like Water for Chocolate and Il Postino (both distributed by Miramax), is documented in the statistics at the end of the chapter.[14]

The dwindling foreign-language market in the US has, in part, been taken over by a burgeoning independent sector. According to Geoff Gilmore, director of the Sundance Film Festival and Institute, in 1993 some 250 low-budget US indie films were made, compared to about 500 in 1995. 'However, you have to remember that only 40 to 50 of these films are getting theatrical distribution, so it's a case of good news and bad news together. There's a glut of product, and an obsession with maximizing profit from the distribution market,' Gilmore explained, adding that it was no wonder foreign-language films are finding it tough in the US.

## Finding a future audience

When the European Film Academy met on 4 December 1993 to discuss Europe's future film industry after GATT, David Puttnam gave a frank address:

'For too many years now we in Europe have been talking to each other in a kind of code. It's time to stop using this polite but ambiguous code and start a more plain, but I hope encouraging, dialogue. If we make a film that nobody comes to see, who do we seek to blame? The distributor, the exhibitor, the critics, the audience, the Americans, the GATT? . . . seldom ourselves! Instead, we've developed to a fine art what could best be described as a "culture of complaint" – combined with something worse, an ever-growing evasion of personal responsibility. After all, isn't it a kind of blind arrogance to believe that "If the general public are too dull and unimaginative to see the splendour of my vision – that's their problem"? The truth is, it's *not* their problem. If the public don't like it, they'll go and see another movie, or maybe they'll just stay at home.

'We cannot evade the fact that ours is a popular medium. It has to be. Being a film-maker is not like being a poet or a musician. It's expensive to make and market a film. Unless enough people come to see it, you'll find it difficult to raise the money to make a another one. If you don't respect your audience, they're unlikely to respect you. It's as simple as that.'

Nearly two years later, during October 1995, the European Parliament, European Commission and Council of Europe staged a '100 Years of Cinema' debate in Strasbourg. The general tone of the discussions were anti-American, nationally obsessed and deeply limited in strategic and structural scope. As one commentator put it: 'It was as if nothing had happened in the last ten years. Things have remained static judging by this meeting.'

If Europe's film-makers are seeking coherent incentives from their political representatives, they will have to fight with considerable more purpose over the coming months than they have managed to in recent years. The future does not look as bright as it might have, given the opportunity at hand during 1994 to shape a viable future. Meanwhile, Europe's polititians are also in danger of losing their way. As the *Economist* reported in early 1996, 'The European Union is in disarray . . . In Brussels, there is a sense of drift.' The thrust of the article was how hard Jacques Santer, the EC's president, was finding it to assert himself: 'He can expect no help from the British, the French or Germans: they may differ on many European issues, but they are united in their opposition to giving Mr Santer, and the body he represents, more weight.'[15] The fudge of compromise and bureaucracy that has so damaged the start of the MEDIA II programme clearly comes from the top.

On the other hand, since the first *Dose of Reality* report was published in December 1993 by *Screen International* and the European Film Academy, certain tangible improvements have been made. Training and development have climbed up the ladder of priorities, and Europe's producers are demonstrating a greater sense of purpose towards screenwriters and the entire development process. National funding systems have undergone considerable changes in policy and practice, most notably in Spain, Ireland and The Netherlands, while the entire French funding system is currently under review at the time of writing.

Most importantly, stronger corporate entities have emerged to take a lead in European production and distribution. The most promising is PolyGram Filmed Entertainment, which is now close to fulfilling its Major Studio ambitions. It is with a view to these areas of progress as well as obstacles that this book explores the state of European cinema.

## Notes

1  The figures come from the IMPACT report, *PACT UK*, 1995. For specific reference, the global film market was worth $53 billion in 1994, compared to $36 billion for the global music industry and $68 billion for the book publishing industry. (*Source*: Hydra Associates).
2  CNC Info, May 1996, Special Edition, p. 69: World Cinema charts; figure for 1994 (see below).
3  *Ibid.*
4  *Ibid.* For specific reference, the market share of foreign films in the US has dropped from a high of 6.4 per cent in 1986 to a low of 0.75 per cent in 1994. (*Source*: CNC) (see below).

**European Union film statistics**

| Date | Features produced* | Market share national films (%) | US market share (%) |
|---|---|---|---|
| 1985 | 403 | 30 | 53 |
| 1990 | 421 | 19.5 | 70 |
| 1992 | 468 | 17 | 73 |
| 1993 | 502 | 15 | 75 |
| 1994 | 466 | 15 | 74 |

*Excluding France-European minority productions (*Source*: CNC)

| Date | Screens | Admissions (millions) | Average admissions per capita |
|---|---|---|---|
| 1985 | 17,150 | 553 | 2.0 |
| 1990 | 19,220 | 658 | 2.0 |
| 1992 | 17,100 | 558 | 1.6 |
| 1993 | 17,330 | 636 | 1.8 |
| 1994 | 17,630 | 640 | 1.8 |

(*Source*: CNC)

5  See *A submission to the European Commission Think Tank on Audio-Visual Policy*, David Puttnam.
6  Claude Berri, quoted in *Empire,* UK, January 1994.
7  For further details on the argument against quotas, see *The Economic Impact of Television Quotas in the European Union*, a paper by London Economics for Sony Entertainment.
8  *Variety,* 27 December 1993.
9  *Felix* magazine, May 1994. Angus Finney: 'Job creation in the audiovisual industry, Power-house Europe?', p. 5.
10  See 'What was GATT about?', Michael Chanan, *Vertigo,* Spring 1994.
11  *Felix* magazine, May 1994.
12  See Patrick Frater's article, 'Lobbying for the Guarantee lottery', *Development Digest*, published by the European Script Fund, May 1995, pp. 4–5.
13  *Felix* magazine, November 1994, p. 8.
14  See chart below:

**USA cinema statistics,**
**charting the collapse of the foreign-language market in the US**

| Date | Screens (millions) | Admissions share (%) | Foreign films market |
|---|---|---|---|
| 1986 | 21,147 | 1056.1 | 6.4 |
| 1988 | 23,234 | 1084.8 | 1.2 |
| 1990 | 23,689 | 1057.9 | 1.4 |
| 1992 | 25,205 | 971.2 | 1.3 |
| 1994 | 26,586 | 1210.0 | 0.75 |

(*Source*: *Variety* and the MPAA)

15  The *Economist,* 'Jacques in a box', 24 February 1996, p. 51.

# 2

# Strategies for Development

**'If carpenters made chairs in the way that [French] screenwriters produce scripts, we would all be sitting on the floor.'**

Jeanne Moreau,
actress and president of the French 'Avances Sur Recettes' support system

**'Part of Europe's problem is that although we have some fantastic film-makers, we have many others who also want to tell their own personal philosophy and poetry. But these film-makers don't know the profession. They don't know how to tell the story.'**

Istvan Szabo, Hungarian film-maker

**W**HEN PEOPLE TALK ABOUT 'development' in most industries, they are normally refering to 'R and D' – 'research and development'. This is best described as an up-front, long-term investment normally involving considerable monies that are unlikely to be returned quickly, or, in many cases, not at all. Nevertheless, long-term planning and the odd truly profitable discovery are deemed crucial to a healthy business operation.

When it comes to the film industry, however, and in particular Europe's independent production sector, development has taken on a much more precarious existence. Few film producers enjoy the depth of resources to invest heavily in development costs such as the acquisition of book options, the research of ideas and mulitiple drafts of screenplays. Those producers who are able to afford the above have often found a revolving credit facility from an investor who is eager to maintain a stake in their current or eventual success, based on their existing track-record. Such support helps to underwrite either all or part of their overhead and development costs.

Before analysing how development support has been organized in Europe, it is important to define what the term 'development' means in the context of this chapter. Development is the entire process preceeding pre-production and while often understood to mean the process of getting to a shooting script, screenplay development is only one part of a process that includes speculative talent hiring, ball-park budgeting, and plans for location and/or studio shoots. Pre-production, on the other hand, involves the locking down and budgeting of the decisions made in development.

Everything from handing out screenplays to executives at Cannes – that is, the costs of photocopying, travelling and accommodation, the wining and dining of prospective investors – comes out of the development budget. In certain cases scripts are further developed in the pre-production stage, perhaps because of casting or director's requirements, or sometimes because a fresh writer is needed to complete the screenplay to the producer and director's satisfaction.[1]

While there are many ways to move a project towards production, one element remains consistent throughout Europe: development is a high-risk stage of film production. There are no guarantees of a project's successful journey from idea through to treatment and draft; or from screenplay to production.

It is a relatively expensive and high-risk area of investment. For example, a European film with a budget of between $1 million and $3 million may cost between $40,000 and $200,000 or more to develop. Films with, by European standards, large budgets of between $7 million and $15 million may cost as much as $400,000 to move through development and into production. However, in reality, far too many European films are going into production too quickly, and at a level of development expenditure often considerably lower than the above figures.

Hollywood, by contrast, invests in development on a much more industrial level. Most of the studios make between 15 to 25 films a year, and each has more than 120 films in development at any one time. Huge resources are ploughed back into the development process. Hollywood spends around 7 per cent of each film's overall budget on development (albeit inflated by the studio's central overhead), when compared to Europe's more characteristic 1 to 2 per cent. And the sheer volume of projects in development at any one time in comparison to those actually made is much higher than in Europe.

A decade ago, the development process within Europe's film industry was a poorly-defined, secondary element in the process of entering film production. One reason why this was the case was due to an overall insufficient level of finance to assist the full development and treatment of script drafts; a situation that tends to 'catapult' the producer towards production and the release of badly-needed production finance before the project is really ready to roll. The European producer's traditional preoccupation with *getting into production* has partly stemmed from the fact that only when producers are in production are they being paid a production fee.

Colin Young, former director of ACE (the European Film Studio), explains: 'European producers are always amazed at the number of Hollywood films put into development but that are never made. People in Europe tend not to abandon films that fail to attract proper film finance; they tend instead to say that they'll make it later, or go on until the bitter end. There's clearly a link in the [European development] chain that's missing. Films can be developed without going into production, but that isn't really in the European film industry's ecology or economy.'

Young's argument has been taken up by other development strategists. David Kavanagh, former head of SCRIPT, and now heading up the new MEDIA Intermediary Organisation for development, the European Media Development Agency (EMDA), was concerned during his time in office at the European Script Fund that in Europe the ratio of projects in development to those that enter production is still far too low. He has made some 'educated guesses' about the volume and value of development activity within Europe. Taking a range of figures derived from a Media Business School book – *Developing Feature Films In Europe: A Practical Guide* [2] – Kavanagh has estimated that the EU has around 3,000 feature projects in development at any one time, against approximately 600 films that are produced each year. Both the European-wide and SCRIPT development/production success ratios are around one in five or six projects. 'Although these figures are very crude, compared to the US studio's one in ten ratio, it is quite clear that the overall number of projects in development is too low in Europe. This figure should be higher, and so too should the amount of money spent on each project,' Kavanagh argues.

### The idea problem

In addition to certain structural problems that afflict Europe's development process, it is instructive to ask more about the kinds of ideas for screenplays that are typically being floated around Europe at the early development stage, and how they are being told. As Hungarian film-maker Istvan Szabo points out: 'If we want to tell interesting stories about our experiences then we have to find another method, because the ones that we've used up 'till now have become boring. If I want to tell the real stories of facism or communism, then I have to go to the people. It requires research. It's very important to tell these stories of Europe's extraordinary experiences, but we need to find a new idea to actually tell them. On a superficial level we've posed every story. But to have con-temporary stories that really travel needs a philosophy of life.'[3]

All too rarely emphasized is the relationship between the writer and the audience. In a briefing paper for a Europe-wide training event, the Festival Film School, screenwriter and doctor Tony McNabb stressed that a writer's 'primary relationship is with the invisible, unknown peo-ple who will watch your film – the audience. To leave them out of your creative equation is to invite failure.' He went on to cite film-maker David Mamet's thoughts on the subject, who argues that it is not a writer's job to be emotional, but to tell a human story that arouses emotion because it is compellingly told.

Mamet suggests that the way to do this is to work at the story's logic, stick to the rules and find a throughline: 'The purpose of technique is to free the unconscious. If you follow the rules ploddingly, they will allow your unconscious to be free. That's true creativity. If not, you will be fet-tered by your conscious mind. Because the conscious mind is going to suggest the obvious, the cliché, because these things offer the security of having suceeded in the past. Only the mind that has been taken off itself and put on a task is allowed true creativity.'[4]

Over the course of MEDIA I and its five-year plan to the end of 1995, it is possible to argue that screen writers who engaged in its training and development projects have become more aware of the commercial demands of the market-place. Many of them are less afraid of intellectu-ally less demanding but commercially successful genres such as comedies, thrillers and fantasies, and there is less emphasis on the turgid 'war-bores' and dull, predictable biopics which dominated previously. These claims are not without foundation, and have been recently backed up by a genre analysis carried out by Christian Routh, formerly of the European Script Fund and now selection co-ordinator for EMDA.[5]

In an extensive survey of the kinds of projects European writers have been working on over the last five years, it became clear that adventure-action, thrillers and fantasy are not at the forefront of their minds, although there have been some changes and improvements.

Routh found that it was very encouraging, from a commercial perspective, that the thriller category has made a steady, if unspectacular increase from 10 per cent in 1989 to 15.4 per cent in 1995. Fantasy enjoyed only a marginally smaller increase (from 5.7 to 9.4 per cent), with a curious blip in 1991, when it inexplicably leapt to 11.3 per cent, while comedy represents the most important shift in the entire survey, having grown from a tiny 4.3 per cent in 1989 to a much healthier 14.8 per cent in 1995. It is significant because analysis of types of films and programmes that are successful with audiences shows that comedy comes out top, albeit that it is a genre that tends to travel badly across borders. Action-adventure had an average of just 1.4 per cent between 1989 and 1995, leading Routh to question why European writers appear to be incapable of creating formulaic but nevertheless blockbuster stories like The Fugitive, Speed, True Lies or the Die Hard films. 'Nobody has ever satisfactorily answered this question, and until they do, Europe will probably remain unable to compete commercially with Hollywood.'

The figures overall show that there has been a better success rate, so far, with those genre categories that are generally considered to be more commercial (and traditionally less European) than the more 'difficult' and conventional European stories. SCRIPT's drama category is perhaps too wide ranging to be able to draw significant conclusions from, but of the others, it is important to note that whereas historical subjects represent 21.2 per cent of the total, the 'hit-rate' for films actually produced is nearly 17 per cent.

By contrast, thrillers account for 12.7 per cent of the total, with a hit-rate of 16.34 per cent; while comedy, which accounts for 9.7 per cent of the total, has a hit-rate of 11.11 per cent. It is worrying that the hugely popular (in audience terms) fantasy genre has fared less well, with only 4.58 per cent getting made, even though they represent 7.8 per cent of the total awards. This may be due to a perceived lack of confidence among financiers, rather than producers, as they are traditionally frightened off by the larger-than-average budgets which the genre generally demands.

This analysis was intended to be a reflection of what is being written for the screen in Europe in the 1990s. If SCRIPT had examined all the 8,000-odd applications received over the same period, rather than just the funded ones, Routh believes that the statistics would have been fairly similar, apart from the following changes: firstly, there would be more war stories, biopics, historical and 'tapestry of dreams' subjects; and secondly, there would be fewer comedies, thrillers and fantasy subjects.

It is interesting to note that this trend is reversed in examining the rates of films produced in comparison to the total number of awards made, where it is demonstrated that there is a higher success rate with thrillers and comedies, and a lower rate for historical subjects.

The results do confirm a theory that has thus far been unsubstantiated, which is that over the course of MEDIA I, writers have become more aware of the commercial demands of the market-place than before. They are generally less afraid of intellectually undemanding but commercially successful genres such as comedies, thrillers and fantasies, and there is less emphasis towards the turgid 'war-bores' which dominated previously.

Despite the improvements, Routh concludes: 'The statistics reveal that writers, writer/directors and indeed the producers who back them, have not gone far enough down the commercial route. There is a long way to go before the European industry is developing the right material to really stand up commercially and take its place at the box office.'

## 'The denigration of the producer and the parallel elevation of the director has been the undoing of European cinema in the past three decades.'

Oscar Moore

Oscar Moore, editor-in-chief of *Screen International*, suggests that producers should be seen as film-makers rather than finance raisers. 'They find and acquire the source material, they hire (and fire) the talent, and they find and secure a film's backers. The denigration of the producer and the parallel elevation of the director has been the undoing of European cinema in the past three decades,' suggests Moore.

Successful creative producers also must know how to read and recognize good scripts – especially if populist screenwriters are to find their work reaching the screen in a form that works for the audience. Typically, the process is devastatingly hard work. As UK writer David Pirie puts it: 'I feel a chill of fear sometimes when I watch American films, thinking how much has gone into the script. When the ending works, you know that it has probably been re-written 70 times.'

## Developing in pictures

When British director Alfred Hitchcock left the UK to go to Hollywood, he remarked that far too many European movies consisted of photographs of people talking. American movies use far less dialogue to tell their story than European movies. The genesis of Hollywood in the 1920s and 1930s centred around silent films, which gradually moved on to talkies. But the majority of the US audiences were illiterate, non-English-speaking immigrants. Hollywood tried to find ways of making stories work for as much of the available audience as possible: hence their techniques tended to rely more on pictures than complex dialogue. Even today, the emphasis is more visual than verbal. A sub-titling agent in Belgium worked out that the average number of sub-titles for an American movie was around 600, compared to 1,000 for a European one.

'The implications of this are extraordinary,' says UK literary agent Julian Friedmann. 'If you examine every scene of a film, it should be with your eyes and ears, but Europeans rarely engage their eyes.' Friedmann points to writing courses held in the US, which are 'far more concerned about form, and are rarely trying to teach dialogue. The problem for European writers is that nearly all think in dialogue. But cinema is a visual medium, and they need to learn to think in pictures.'

And thinking in pictures has to start early in the development process, long before the actual writing of the screenplay.

## The European theory

'If Europe is to have a film industry worth anything at all, then we must have a philosophy, an aesthetic, a vision, a dream, *a story*, of our own,' argued Stephen Cleary, head of development at the UK government-backed film support body, British Screen Finance, in an address to Dutch film-makers in September 1995. 'We must have writers who know the principles and foundations of European storytelling, which cannot be the same principles and foundations that Hollywood uses.'

Cleary argues that there is a need to develop a European script theory, as opposed to American script theory. By American script theory, he is referring to a way of analysing and defining scripts which makes it possible to write and produce movies on an industrial scale for a mass audience. Cleary is concerned that 'today in Europe, national film institutions, national broadcasters, and, through some areas of the

MEDIA programme, European film bodies are throwing their doors open to theorists to teach, usually in a half-baked, second-hand, badly argued way, an American way of defining writing which is of little benefit to European film culture. The key side-effect of such activity is to slowly eat away at the identity, confidence and possibilities for screenwriting in Europe.'

To go one step further, and define what the overall differences are between American and European screenplays is problematic. Cleary argues that 'we should recognize that European cinema is in no way similar to American cinema. It does not *explain* the world to its audience, it comments on it. In Europe, we used art to to explain the world to ourselves during the Renaissance, we're older, more tired, a little more frightened than America, but we've seen more. And because of what we Europeans have done this century, because of the people we've killed and the nations that we've destroyed, we can tell no stories of innocence. We cannot write, and it is not our destiny to write, The Lion King.

'If you had to try to characterize American cinema, and American screenwriting in one word, a good word would be *active*. I don't think European screenwriting is active in the same way, and when it tries to be, it ends up looking like a fat uncle playing volleyball on the beach. In some sense, and I don't mean in the plots of the stories it tells, European script theory has to be reflective.

'It also has to find a way of embracing complexity and diversity because it must allow for language – and not by using the American solution of having as little dialogue as possible – and cultural differences. The idea is not to make everyone European in the way that Hollywood sets out to make everyone American. We must find ways of writing and finding stories which accommodate difference, which understand it to be a good thing, not an obstacle to pan-European marketing and cross-border poster campaigns.'

In reply, critics of Cleary argue that certain of his basic generalizations are too simplistic. They point to the principle of 'entertainment' above all else, and that means good stories that work for audiences. European films may well be more ideas-driven, often intellectual and culture-specific but all too often lacking in universal value. It is only the exceptional European screenplays that really help the resulting film travel across borders.

## The practical advice

Rather than just stick to theory, Cleary does argue for certain points on a practical level. 'Firstly, we must not be scared of screenwriting. I notice in Europe a real lack of confidence in both writers and producers when talking about scripts. This is coupled with a desire to find someone else to tell them what their script is, and whether it is any good. I have noticed this all over Europe but I think it's particularly true in smaller countries where, even within Europe, they feel that their language and culture is under threat. Thinking and talking intelligently about scripts is not an Anglo-Saxon gift – anyone can do it – and it's not a talent the British have above other Europeans. In continental Europe I find that British opinions about scripts are often treated with an exaggerated respect, as if we had access to some secret. All that we have is a structured environment to work and think in, and a film culture that takes screenwriting seriously, sometimes too seriously.

'So what Europe needs to do is to find ways of spreading confidence and the idea of the seriousness of screenwriting. Here, film institutions and TV stations have a large responsibility. Film development, script development and TV-series development is not simply a process of giving out money. Writers need encouragement, intelligent consideration of their work, and detailed script guidance. This doesn't happen anywhere near enough.'

Cleary, like many other development professionals and agents, is concerned that the majority of Europe's writers for cinema are isolated and disconnected from the main pump engines of the film industry. Few are 'networked' into the channels that would help move their projects through development and into production. (Those that are, are in extremely high demand.) Few European writers for cinema work in teams, or even in pairs. This is a major contrast to Hollywood, where it is not unusual to find that considerable numbers of writers have worked on a film screenplay, albeit often on separate drafts.

Above all, screenwriters often lack close and trusting relationships with film producers. Writers in Europe (and America, incidentally) find it hard to identify and develop the right links, productive introductions and stable conditions to work effectively. The results of strong relationships are formidable. The most dynamic new writer-producer-director team to emerge this decade is the John Hodge, Andrew Macdonald and Danny Boyle team (Shallow Grave, Trainspotting – see Case Study 1).

They have made a point of staying together rather than taking individual Hollywood jobs. They also share a joint credit for their films, emphasizing the team approach rather than the film world's typical hierarchies.

The relationship between producer and director is also essential to the process of developing. During the writing, development and production of Jean-Jacques Annaud's The Name of the Rose, the writer/director of the complex production forged a highly productive relationship with the film's German producer, Bernd Eichinger. Together, they fought to raise the $30 million budget and ultimately produced one of the most successful European films ever made. 'I have never found that my producers are my enemies,' explains Annaud. 'They are fighting for me, so I have to fight with them.' (See Case Study 4.)

Other professionals agree. For example, UK writer/director Terry Jones argues that a good producer can help a writer and director have more freedom, not less. He also stresses teamwork, but warns that the relationship between the writer and the director has historically been difficult. 'Directors have treated writers very badly in the past, to the extent that some producers have had to go in and do something about it,' says Jones, pointing out that during the 1970s many directors seemed to think that they were the only elements to a film that really mattered. 'Directing a film is much easier than writing it,' he argues. 'The director is really answering a multiple-choice exam, while the writer is staring at a blank page every time they write.'

There is, however, evidence of new teams coming through. In addition to the Shallow Grave and Trainspotting team, during 1996 a Swedish team of young film-makers saw their Lapland thriller, Jagarnar (The Hunters), take more than $6 million at the domestic box office. The screenplay was co-written by Bjorn Carlstrom (also the producer, along with Joakim Hansson) and the director, Kjell Sundvall. In a case study at the Festival Film School in Gothenburg in February 1996, they stressed the need for teamwork in creating strong films for audiences.

The theme of a team approach, compared to the director-led *auteur* school of film-making, has been taken up by a new development and training centre, the Maurits Binger Film Institute in Amsterdam. It opened in September 1996 with 15 new, talented international film-makers attached (alongside five 'active' observers), and aims to bring more market-driven, commercial principles into the development process. Feature films and single TV plays are being developed under the Institute's wing. Director Jeanne Wikler points out that one of the key services is to bring writers back in touch with the industry. 'They're much too isolated – and they'll benefit from a meeting-place like this. And it's the younger generation that will be able to break through that isolation barrier,' says Wikler.

## The treatment catch

Part of the problem facing European screenwriters and their resultant scripts, however, has to do with the production system. Screenwriters cannot work well in isolation; they need feed-back, collaboration, and a sense of direction to their work. There are serious doubts within the industry about the strength of screenwriting across Europe, not just within the UK. These doubts do not just stem from talent-gaps, but from critical gaps within the industry's development infrastructure.

Some of these problems begin very early in the development process. Certain literary agents who represent screenwriters are not convinced that the *way* writers are paid (both in Europe and in North America) help the development process. Julian Friedmann argues that there is a fundamental problem with the standard Writers' Guild agreement. It has seven stages of payment, two for the treatment (commencement and completion), two for the first draft, two for the second draft, and one on principal photography. These break down normally into 10 per cent on commencement of treatment, 10 per cent on treatment acceptance, 20 per cent on the commencement of the first draft, 20 per cent on delivery, 10 per cent on the second draft, and 30 per cent on the first day of principal photography.

'The point I'm making is that everybody who has had experience will accept that in order to produce a really good script, screenwriters would need to invest anything from 40 to 70 per cent of their time to do the treatment, and yet this stage is only attracting 20 per cent of the money. As a result, it is demoted in the mind of the writer; who understandably wants to move on to the properly paid part of the development process: the script. You can't ask a writer to spend 70 per cent of the time it takes to write a script only working for 20 per cent of the overall fee.'

Writers also generally dislike writing treatments, which are extremely demanding, creative blueprints that require a lot of work. There is an unhealthy currency that stems from the treatment problem, Friedmann suggests. It leads to producers saying 'We'll sort the story's problems out in the script', or them saying that the treatment does not work, so they won't put the project into development. In addition, no film-schools and feature screenwriting training programmes teach treatment writing, an omission that is discussed in Chapter 3.

## The French approach

Feature-film-making in France is now emerging from beneath the shadow of the 'Nouvelle Vague' – the New Wave period of the 1960s. In an *auteur*-dominated environment, feature-film development was an idea in a director's head, rather than a team-driven process involving the producer's input, let alone a script editor or co-writer. Producers tended to become marginalized by the French *auteur* system, and their skills were largely reduced to raising money for the director. One of the main results of this trend was to breed producers who were invariably underskilled when it came to script commissioning, reading and editing. A perfunctory attitude towards pushing films quickly into production was predominant, with major implications for the relative health of French feature-film development.

But it wasn't just producers who fared poorly under the New Wave. Professional screenwriters also tended to be seen as little more than adjuncts to the all-powerful director. The result was that the standard of screenwriting remained low. 'If carpenters made chairs in the way that [French] screenwriters produce scripts, we would all be sitting on the floor,' Jeanne Moreau, actress and former president of the French 'Avances Sur Recettes' support system, commented after spending a year reading Avance applications.

As I have argued in *Developing Feature Films: A Practical Guide,*[6] the above problems have been encouraged and exacerbated by the structure of subsidy support in France. The majority of the support is provided to film productions in such a way that it tends to reward film-makers when actually in production, but not at the development stage.

Legal demands have also had a significant impact on film development and the respective roles of the writer/director versus the producer. French law asserts the primacy of the director through 'droit moral', or 'moral right' over the copyright of the material. The consequences of the director's enhanced power has had problematic results. For example, scripts could be under-developed on the grounds that it was highly probable that film directors would change them during the shoot anyway.

Nevertheless, attitudes towards development and its support has started to take on a larger and more prominent place within the wide array of subsidies and incentives administered by France's Centre National de la Cinematographie (CNC). Top CNC official Elisabeth Fleury-Herard, speaking at the Paris Development Conference in June 1995, described the Aide Au Developpement (AAD) scheme as 'becoming more and more fundamental' to the body's work. After what has been effectively an 18-month experimental phase for the AAD since early 1993, the CNC is expanding development aid and has given it a formal legal footing.

By mid 1995, development aid had been granted to a total of 55 companies with aid varying from FFr100,000 to FFr900,000 ($19,000 to $171,000) in the case of Les Productions Lazennec, which presented a slate of five projects for support. Approximately half the awards made have gone to companies developing one project at a time.

## The French future

By the end of 1995, development had emerged as one of the CNC's key priorities following a secret meeting between the centre's Marc Tessier, the minister of culture, Phillippe Douste-Blazy, and French industry representatives. The meeting held outside Paris at Champs-sur-Marne in November 1995, agreed that the CNC would set up seven working parties on the industry, which will report within the next 12 months. At least two of the working groups will focus on development issues.

The first CNC working group examined the Aide Au Developpement fund, and its possible financial and practical expansion. By that stage, the AAD currently had an annual budget of some FFr10 million ($1.9 million), which is sourced separately from, but adminstered by, the CNC.

The working group also looked at ways of increasing the total amount of its financial resources and examined the possibility of making advances to producers that are non-refundable in cases where projects are abandoned. The group also considered the creation of a separate Aide Au Scénario, which would be allocated by AAD adminstrators to individual screenwriting projects (see Chapter 6).

## Policies towards development

In the 1994 EC Green Paper on audiovisual policy, a diagnosis of the structural shortcomings of the European programme industry argued that: 'At the creation stage, European projects are handicapped by a lack of development. This is the crucial stage where original ideas must be reworked and geared' towards wider audiences.

The diagnosis went on to argue that it was 'regrettable that some public support mechanisms are unduly restricted to domestic production and do not give sufficient incentive to work for European and transnational markets. This creative/development stage is essential: even with the most sophisticated distribution mechanisms, if no account is taken of the audience's tastes and demands, the European film industry will never be competitive.' Hence, support for development activity was underlined as a priority sector for the future building of the European audiovisual industry.

MEDIA I's development project, the European Script Fund, enjoyed a strong professional relationship to the film industry from 1989 to 1995. (See Notes for SCRIPT's track-record in statistical form.) In addition to awarding repayable loans to companies, teams of producers/writers and directors and single writers, the fund built up considerable resources in additional areas such as script reports and 'financial engineering', the latter dealing with projects' sales potential to international distributors and private finance in addition to the obvious public subsidy sources. Both areas of servicing have been praised by recipients, and the script report process has, in some cases, been copied by other European funders. The financial engineering also reflects the extent to which financiers are less interested initially in the financial package of independent projects, and most concerned with the creative package – the experience and identity of the director, writer, cast and the appeal of the screenplay – and whether the producer is clearly focused about the project's intended market.

## The ACE approach

The ACE programme became, in 1993, the first permanent development centre for European feature films. ACE is a Club of European Producers' project, backed by significant financial support from Canal Plus, PRO-CIREP, British Screen, Channel 4, BBC, Department of National Heritage (UK), PACT, the Nordic Film and TV Fund, Filmboard Berlin-Brandenberg and Ville de Paris.

Taking media consultant Neil Watson's 1992 European Film Studio Feasibility Study to its practical conclusion, ACE was built on the belief that 'the creative and financial planning for a project should proceed in tandem', and that the producer is the central nodal point of the project's development. The producer should become the essential bridge between the creative work of the writer and director, and the audience.

Although ACE is primarily a development initiative rather than a training programme, the MBS hoped that ACE would groom articulate, audience-sensitive film producers who possess an understanding of Europe as both a cultural and commercial market, fostering a generation of producers who will galvanize Europe's film industry.

Such an ambitious approach, however, was always bound to encounter obstacles, and ACE was caught in something of a 'Catch 22' situation. For example, a couple of the early ACE producers explained that they had misunderstood the role of the godparents – eminent producers such as Puttnam, Dieter Geissler and Rene Cleitman – whom they felt didn't put much weight behind their siblings' projects due to their own busy schedules. Observers pointed out that ACE might be seen as a device for these producers and supporting institutions to simply cherrypick the cream of Europe's younger crop of talent. The record, however, has shown that no godparents have been acting in such a self-interested way, as the direct picking up of projects has not materialized. Ironically, it wouldn't necessarily have been a bad thing in any case. Meanwhile ACE has carefully monitored feedback and criticisms, and correspondingly fine-tuned the programme.

Any development project takes a long time to work, as individual projects take from two to over five years to reach production. Judging ACE on acceptance/production ratios is irrelevant. What is more important is the positive change in attitude that ACE signifies. As director Colin Young points out: 'ACE's in-house attitude is that we would rather ACE projects expose themselves to risk investment than just tap finance from subsidies and TV licences. Our projects are encouraged to meet the market.' For how much longer looked debatable at the end of 1995, but fresh support from a number of new sources, including the Nordic Film and TV Fund, has secured ACE's future. If Europe is to improve its approach towards development and the marketplace, projects such as ACE will need all the support they can raise.

## Training the writers

When MBS research was carried out by Watson in 1991/92 for the establishment of ACE, the European Film Studio, there were (albeit with the exceptions of the UK and, arguably, France) 'serious concerns about the shortage of high-quality writers in every territory. This stems from the heritage of the *film d'auteur* in which the director and the writer is usually the same all-powerful individual unwilling to relinquish or share his or her creative leadership merely for the sake of a wider audience. Until Europe encourages the development of a substantial stable of writers, it will remain difficult to break the tyranny of the *film d'auteur*.'

The European Film Studio feasibility study went on to stress the need for better-quality writing, and the need to keep talented writers interested in continuing to write screenplays, and not 'grab the first opportunity to become second-rate directors'.

There lies some of the reasoning behind the range of producer and writing training programmes designed to aid development – including MEDIA I's EAVE, SOURCES, the Media Business School's involvement in ACE, and some of the larger screenwriting courses taught in Europe, including France's Equinoxe and the Frank Daniel Script Workshops.

Even Germany's development and training strategies towards screenwriting have undergone considerable changes in the past few years. When the NRWF's Dieter Kosslick joked at the June 1995 Paris Development Conference that 'German films are the ones famous for going into production on first draft', he wasn't completely exaggerating. Screenplays originating in Germany have, over recent years, been more concerned with attracting subsidy support than ultimately reaching an intended audience. Screenplay editing has been, until lately, an untaught and unknown skill, while work between producers and writers has not been as productive as it has to be if development is to lead to effective production and beyond. However, the larger German filmfunding bodies have taken note of the need for development support – not just in the form of writing and pre-production loans, but also in terms of training, writing and development.[7]

Not all agree with the American-influenced screenwriting approach employed by Frank Daniel and other training courses. Stephen Cleary, head of development at British Screen, recently argued that the whole approach to writing and training is misplaced in Europe, but that does not mean that Europe should accept American screenwriting gurus at face value. Cleary is particularly suspicious of what he sees as American script missionaries, who preach Hollywood mantras about stories and structure: 'What Europe needs to do is to find ways of spreading confidence and the idea of the seriousness of screenwriting. Here, film institutions and TV stations have a large responsibility. Film development, script development and TV series development is not simply a process of giving out money. Writers need encouragement, intelligent consideration of their work, and detailed script guidance. This doesn't happen anywhere near enough.'

Cleary argues that there should be some sort of support for writers independent of producers and directors. Institutions should identify, commission and develop scripts with writers alone. 'This would force the institutions to work out their policy on script development, work out their own script theory, train development staff and devote significant resources to development within their institutions.'

## The new development organization

In June 1996, the former SCRIPT team under David Kavanagh was successful in its 'European Media Development Agency' (EMDA) application to manage the new MEDIA II Intermediary Organisation (IO) for development.[8] The IO will technically assess all development and company applications, and make recommendations to the jury of professionals, who are appointed by Brussels. The Commission makes the final decision on the advice of the jury. EMDA will handle applications for fiction and documentary development; company support, animation, new technology and audiovisual heritage. (The last three will overlap with the 'Industrial Platforms', which will be established to cover expert advice on these respective areas, and also give recommendations to the development jury.)

While the continuity of EMDA's management team following the depth of experience gained during MEDIA I is positive, there were some questions remaining during mid 1996 about the new IO. The Commission's guidelines made little sense, most notably on points such as loan repayments. Kavanagh was unsure to what extent the old SCRIPT team would be able to employ services such as script reports, an area he views as vital to the role of a development agency. On the plus side, consultant Bernie Stampfer is remaining with the team to handle financial engineering. Kavanagh is also hoping to increase the number of applications from twice-a-year to three times or more, on the simple grounds 'that it doesn't make sense to the industry. It's no good having producers set to buy the option rights to a novel, and then turning round and saying: "I can't sign for six months because my development application won't be known until then!".'

In addition, the new development funding will not deal with single writer loans anymore. First-time writers without producers have been moved across to the training area. It remains to be seen, however, whether young writers will actually be given development loans from the training IO, or whether this area will be short-circuited by Brussels completely.

EMDA's emphasis is on team (producer/writer/director) support and company loans. The latter will be broader-based than the previous Incentive Funding system for independent companies. 'We've already had applications from companies with projects in more than one area. Companies have been looking for fiction support and CD-Rom development support; and drama project support alongside their normal documentary slate, for example. The good thing is that companies are coming to us with their strategies, rather than having to bend their practices to suit the rules,' says Kavanagh.

## Putting theory into practice

Development as a serious industrial activity has clearly improved over the past decade. However, whichever way Europe moves in terms of practical support, there is a sense that it also needs to find a new creative direction now that *auteur* theory has lost its way. Writers need to be brought towards the centre of the industry, rather than left on the sidelines. As German director Wim Wenders explained at a European Film Academy–SOURCES[9] debate in Cannes 1995, 'We are looking for maybe different models to replace the *auteur* system. We don't have to look round too hard, because there is a model that we can see works very well: one where the director, the producer and the writer are very distinct professions.' Within this triangle, Wenders suggests that the weakest link remains the writer.

'It's crucial that the screenwriter in Europe doesn't disappear in the credits. We have to convince screenwriters, by the way that they are represented in the process of film-making as well as by the way that they are rewarded financially, that they don't necessarily have to turn to directing themselves in order to feel good about their job.'

## Notes

1 For a wider description of development see *Developing Feature Films In Europe – A Practical Guide*, by Angus Finney, published by Routledge for the Media Business School, August 1996.
2 *Ibid.*
3 See *A Dose of Reality: The State of European Cinema*, Angus Finney, 1993, chapters 1 and 2.

4  The Festival Film School, Gothenburg, Sweden, February 1996. Produced by the MediaXchange for the Nordic Film and TV Fund. (See Chapter 3.)

5  See 'The Genre Survey', *Development Digest*, pp. 8–11, January 1996 (copies via EMDA, 39 Highbury Place, London, N5, UK).

6  See *Developing Feature Films In Europe: A Practical Guide*, by Angus Finney, *Ibid.*

7  German screenwriting, Martin Blaney, *Development Digest,* Issue 5, November 1995.

8  The Commission has established four IOs for MEDIA II: Development; distribution; training; and a management IO. The first three will have juries of professionals of up to 15 people. The IO gives both the jury and the Commission (which ultimately controls payments, which will come from the Management IO) technical assistance on each area. At its simplest level, the IO chooses the applicants, which the Jury approves. The money is then paid by the Management IO.

9  SOURCES was a development project under MEDIA I called Stimulating Outstanding Resources for Creative European Screenwriting. It was headed up by Dick Willemsen and the development/training sessions were run out of Amsterdam.

### Figure 1: Survey of total script applications and projects funded
### (October 1989 to December 1995)

| Country | Applications received | Total funded | Teams funded | Writers funded |
|---|---|---|---|---|
| Austria | 99 | 14 | 14 | - |
| Belgium | 322 | 48 | 36 | 12 |
| Denmark | 151 | 37 | 35 | 2 |
| Eca* | 8 | 2 | 2 | - |
| Finland | 56 | 12 | 11 | 1 |
| France | 1441 | 173 | 135 | 38 |
| Germany | 858 | 107 | 84 | 23 |
| Greece | 337 | 61 | 45 | 16 |
| Hungary | 46 | 15 | 10 | 5 |
| Iceland | 78 | 16 | 13 | 3 |
| Ireland | 564 | 76 | 62 | 14 |
| Italy | 1025 | 100 | 77 | 23 |
| Luxembourg | 11 | 5 | 5 | - |
| Netherlands | 219 | 38 | 33 | 5 |
| N. Ireland | 16 | 3 | 1 | 2 |
| Norway | 33 | 7 | 5 | 2 |
| Other | 99 | - | - | - |
| Portugal | 142 | 31 | 26 | 5 |
| Spain | 584 | 99 | 76 | 23 |
| Sweden | 51 | 7 | 4 | 3 |
| Switzerland | 93 | 22 | 21 | 1 |
| UK | 2598 | 200 | 165 | 35 |
| **TOTAL** | **8801** | **1073** | **860** | **213** |

*(Source:* European Script Fund)
* European Co-Production Association (no longer running).

**Figure 2: Single project team statistics (1989 to 1995)**

| | |
|---|---|
| Applications received* | 8841 |
| Projects supported** | 971 |
| Projects completed 1990–93 | 30 |
| Completed 1994 | 32 |
| Completed 1995 | 22 |
| In production 1995 | 15 |
| In post-production 1995 | 18 |
| In pre-production with start dates | 24 |
| **TOTAL** | **141** |

\* Including writers up to 1994
\*\* Since Jan 1991
(*Source*: European Script Fund)

**Figure 3: Incentive funding statistics (1991 to 1995)**

| | |
|---|---|
| Companies awarded IF* | 121 |
| Projects delivered (2 years+) | 52 |
| Projects entered production | 17 |
| (Single projects delivered) | 471 |
| (Single projects entered production) | 117 |

\* 119 awards have been made. Four of these were repeat awards (i.e. to the same company, including Gemini, Scala and Tele Images.)
(*Source*: European Script Fund)

**Figure 4: Development loan-to-production success ratio**
**(A comparison of single and incentive funding)**

| | |
|---|---|
| Incentive funding: | 32.72% |
| Single team funding: | 24.84% |

(*Source*: European Script Fund)

# Training for the Future

> 'One of the greatest weaknesses of the European film business is
> that not enough producers actually know how it works.
> It is a business, it is hard work, and you need to understand it all.
> It's only by taking this approach that you learn to make a
> commercial product with other people.'

Jake Eberts, Allied Film-makers

> 'What Europe needs is not just one centre of excellence nor lots
> of smaller bodies. It needs six or seven powerhouses,
> like the American training centres of excellence.'

Bjorn Erichsen, Danmarks Radio MD of TV and
former Principal of the European Film College, Ebeltoft

FILM-MAKING, like any other industrial activity, requires a fertile breeding ground for technical and creative talent to develop. However, training in Europe should, arguably, have been placed higher up the list of priorities than it has been over the past decade. Training has a direct effect on Europe's ability to consolidate on an existing skills base, and upon its creative and industrial growth potential. As the UK Government recently stressed, 'The broader the talent-base within the industry, the more cost-effective and efficient it becomes – good training has as great an impact on costs as it has on quality.'[1]

The current heavy expansion in the supply and demand of audiovisual programmes has led to the European audiovisual market-place growing at a rate of more than 6 per cent a year in real terms. This rapid expansion of employment opportunities and demand for highly skilled professionals was underlined by the European Commission's White Paper on growth, competitiveness and employment, which concluded that a backbone of highly qualified professionals would be required to meet the demands of the industry.

Training raises a number of supplementary issues, some of which stem from historical trends and tendencies – such as the former stranglehold trade unions have had in technical training responsibilities – while others concern the differences between national and pan-European employment and training strategies. At the same time, concern has risen about who actually carries out training, and which centres are properly equipped for the job.

As the Commission's MEDIA II paper, *Audiovisual Policy – Stimulating dynamic growth in the European Programme Industry* made clear, 'Vocational training has nowadays come to be an issue outside its traditional school and university domain. Rapid changes in the economic and technological environment require not only high-quality initial training, but also regular continuing training throughout working life to preserve competitiveness. This is a matter for all those involved in the industry – firms, training centres, professional associations, the authorities – whatever their level of involvement. They must each play a part within an overall strategy.'

Quite how this alleged 'strategy' is taking shape is still under debate. This chapter explores the key national and pan-European trends, and seeks to help the younger entrants find their way through the various industries' starting blocks.

## The union background

Finding a way into the film industry presents to most a vague maze. Successful navigation continues to have less to do with academic qualifications and more to do with having technical skills and then making practical contacts and finding incidental work that leads to employment. Clearly there is a difference of approach between the craft and technical areas of the industry, and the creative/managerial roles, such as writing, producing and running independent companies.

Historically, the craft section of the industry has been dominated by trade unions, which in some territories are fragmented down to the carpenters (Ireland). The over-riding aim of the up-and-coming hopeful was to find a way into the appropriate union. Trainees had to win the support of existing members before being signed up, and would then spend a minimum of two years before being able to move up in grade. As

Josephine Langham makes clear in her book, *Lights, Camera, Action! Careers in Film, Television, and Video*,[2] the UK union structure, 'for all its faults, ensured excellent on-the-job training'. While she concedes that the union structure was also irrational, restrictive and unfair, it worked very effectively: 'The slow pedestrian grind through a union apprenticeship produced some of the most skilled technicians in the world. Film is an extremely expensive medium and mistakes can be distastrous. Trainees started at the very lowest levels where they could do no harm . . . No further education college or film studies course could offer better.'

## The UK education trap

Some of the key problems facing training in the UK lie in political and general weaknesses in the British education system as a whole. Unlike the United States and countries such as France and Germany, the UK had rarely integrated its university degrees with vocational training opportunities. The UK's universities tended to remain arrogantly dismissive about taking a vocational approach and shunned work-placement schemes and practical links with all industry.

Back in 1984, the UK Government commissioned a report, *Competence and Competition,* which pointed to the UK's lack of training and skills when compared to other European countries. By 1988, 63 per cent of the UK workforce had no vocational training at all, compared to 38 per cent of the Dutch, 26 per cent of the German and 53 per cent of the French workforces. As Langham observes: 'More than 70 per cent of British workers who will be in the workforce in the year 2000 are already in employment and most of them are unskilled. They are totally unprepared for the market of tomorrow.'[3]

Gradually, however, the UK higher education bodies started to recognize the demand for more practical training against the backdrop of new technology demands. A change in public policy led to the introduction of the National Vocational Qualification (NVQ), a post-16-year-old training programme designed to bring further education, training and employment much closer together. Employers have been encouraged to become much more involved in training as a result of the NVQ and a range of other training initiatives.

If the above overall criticisms appear particularly harsh on the British system, then it is worth noting that even the Government has been forced to reappraise its efforts. Britain's $2 billion overall training programme was recently investigated by the Department of Education and Employ-ment, which found growing evidence of fraud. According to a report in the *Guardian*,[4] 'falsification of attendance records, duplicate claims, forged certificates and claims for people who never attended courses' were uncovered and published in a National Audit Office report pub-lished in June 1996.

Most damaging of all was the UK's first skills audit, published on 13 June 1996 following a White Paper entitled *Creating the Enterprise Cen-tre of Europe*. The audit compared the UK to its key economic rivals, and placed it at number 16 in the gross domestic product (GDP) table, behind 11 other European countries. Vocational courses were lacking in credi-bility and even the country's relatively high proportion of graduates are now being overtaken by France.

Overall, the rate of technological change and increasing international competition is requiring a new demand for a properly skilled workforce, which is proving problematic for a country with an estimated six million people who are functionally illiterate.[5]

## The German approach

The weakness of the UK approach has been highlighted by Germany, where under the former Federal Republic, a highly vocational and tech-nically-demanding approach was employed in higher education. This has more recently been expanded post-reunification through specific training schemes in the German Laender.

For example, Ausbildung In Medienberufen (AIM – the Co-ordination Centre for Training in Media Occupations) has been set up by the VFAW (Association for Promotion of Education and Training in Media Business in North Rhine-Westphalia). The objective of such groups is to collect infor-mation about all media occupations, then making it available to both the public and specialized bodies. In addition to finding individual placements, AIM advises companies on education and training of their employees.

'There is hardly a sector to compare with the media for its variety of different career profiles,' says AIM. 'The sector moves fast, the pace of technological change is rapid and more is expected of new entrants all the time', and the service aims to give a better 'fit' with current trends in the media business than have previously been available.

Since 1994 a Hamburg-based professional training organization, Bil-dungswerk Medien, has run three-year courses targeted at film, TV, video production houses, post-production houses, labs and TV stations. The student attends technical college for 13 weeks, and the other 39 are practical training in the workplace.

The German Federal Film Board (FFA) also provides project funding for professional training. Around $320,000 was awarded for 13 different measures, ranging from group in-house seminars to individual  grants. The German film law specifies that projects should assist technical and junior business staff in employment opportunities.

## The freelance problem

Training has clearly suffered from the increasing casualization of the film and television industries over the past decade. The key challenge is how to handle the training (and re-training) of a predominantly freelance workforce successfully. According to research by Skillset, the UK training body for the audiovisual and media industries, some 60 per cent of the workforce in TV, film and video are freelance. (Skillset is managed and supported by PACT and funded by the BBC, C4, ITVA, IVCA, AFVPA and the Federation of Entertainment Unions.)

Of those freelancers who work in feature films, 90 per cent of those who have undergone training while working on films have paid for it themselves. The freelance workforce is predominantly composed of middle-aged people whose skill levels are dropping further and further behind the demands of a market driven by new technology. As Skillset puts it: 'The skilled workforce of today was, on the whole, trained yesterday. Unless serious thought is given to the funding and organization of structured new-entrants training, the industry will experience significant difficulties in the future in relation to its ability to compete with a world market.'

Although Skillset has made strong inroads into supporting and highlighting practical training programmes in addition to overseeing new NVQ and job placement schemes, the organization is deeply concerned about what it sees as a continued 'lack of training which could kill off the industry'. But it is not just training at issue: it is also a question of who does the training. One of Skillset's roles has been to act as a 'quality watchdog' over new training centres (a crucial function that is relevant to all European training bodies). As Kate O'Connor, Skillset's Scottish NVQ project director explained, when it comes to wanting to set up a centre 'what people don't realize is that you really do have to think about how you are going to offer these qualifications, how many candidates you can cope with, whether they are permanent staff or freelance, new entrants or fully experienced; how many assesors you will have and how the funding is going to be arranged. We expect potential centres to put forward proper business plans.'

By the end of 1995, Skillset had established a network of centres across the UK that ranged from training organizations which provide workplace assessment for new entrants, employers' organizations and regional/ open assessment centres for freelancers. Despite all the problems facing people working in film, there is no question that Skillset has had a fundamentally constructive effect on employment and training issues in the industry in the UK.

A considerable level of Skillset's finances comes from the Independent Production Training Fund, which was created in 1993 to recognize the obligation of the British independent production sector to the future training needs of the industry. The Fund has raised support by implementing a levy, set at 0.25 per cent of the total overhead and direct budgeted costs, on all productions whose contracts were signed after 1 January 1993.[6] As producer Timothy Burrill points out, 'for independent producers to have voluntarily accepted the need to raise money for training is a remarkable achievement'.

## The French situation

The equivalents to Skillset and the Independent Production Training Fund are less prevalent across Europe than might be expected. Germany, as previously mentioned, has a more fragmented, regional approach;[7] while France is more centralized. France benefits from a substantial number of film schools in both the public and private sectors, all of which provide technical as well as creative training. Unions and the Centre du National de la Cinematographie (CNC) insist on certain skills levels before work permits are issued.

The large number of films made (around 130 per annum) and the established system of using trainees on productions means that opportunities for on-the-job experience are good in France. In the television sector, the main broadcasters are required to sub-contract the vast majority of their production, thus increasing the emphasis on freelance work.

## The Irish situation

Ireland has taken a more pro-active role in recent years. A statutory committee (STATCOM) commissioned a report into training and the audiovisual industry, and subsequently established a National Training Committee (NTC) to administer and disperse a $4.2 million three-year fund, which started in late 1995. Seven of the key state bodies involved in film and television, including RTE, the Irish Film Board and the Arts Council, are on the NTC's board.

The 160-page report, overseen by Mary Lyons, is an excellent example to any government needing to review its training priorities in the audio-visual sector. It identified producers and screenwriters as a priority area, alongside operational areas such as camera/lighting, production design and post-production. In the executive summary, a key criticism (that has much wider implications for all of Europe's audiovisual training) was made of the existing structures: 'There is dissatisfaction with current media education provision because it is primarily focused on educa-tional objectives. There is a widespread view that current third-level media education does not prepare people adequately to work in film and telelvision. Provision for continuing professional development was reported to be virtually non-existent.'[8]

Prior to (and following) the setting up of the NTC, Film Base – which is on the NTC's board – has done excellent work in co-ordinating train-ing programmes and helping initial stages of development for young film-makers and new talent, operating in a slightly similar way to the New Producers Alliance in the UK, although its membership covers all sectors of the industry.

Little attention, however, was paid to training in the Indecon Interna-tional Economic Consultants' report on Section 35 incentive and, cru-cially, its 'recommendations on how to develop the contribution of the film industry in Ireland'. (This was probably due to the existence of the STATCOM report.) The report, entitled *A strategy for success based on economic realities; the next stage of development for the film industry in Ireland*, was presented to the Department of Arts, Culture and the Gaeltacht in December 1995.[9]

Nevertheless, the report did recommend that Irish film companies should be developed and upgraded in terms of their 'strategic manage-ment resources', and that the industry 'should urgently enter consulta-tion with the trade unions to address the issue of labour-market entry restrictions and inflexibility in labour-market practices'.

The latter was a sensible point to raise, as the restrictions on joining union membership and issues over the nomination of individuals had been damaging the industry for many years. By the summer of 1996, the carpenters and painters unions had agreed to join an industry committee that oversees low-budget film deals, ranging from $500,000 to $3 million.

## Selecting courses

The advent and proliferation of the media studies course, although not exclusively targeted to the audiovisual industry, has been a further training development. With the cut-back in union power, the more practical elements of these courses are providing useful introductory training elements in an otherwise poor preparation schedule for young film industry entrants. Most courses combine film and communications theory and practical experience through work placements and production activity. However, applicants should check the respective curricula and status of courses with great care. The reputation and links with the film and television industry vary widely, and it is often best to talk to former students before applying. Some of the institutions attract people better qualified to run a travel agency than a professional place of learning. And as the Irish STATCOM report points out, the educational aspect has often overshadowed the practical use of such training schemes. One of the best indicators of a course's success is the number of students who leave to go to jobs *before* they complete the course.

## The film school approach

Media studies courses at universities and academic institutions are quite distinct from dedicated film schools, most of which are exclusively postgraduate institutions. Both are highly competitive and heavily oversubscribed. Across Europe there has been a strong training element fulfilled by top institutions, including the Munich Film School; the German Academy of Film and Television in Berlin; the Film School at Potsdam-Babelsberg; Copenhagen's National Film School of Denmark; the Paris-based FEMIS; and the UK's National Film and Television School (NFTS) and the Royal College of Art. The co-operation between schools has increased considerably, with CILECT (Centre International des Ecoles de Cinema et de Television) and GEECT (Groupement Europeen des Ecoles de Cinema de Television) playing a role in co-ordinating joint activities, exchanges and show cases for the students' work.

Film schools offer degrees, others diplomas or vocational certificates. Some, like the Danish Film School, insist that students choose a specialism, while others allow the student to roam around picking up a range of skills. In the UK, most of the top courses are accredited by the Broadcasting, Entertainment, Cinematograph and Theatre Union (BECTU). The union is particularly keen to ensure that accredited courses have strong relevance to the demands of the industry.

However, once out on the streets, many students end up entering other sections of the audiovisual market rather than film *per se*. The lack of strong contact between students and jobs is an area that the Karlsruhe-based European Institute of Cinema, under the direction of film-maker Edgar Reitz, has identified as a key area of concern. The Institute has put forward a proposal for a film-student placement scheme which would allow for certain graduates to work on fully-fledged feature films as assistants by way of a working apprenticeship. The cost would be borne by the Institute, not the production. Students would have to work outside their home country in an effort to help enlarge horizons and Europe-wide experience. The concept is potentially quite strong – especially if the right films and producers are selected – but the scheme was in a working paper stage during the summer of 1996 and will need considerable industry support to move forward. Taking on students is not exactly the first thing on a film-maker's mind when making a film.

### Teaching producers?

Exactly where producers fit in to Europe's film school training concept is a moot point. Speaking at a seminar at the European Film Academy's Strategies for Survival conference in Berlin in June 1996, Sundance director Geoff Gilmore felt that European film schools tend to focus too much on directors.

> **'Film directors and writers want to make films anyway –
> they can't help it. What you need to do is push producers,
> and make them the elite of your schools.
> They need to know what a good story is,
> how script editing works, and how to read.
> They also need to realize that the word "money"
> is less appreciated in Europe,
> and that's where so many students go wrong.'**

Geoff Gilmore, Sundance Film Institute

In the same session, Reinhard Hauff from the German Academy of Film and Television pointed out that even when his students leave the school, 'the professional world seems very foreign to them. Many of them don't want to leave, but we throw them out because they have to run by themselves.'

Hauff was particularly critical of the lack of contemporary stories being told by young European film-makers: 'We have enormous inner-city conflicts and social problems on our doorstep, but rarely do we find this life in our films.' He hoped that Europe's schools would experiment by bringing in professionals from outside just the film industry in an attempt to widen people's views of the world. 'Film schools as academia are no good to anyone,' he concluded.

What was worrying in the session (with the exceptions of the above names), was the level of complacency about so-called 'standards' and 'excellence'. Good, interesting short films which are subsidized are all very well, but learning how to deal with real film-making challenges with real money is a more exacting training. As US film-maker Hal Hartley put it in a different session in Berlin, 'You have to learn that you pay for everything, no matter where it comes from.'

## The UK situation

The UK's NFTS has undergone something of a revolution over the past three years under its Danish head, Henning Camre. The previous regime under Colin Young tended to allow students to continue to complete their student films for many months, and in some cases, a number of years after their official course time should have been completed. It is now no longer possible to switch discipline, and the intake has become much more balanced, meaning that for every director there is a sound engineer, a sound recordist, an editor and a cameraman. David Puttnam, who recently stepped down as chairman of the School, explained that 'the NFTS has, rightly in my opinion, returned to re-emphasizing a proper, academic curriculum that students are now required to follow. There is also a new emphasis on television, and overall the School is responding to the changing nature of the industry.'

The School plans to move to the Ealing Film Studios within two to three years, with the support of a Government grant and other public sources worth more than £2 million ($3 million). Up to £25 million ($37.5 million) will hopefully be forthcoming to put the Ealing plans into practice. The move from Beaconsfield (some 25 miles outside Central London) to Ealing has major implications for the School. In addition to helping the organic changes above take root, the move addresses one of the more bizarre elements of the previous institution.

As Puttnam put it: 'The NFTS is one of the few graded institutions in the UK that closes at five or six o'clock in the afternoon. It was a daft and ludicrous idea that everyone had to catch a bus and go home.' Puttnam hopes that the new Ealing site will lead to effectively two forms of school time: one practical and academic schedule during the day, and a further evening learning space for lectures, screenings, projects and discussions. He's confident that the NFTS has the potential to become 'one of the premier influences over the way in which Britain and Europe develops into the twenty-first century. There is no question that we are training the messenger, and the nature of those messengers is going to have a lot to do with what the message is. That is a crucial responsibility for the future.' The NFTS has campaigned valiantly to continue to match its Government's DNH grant [£1.85 million in 1996], but raising the other 50 per cent from the industry has proved difficult. However, a strengthened board with top industry ties should help the battle.

Beyond the NFTS, there is a range of other strong training centres, albeit less ambitious in scale. The Royal College of Art, for example, has a vastly smaller budget compared to the NFTS, but still manages (among other services), to give an excellent grounding to a group of potential film producers. Its production course has gained a strong reputation under the control of Mark Hubbard, who takes a very practical, market-driven approach to training. Every year a group of the production students go to Cannes, and every year they receive a tremendous shock at the reality of the market-place.

### On-the-job training

The most valuable way of entering the film industry is through on-the-job formal (and informal) placement training schemes. The funding and structure of new entrants' training tends not to be organized in a formal manner. However, some bodies have come up with new ideas. The New Producers Alliance (the NPA, the 1,200-strong UK body of young film-makers) made a proposal to the National Heritage Committee in March 1995 that suggested the following: Established producers should be offered a financial incentive to employ aspiring producers by way of a subsidized job-placement scheme. A similar proposal was made for writers by the Writers' Guild. The NPA argued that at any one time there are likely to be at least ten individual UK producers willing to offer placements, and that they are bound to be over-subscribed if the scheme got off the ground.

On the assumption that ten producers participate, each with two trainees, for an average period of nine months training and a wage of £100 to £120 ($150 to $180) per week, the NPA estimated the likely cost of the scheme to be around £85,000 to £90,000 ($128,000 to $135,000) a year. At least part of the scheme could fall under the EU's MEDIA II training section, or other initiatives designed to stimulate business training and employment. 'It is initiatives such as these which will generate a new vitality in the British film industry, equipping our young producers to achieve success,' argued the NPA in a briefing note. Such a scheme would not only be beneficial in the UK, but also in other territories. And there is no reason why a cross-border version could not be pioneered. The Motion Picture Academy of America, meanwhile, has already offered Hollywood Studio placements as part of its Round Table discussions with the European Producers Club and other bodies. More co-operation on this level would go some way to bridging the inevitable gap younger producers across Europe face when trying to make the leap into the industry.

## The European dimension

While film schools and university courses abound across Europe, few if any teach about the way the audiovisual market operates on a pan-European level – or an international one, for that matter. In the Commission's MEDIA II paper, the following shortcomings in existing training were identified:

- Training for the career of a producer (including the development of a production project, drawing up a financing plan and marketing strategy, etc.) is virtually non-existent on traditional courses.
- The same applies to distribution, transmission and operation, for which there is hardly any specific training in Europe.
- Vocational training on new film and television technologies (including digital techniques, multimedia, interactive TV, etc.) is rather haphazard, since it is usually provided on a one-off basis by the industry in the form of on-the-job training, workshops and seminars.

MEDIA II's training wing will have access to ECU45 million ($56 million) over a five-year period to the end of the year 2000. The money is in the form of non-returnable grants, which will cover up to 50 per cent of the training budget, and in special cases, 75 per cent.

Media Research and Consultancy Spain (MRC) is the new Intermediary Organisation (IO) responsible for recommending projects to the Jury and the Commission, and is run by former MBS manager, Fernando Labrada. In the light of Europe's perceived shortcomings in certain key areas of the industry, the main modules will be courses in Initial (meaning younger, first-time professionals) and Continuing (meaning further, higher level) training. Rather than concentrating the money on certain key centres, it will be spread across a number of initiatives, courses and institutions.

According to a MEDIA II newsletter in June 1996, Masters degree courses and short courses will be offered through 'Initial' training; and in-house training, and training programmes based on production projects as well as short courses through 'Continuing' training. The new principles behind these courses are: to increase the level of management training on the audiovisual market; training in new technologies; and a greater level of networking between Europe's existing vocational training centres. Screenplay techniques are included in the new MEDIA II training programme, rather than being run through the Development IO.

There is only one call for projects for training each year. A priority will be given to projects that have transnational elements in their programmes, either by teaming up with other institutions in the EU or by providing access to courses for European professionals.

While recipients of MEDIA II training support were not announced by the time this book went to press, it was understood that 34 different groups were to receive support. Some of the former MEDIA I programmes had been told by the Commission that they were likely to be backed, but precisely *which* ones was still unclear by September 1996.

## Additional support

In addition to the MEDIA II training system, $2 million over a five-year period has been donated by America's Motion Picture Academy (MPA) to European training programmes. Half was directed to Denmark's Ebeltoft-based European Film College's new Media Training Centre, and half was being supervised by the MEPs, Alan Donnelly and Mary

Banotti, and subsequently delegated to the European Producers' Club to put into practice.

Unfortunately, the presumptuous earmarking of the EFC share prior to a Cannes 1995 meeting to discuss the $2 million fund's application irritated the European Producers' Club. Puttnam argued in a prepared memo that for the College to hold an international chair in collaboration with the MPA was not necessarily the right move. He argued that Ebeltoft does not have a 'permanent faculty or curriculum at the right professional level', and went on to state a case for London, Paris and Berlin to become Europe's three main 'shared' training chairs, with a role also for Ebeltoft. Again, unfortunately, the memo was subsequently circulated by a third party after both Donnelly and Puttnam had resolved their differences.

In a letter, Bjorn Erichsen, the College's principal at the time, made it clear that the School's business plan for a Media Training Centre (MTC) was based on the fact that 'there is no permanent faculty or curriculum for professional training at the right level anywhere in Europe. This is precisely why we have stepped forward with detailed proposals to fill at least part of the gap.'

The plan is to combine the undergraduate international film school that the School currently runs, with a new facility, the MTC, which would be solely for the use of professionals and postgraduates. The centre will develop three main faculties: business skills; new media; and script development and writing. There will also be training facilities for trainers, and plans are under way for a European equivalent of the Sundance Institute to be set up at the centre.

Erichsen also pointed to the College's track record and strengths: 'We provide one thing the national schools do not offer: The European dimension. Our last intake of 106 undergraduate students came from 27 countries.' Between May 1993 and September 1995, nearly 4,000 professionals participated in 60 training events, including workshops, seminars, conferences and roundtables.

Once the row had settled, Puttnam suggested that the role of a European version of the Sundance Institute would actually suit the European Film College very well. 'What Ebeltoft cannot claim is that it is in the right position to become the UCLA or USC of Europe, because that's not how it can function. UCLA and USC function well because they are down the road from Hollywood, so a fantastic roster of lecturers, visitors and guests can take an evening off and drive up to the Schools and do the job. Sundance could never offer that level of integration, and neither can Ebeltoft.'

However, once the European Film College's Media Training Centre is up and running at full speed by 1997–98, it could serve as a useful industry focus for professional training needs and skills, but it will need to overcome the problem of encouraging top professionals to return to the College on a regular basis. On a wider scale, Erichsen feels that the direction MEDIA II's training system is taking is wrong. The spreading of financial support to possibly more than thirty to forty training entities will simply fritter the opportunity (and the money) away. 'What Europe needs is not just one centre of excellence nor lots of smaller bodies. It needs six or seven powerhouses, like the American training centres of excellence. We need to concentrate our resources, share our knowledge and build up research.'

Others disagree, suggesting that if enough larger training projects are granted support via the Training IO, a critical mass will be achieved. What is clear is that the overall programme will be delegating far more of the responsibility to contractors than previously. Quite how those contractors will be monitored each year remains unclear.

## The future of training

On nearly every level, including the political, corporate, strategic and practical, training is clearly an acceptable horse to back. The key problems, however, appear to lie in who will fork up the money; and what freelance professionals can do about developing their skills. Despite the ECU45 million ($56 million) from the EU, and additional monies from the MPA and other national sources for domestic schemes, the truth is that there appears to be a lack of an over-riding strategy for audiovisual training in Europe. If the European audiovisual market is set to create more than two million new jobs over the coming decade, then the training implications are very large indeed. And they are yet to be adequately planned, let alone answered.

## Notes

1 National Heritage Select Committee Report, June 1995.
2 Josephine Langham, *Lights, Camera, Action! Careers in Film, Television, and Video*, BFI Book Publishing, 1993.
3 *Competence and Competition: Training and education in the Federal Republic of Germany, the United States and Japan*. An Institute of Manpower Studies report for the National Economic Development Council and Manpower Services Commission, London, MSC, 1984.

4 The *Guardian*, 'Ministry hits back as fraud undermines training plans', 13 June 1996, p. 7.
5 The *Guardian*, 'Britain trails rivals for want of skills', 14 June 1996, p. 6.
6 Details from PACT, Gordon House, Greencoat Place, London SW1, UK (Tel: 44 171 233 6000).
7 See *Cinema in the Federal Republic of German* (new edition), Hans Gunther Pflaum and Hans Helmut Prinzler. Training Facilities, 1993, pp. 218–221, 1993.
8 *The Independent Film and Television Production Sector in Ireland: Training needs to 2000*, STATCOM report prepared by the Training and Employment Authority. Project Manager: Mary Lyons. 1995.
9 Department of National Heritage, Second Report, 8 March 1995, Volume One; minutes.

# 4

# Casting and Stars

'You have to be pragmatic when you cast a project.
If a star is capable of creating the right level of revenues,
then they are worth the money we pay them.'

Stewart Till, PolyGram Filmed Entertainment

'European stars suffer from the dreadful poppy syndrome:
The press builds you up and just when
you're about to flower, they chop off your head.'

Jeremy Thomas, film producer

THE EUROPEAN FILM INDUSTRY currently suffers from an almost total lack of film stars capable of wielding box-office clout across the European continent, let alone the world. Stars are an essential ingredient in making cinema reach people. They attract finance, press coverage, hype, *frisson*, and above all, audiences to come to the cinema.

Historically, Hollywood has always acted as a magnet for talent and a pay-master for the faces that drive ticket sales. And yet precious few stars are truly 'bankable' in today's Hollywood market, and even the top marquee names cannot insure against a film's box-office failure.

Of today's $20 million elite club, whose leaders include Tom Cruise, Arnold Schwarzenegger, Jim Carrey, Sylvester Stallone, Tom Hanks and Harrison Ford, the latter is seen by the industry as one of the safest, best bargains available. Ford, whose average price per film has risen to $15 million in recent films, has starred in seven of the top 25 films of all time.

What does this say about Hollywood's continuing obsession with the birth, building and bolstering of its stars? Firstly, stars have always formed a central plank of Hollywood's economy, a role that shows no sign of decreasing. Secondly, their prices are likely to continue to rise in a game of copy-cat one-upping, fuelled by aggressive agenting and Hollywood's hunger for greater box-office revenues. In these senses, stars represent the price of doing business, but they are also a very expensive, unguaranteed insurance policy.

Above all, Hollywood's willingness to pay such huge amounts may appear to some as a strange business practice, but the irony that is worth remembering is that the star 'franchise item' is still focused, after all, on a person. Indeed, as one observer put it: 'Real movie stars are the kind of people that when you sit down to dinner you don't know if they're going to fuck you or fight you. It's about being an unpredictable human being.' Whatever their idiosyncracies, stars in Hollywood inevitably attract considerable layers of business activity around them. Tinseltown's agenting and managing system has aggressively inflated both their worth and their mystique, the latter through the guarded management of the press and publicity machine.

This Hollywood focus on a star-driven industry is completely at odds with Europe's situation today. With certain exceptions (most notably from the UK), Europe's feature films seem clogged with an array of domestically renowned actors, many of whom are struggling to win vague recognition from neighbouring countries, let alone international fame. And as this chapter explores later, the language factor allows for British talent to move with ease to an English-language run Hollywood structure, but effectively blocks nearly all non-English-language speaking stars from crossing over to the international market. The lack of a pan-European star system has major implications for an industry struggling to hold on to audiences against the powerful onslaught of Hollywood.

### Star-struck?

So what is a movie star? According to Polish director Krzysztof Zanussi, 'the definition of a movie star is very simple: it is somebody whom we all know, whom we all admire, and whom we all identify with. Stars are vehicles to express our feelings and emotions. We want to be like them. For one evening, they are us.'[1] Europe's television stars tend not to cross boundaries, which leaves film stars as the only points of reference for pan-European audiences, Zanussi argues.

Hungarian director Istvan Szabo, expanding on his philosophy about film stars discussed in the original *Dose of Reality* report, argued in an Ebeltoft Lecture in October 1995[2] that cinema is about a human face.

Hence 'it can't really be an accident that the audience asks: Who is the star? Who is this person who represents, who wants to show our life? I don't think that it's accidental that the star system was born through the cinema.'

The basis of the star system is our need to be represented: 'To have a feeling of security. To have our dreams and ambitions acted out for us. All this is happening in America: the star system is an invention of America.' Szabo points out that cinema, as a piece of propaganda for the positive American way of life, works completely differently in Europe. 'European films represent losers. Every European hero carries inside him [sic] the experience of collapsed empire, lost wars, revolution . . . The real problem is that we don't have a philosophy about the future, and that is why our stories are only about losers.'

Others, such as British Screen's Simon Perry, agrees with parts of Szabo's analysis. Perry suggests that 'the public want to go to the cinema to be with someone for a certain, anticipated experience.' For a star to flourish, he or she needs to enter an unconscious 'deal' with the audience. Fine critical performances are quite distinct from a star giving something emotional to the audience directly through the camera. And it often follows that a star will carry out a similar version of this complicity off-screen, when they are in the public eye or dealing with the press. Why? 'Because they want to be loved. They are hungry for it. Actors don't necessarily give a damn, and often clam up at those very public moments when something special is demanded of them,' Perry explains. 'It takes a certain connivance with the audience and the wider public to reach real stardom, and that's not a very European approach.'

From a marketing perspective, the link between the star and the audience is critical, as audiences know little about a film before they see it. Stars are a kind of 'brand-name recognition', suggests Caitlin Buchman, a former Hollywood agent with Triad Artists and now consultant. 'There's a way of constructing a movie star's career that allows the audience to know that they're going to have a certain kind of experience from the film. If you want to create a film industry, then you've consciously got to encourage stars to emerge.'

### The television system

Many European countries have sophisticated television star systems whose members are guaranteed the oxygen of press publicity in tankfuls.

Certainly popular drama and soap operas attract the same level of interest and have the same cultural centrality in the UK as Hollywood has in America. The tabloid papers and TV cultures run a form of populist collusion, feeding off each other's stars and the surrounding gossip. And there are TV stars who have an audience figure on their heads. Ask any UK broadcasting executive how much Richard Wilson or John Thaw are worth, and the answer will be 'ten million plus'. In addition, television stars benefit hugely from the regularity of their exposure, especially those that specialize in weekly drama or sitcom.

Part of the answer to the question, 'What is a film star?' is that the creation of a star system is a direct result of marketing – the selling of a product. What Europe's commercial section of its film industry needs to start addressing is the demand for the sophisticated creation of an appetite for actors with star potential. Once this taste is established, Europe's film-makers and shakers need to stick with the talent, and become less inhibited about selling its icons to the public. This requires money and market-driven support, but there is a further factor that seems to prevent this phenomenon from taking off.

One of the key reasons why Europe is not producing stars lies in the simple economics of the film business. It is almost impossible to make a feature film on a budget that can be recouped successfully in a single European domestic market. Among the few examples of films that perform well enough in their own territories for this to be feasible are comedies. The problem, however, is that comedies hardly ever succeed in travelling across borders. Germany's Otto series, starring Otto Waalkes; the Dutch Flodder series; the Italian comedy Johnny Stecchino, starring Roberto Benigni (which took more than $25 million domestically, and flopped abroad); and most recently, Der Bewegete Mann, which is now being remade by producer Bernd Eichinger into English, are all prime examples of comedy's failure to appeal across a domestic border.

Foreign-language films that do perform well across borders don't necessarily depend on star pulling-power. Rather, they are often films that are more emotionally resonant and universally accessible, including Il Postino, Cinema Paradiso and My Life as a Dog. Il Postino also benefited from a heroic marketing campaign by Miramax Films, which successfully backed the film for top Oscar nominations rather than settle for the foreign-language nod. The result was a worldwide box-office gross of more than $70 million.

Beyond specific genres, the nationally fragmented nature of much of

Europe's industry works against the creation of star power. In contrast to the studio- and agent-dominated Hollywood environment, Europe suffers from, at best, an ad-hoc, hand-to-mouth approach. There are no mature pan-European agent or distribution systems (see Chapter 8), although both areas are amply filled by equivalent American entities where Hollywood feels they are profitably appropriate. As ACE's Colin Young puts it: 'There is clearly a reluctance on the part of the [European] producer and agent to commit to talent who will be big later in their careers. This investment process is crucial to help a production system to work effectively.'

## The 'Nouvelle Vague' legacy

If the European film industry is failing to create stars today, how did it manage during the New Wave period of the 1960s, when it seemed to make stars out of both directors and actors? Figures such as Jean-Paul Belmondo, Brigitte Bardot, Alain Delon, Marcello Mastroianni and Gina Lollobrigida enjoyed successful followings across Europe and attracted attention in the US as well. But somewhere along the line European cinema culture stopped wanting to create a cinematic version of the boy or the girl of the year.[3]

More specifically, Europe's glaring lack of what Hollywood calls 'star vehicles' – films with high-profile, strongly written lead roles – is of no help in promoting its talent. Indeed, Sophia Loren virtually launched a 'back to basics' campaign at the Berlin Film Festival in 1994, where she argued that 'the crisis throughout the European cinema is due to a lack of really good stories and strong scripts. Without these, the public isn't likely to want to come and see our films.'

But the rose-tinted spectacles of nostalgia don't necessarily help to put the current problems in perspective. How genuinely successful were *auteur* films with audiences? Some argue that *auteur* cinema failed to live up to the expectations aroused for audiences by the often exaggerated claims of the critics. And even when new stars were established, the press would all too often praise them to the skies only to pounce on their personality or private life in an effort to topple them from their pedestals. This negative cycle is described by UK producer Jeremy Thomas as 'the dreadful poppy syndrome – the press build you up and just when you're about to flower, they chop off your head.' Can Europe's newspapers, magazines, and – most influential of all – television, be encouraged to be more strategically supportive of new talent?

**'Killing someone's career is more interesting than promoting an actor over a longer period of time, and more fun than discovering them. And it sells newspapers more quickly.'**

Simon Perry, British Screen

Across most of Europe, the press is a more powerful tool than the cinema business. Newspapers and magazines are not dependent on cinema for advertising income at the same level as North America; while film journalists (with the exception of critics) tend to see themselves as distinct and separate from the cinema business. This was demonstrated very clearly at Critical Times, an event at the European Film College in June 1995, where key figures in the European press and the film industry were brought together to discuss their respective roles and explore the fact that they are often working at cross-purposes to each other.[4] Producers and distributors remained profoundly suspicious of the press's motives when covering the industry. As Simon Perry put it: 'The American Press corps sees itself as very much part of the cinema industry, but our European journalists – and most notably the British – seem to see their roles as troubleshooters.'

## The tabloid 'truths'

Sometimes the tabloids get there before an actor's career has barely started. The press treatment of Jean-Jacques Annaud's The Lover, which starred a new British actress, Jane March, is a case in point. Talking at the December 1993 European Film Academy Master Class, A Bag Full of Tricks, about the release of the French hit across the world, Annaud explained that there was a clear pattern to the movie's success: 'Latin countries liked it, Asian countries loved it, and Anglo-Saxon and German territories didn't care for it.' Part of the problem was that Guild Entertainment, the distributors in the UK, 'saw the film as provocative, something to do with sex which was nasty and dirty, so that was how it was advertised to the public.

'The worst [territory] was the UK. The actress was woken up in her hotel in Paris the day the film was released in France. Fifteen photographers from the trash tabloid press had come to take pictures, hoping that she would be with three lovers, a dog, a pig and a horse having sex in her hotel room, because the whole question in the film was: Did she or didn't she? The poor girl was born in a little place called Pinner, so the headlines became: "Pinner Up!" or "Sinner from Pinner!"'

When Annaud started to do press interviews in other territories that read the UK press, they already knew about the coverage and the angle it had taken on the film's new female star. 'It's terrible sometimes when you see the promotion going wrong, but it's because the public wants it this way,' he suggests. In the end, however, he believes that the problem lies in the relationship between the film-makers and their audience: 'It's a weakness for film-makers to blame distributors, producers or financiers. I think the problem is to do with ideas and style. Whenever I fail, I blame myself.'[5]

## The ambivalence barrier

Even European actors who have made it in North America feel ambivalent about what it means to be a star. For example, Swedish actor Max von Sydow has starred in European films and featured in many Hollywood films. He suggests that a star is 'born just at the very moment when the right person appears at the right time in the right film. That is less a matter of talent than charisma. The audience wants to be able to identify with the star. In America, the film industry lends a helping hand at times. Stars there are also formed by their producers and PR agencies. Film-making in the US is very much a business. In Europe, where film-making is regarded as an art-form, this is more difficult. The public is much more critical of actors, and often actually doesn't allow them to become stars. And we European actors – especially if we come from smaller countries – have also developed within ourselves a different kind of consciousness. I can quite easily accept being called a star in America, but I feel quite uncomfortable when people in Europe call me a star.'[6]

The will to play the star game is missing across much of the European continent – and it is hardly surprising. When a new British actress recently emerged to stardom on the back of a bunch of Hollywood movies, malicious stories flooded the British press about her childhood, her temperament on set, and how she recently sacked her agent for a bigger one. Such press is hardly an incentive to become famous, but it goes with the territory. At least the star in question has a shrewd idea about her image, and took cover as any sensible person exposed to the critical public limelight would do. The same cannot be said of many of her contemporaries. And to judge from some astonishingly unpolished press conference presentations over the past years at the major film festivals,

Europe would appear to specialize in actors who refuse to indulge in star-like behaviour.

'We need to have people who want to be stars. You cannot only make them,' Wim Wenders argues. 'It's incredibly hard work to be a star and you have to be ready to do that work. That's so much more of an American tradition. A lot of European actors who mostly have a theatre background are not ready to do that work. And you cannot blame them, because some of that work is destructive. Success is almost a reason to be punished in some European countries, where stars get overly criticized and hurt, and then withdraw and go back to the theatre. In that atmosphere, it's difficult to become a star.'

## The business of casting

From a Hollywood perspective, when it comes to choosing the star, the key factors are whittled down to three basic elements: 'One, they're really good acting a particular role. Two, they put bodies in seats. And three, they're willing to go out and work for a movie,' said former MCA chairman Tom Pollock. 'Of the three, number two is most important.'

Playing to the audience and its expectations is clearly a defining part of Hollywood stardom. Even those who don't conform to any star models find that the system is obsessed with their changing fortunes. Post-Unforgiven's Oscar haul and $100 million US gross, Clint Eastwood could command multi-million dollar fees on In the Line of Fire ($102 million US gross), while opting to take a director/actor handle on A Perfect World for a gross percentage of the profits and no up-front fee. His 'price' is based only partly on his lengthy track record, but more importantly, on the status gained or lost from his *previous* movie.

This notion of 'current status' and its constant redefinition is on the tip of Hollywood's agents' and executives' tongues on a daily basis. Specifically, the Eastwood myth has also climbed thanks to his directorial and creative development, rather than from help from the marketing hype used to create younger star specimens. And while the key business role stars play in the overall system is not new, their salaries have been rising consistently over the past decade. Given that today's Hollywood studio budgets are averaging around $37 million, up at least $10 million from 1990, A-list stars are perceived to be one of the main areas of film-making costs which have pushed budgets upwards.

Larger European-financed films and their key casting decisions come down to economics very similar to Hollywood's. 'You mustn't get hung up on the philosophy surrounding stars,' warns PolyGram's Stewart Till. 'You have to be pragmatic when you cast a project. Do you want to pay X million for Meg Ryan in French Kiss? Will it add to the pre-sales and the distribution revenues by at least that amount? If a star is capable of creating the right level of revenues, then they are worth the money we pay them.

'PolyGram was incredibly pleased about Andie Macdowell being cast in Four Weddings and a Funeral. But we had not been so wildly pleased about Hugh Grant. And yet while 95 per cent of the excitement was Andie, the reality when it came to the release of the film was that they were attracting attention on at least a 50/50 basis.'

There exists a direct correlation between which actors are in a film, and how a producer can position that film in the market-place. If the film does not have a 'bankable' name or an interesting combination offered by the two lead roles, experienced producers and sales agents suggest that it will need some other kind of 'USP' – unique selling point – to reach the market-place and find an audience. This is a crucial area of project preparation. Unfortunately, the answer the majority of the market-place seems to accept – sometimes to its strategic and financial detriment – is that American stars are still the safest bet when in reality they are completely inappropriate. A recent example was the potential casting of Bill Paxton for a Finola Dwyer-produced film of Douglas Kennedy's novel, Dead Heart. None of the film-makers felt that the actor was really right for the material, but Samuel Goldwyn were looking for 'insurance' for their risk to, arguably, the creative damage of the project. Paxton's recently gained clout meant that Goldwyn could bank on the film 'opening' in North America.

On the other hand, the overall reliance on US actors *per se* is under re-appraisal. 'If you look at many British actors who are doing very well today, many of them started on those low-budget features of around £1 million or so. It's absolutely crazy for producers of these smaller films to think that by putting an American name in a European project, it's going to help it. All it does is block indigenous talent from moving up the ladder,' says a London-based talent agent.

## The seller's viewpoint

International sales agents are also unimpressed by low ranking American names. 'This sort of casting is inane,' complains J&M's Mike Ryan. 'It's like putting Forest Whitaker in The Crying Game. That was just daft, because it didn't get them a deal anywhere. These kinds of films should be made true to their cultural roots.' But even using indigenous actors creates problems. 'When J&M comes across potential UK films, we often have a real difficulty selling them in the international market on their casting. Take an example: Paul McGann. He's very talented, but what can I do with him? Does he get me a pre-sale in the rest of the world or North America? No.'

On the other hand, specialist sales companies who handle foreign-language films are generally more concerned with the quality of the material and the track-record of the director than specific casting decisions. CiBy Sales have faced few obstacles pre-selling a host of director-led films, including Mike Leigh's Secrets and Lies, which most distributors snapped up well before its successful outing at the Cannes Film Festival in 1996. This was despite lacking actors approaching an international, bankable 'name'.

Just as non-English-speaking actors in English-language material can be an obvious hitch, so too can the casting of English actors in foreign-language films. With the exception of an actress like Kristin Scott-Thomas (Autobus, Four Weddings), who is flawlessly fluent in French, casting a 'name' is simply detrimental to the material unless that character fits a specific English-speaking role. Carole Myer, former head of The Sales Company, was happy to see Julie Christie pass on Antonia's Line, because in her mind the film was always going to be stronger in its own Dutch language than in English, even if the sales potential was to be drastically reduced (see Case Study 8).

A dissection of the structures of the European and North American approach helps to illustrate this. German producer and former actor Dieter Geissler explains that when a North American international distributor (i.e. sales company or studio) 'compiles its guarantee list for a film, the prices demanded are based first of all on the film's genre and the prominence of its leading actors, and not – apart from a few exceptions – on the name of the director. In Europe, the emphasis is almost always on the director. The price of a film in each different licence area is based essentially on the respective television profits and not on possible cinema success. While the American distributors aim for profits running into millions of dollars, their European counterparts must content themselves with six-figure sums. If we don't succeed in recreating European stars, European film is going to become even more stunted in the TV-film mode, and the Americans will be left with an open field at the box-office.'

## The British–Hollywood axis

Hollywood has never had a problem attracting stars and directors from Europe and the rest of the world. Even the rare European stars who are breaking through today tend to have been created by Hollywood rather than by Europe's own film culture. Take the recent spate of British and Irish actors who have risen to international fame on the back of Hollywood exposure and Academy Award success.

The impressive list includes Daniel Day-Lewis, Gary Oldman, Emma Thompson, Hugh Grant, Anthony Hopkins, Jeremy Irons, Miranda Richardson, Alan Rickman, and, most recently, Liam Neeson, Tim Roth, Ralph Fiennes and Julia Ormond. The majority of these actors have arrived as a new generation – following on from a smaller range of actors in the Bob Hoskins, Gabriel Byrne mould, and older stars such as Michael Caine, Sean Connery, Terence Stamp, Julie Christie, Richard Attenborough and Albert Finney.

This new generation offers at least three or four stars – Day-Lewis, Fiennes and Grant included – for whom a Hollywood studio is prepared to put up to $40 million. British actors have never had that sway with the studios previously. Most of the above started their careers in television, the theatre and smaller British films before making their way to Hollywood, and some of them are still happy to work on independent (as opposed to studio) projects.

The exploitation of low-budget UK movies that won distribution and attention in North America has also assisted the rise of these new stars. Take the Oscar-winning Day-Lewis (My Beautiful Laundrette, My Left Foot) and Grant (Four Weddings), both of whom climbed on the back of the American marketing machine. Miramax Films' role as an aggressive independent distributor and outstanding marketeer has also been a key factor in their advance. After the public's appetite was whetted, the studios then set about forcing these talented actors down the throats of the media – a kind of catapulting into the Hollywood global star system – which, via its global tentacles, has promoted them to international fame. It is unthinkable that their names would be known across the world today if it had been left to the marketing forces of the British industry.

There is also a much younger flock of English-speaking actors who are just arriving. They include Ian Hart (Backbeat, Land and Freedom), Ewan McGregor (Shallow Grave, Trainspotting), Tara Fitzgerald (Hear My Song, Sirens), Kerry Fox (Angel At My Table, Shallow Grave), Jeremy

Northam (The Net, Emma) and Kate Winslet (Heavenly Creatures, Sense and Sensibility). According to one top London talent agent, 'at a certain budget, these actors in themselves become financable. Take Colm Meany (The Commitments, The Snapper), who if you put in a decent film, Miramax will pay for, because they're part of Harvey [Weinstein's] family.'

Producers of films in the English language are starting to enjoy a wider and (at the right level of budget) more bankable choice of actors than ever before. But still their relationship with the talent agents remains strained and suspicious. ICM Ltd's managing director Michael Foster suggests that this is due to the special position that agents find themselves in. 'The closeness to actors and stars frightens producers because they recognize talent as the element that will green-light the film.' And neither Hollywood studios nor independent investors will green-light a film without key casting locked into place.

## The French system

France is the only other European country that has a star system, and it is far less dependent on Hollywood than the UK's. In France, a producer can set up films with actors who have a value attached to their names. While the majority of French film funding comes via television, cinema is absolutely central to the nation's cultural life. The press and public attention paid to the likes of Catherine Deneuve, Daniel Auteuil, Emmanuelle Beart, Isabelle Adjani, Sandrine Bonnaire, Irene Jacob, Charlotte Gainsbourg, Romaine Bohringer, Sophie Marceau, Juliette Binoche, and, of course, Gérard Depardieu, is very high indeed.

Each day, considerable numbers of pages of Le Monde and other newspapers are devoted to cinema; entire magazines are based on the film industry, with photographs, puff pieces and so on, while television offers more cinema magazine programmes than any other European country. Quite distinct from the role that critics play, France has a populist press that simply reflects the place that cinema enjoys in its everyday life. The industry, in turn, feeds on all the attention and hype – including Europe's premier film festival at Cannes – and exploits it to keep the machine well oiled.

But what works in France does not help to push Europe as a whole any further down the road towards solving its star problem. One reason is that few French stars travel successfully. Even such a talented actress as Juliette Binoche – winner of the European Actress of the Year Felix for

Les Amants du Pont Neuf – commands no real weight on film projects outside her native country. Sales companies point to her uneven performance in Louis Malle's Damage, suggesting how hard it is for French actors to move across into English-language films. The brutal point is that even if they can speak English, it will be with a limiting accent that directly affects their international box-office status.

Even Depardieu, despite more than 60 films over the past 20 years, encounters considerable resistance outside his home territory due to the language barrier. Independent film distributors claim that although Depardieu is the only major non-English speaking star on the international market, his name alone cannot open a film. His English-language version of Mon Père ce Héros performed only moderately in the US, and his box-office figures for English-language films in general have tended to be significantly lower than for French-speaking ones (with the exception of Green Card). Ridley Scott's 1492: Conquest of Paradise was a hit in France – where Depardieu spoke French – but performed rather less impressively in the US and the UK. Over the past two years he has been reading an increasing number of English language screenplays and is concentrating on improving his English-speaking potential. The implication is that Depardieu's reach will be limited if he remains bound by his native tongue.

'The problem, loud and clear, is that French (and most continental) actors don't speak English well,' says one agent. 'The jury is out on Sophie Marceau (Braveheart), Jean Renot (Leon) and Irene Jacob (Victory), but Depardieu and Binoche, for example, have clearly struggled in the English-language films they've done.' Emmanuelle Beart (Mission Impossible) could be added to the list. Often praised for her French-language performances, her role opposite Tom Cruise attracted the few negative critical mentions of an otherwise much-admired blockbuster. Marceau may find more critical recognition in William Nicholson's Firelight, a moving period film fully funded by Disney and due for release at the end of 1996, alongside the title role in Anna Karenina, also in the English language.

There are French actors who might have become bankable international stars but who haven't quite made it. Isabelle Hupert, albeit recently playing a key role in Hal Hartley's Amateur, has never managed to cross over to Hollywood successfully. Others, like Christophe Lambert, have managed to carve out a mainstream 'niche' in science fiction and action films; but Lambert remains more of a video household name than a theatrical draw.

## Casting careers

The factors against foreign-language actors making it into the star category are many. Part of the problem is that there exists a string of clichéd expectations of foreign acting roles in Hollywood movies, starting with the fact that foreigners are always cast as villains. Take Alan Rickman and Jeremy Irons, who both played bad guys in different Die Hard 'instalments'; Sean Bean, the terrorist in Patriot Games; Nigel Hawthorne, the wicked ruler in Demolition Man; Jeroen Krabbe, the double-crossing doctor in The Fugitive; Armin Mueller Stahl, the murderous father in The Music Box; and Gary Oldman, who seems happy to blend Dracula with murderous villains and corrupt cops at every moment, and who, with the exception of his commercially unsuccessful portrayal of Beethoven, hasn't played a true hero for many years.

Agents tend to be critical of their rivals' career planning. Some suggest that many European actors spend too long in negative roles, and never make the crossover to the good guy. Opportunities, however, to play top heroic or postive roles are rare. This kind of planning is about building a franchise. According to Caitlin Buchmann, former Triad Artists agent and now a Los Angeles film development and packaging expert, 'Every actor or star is a franchise. Smart actors consider their icon to be a separate entity from their person. They manage that icon like anyone would manage a franchise. Disney is a good example of a studio that has a library of characters that they protect, exploit, and top up. Disney protects Mickey Mouse. The studio doesn't put Mickey in a pornographic piece because it understands that Mickey has no value in the family market after the animated skin-flick comes out.'

Certain agents are privately concerned about a talented young actor like Ralph Fiennes, who some suggest has done one bad guy too many. 'Ralph should never have done Strange Days,' suggests one agent. 'That was a very bad choice. If you go back and look at his track record, you'll see that he was dark, evil and brooding in Wuthering Heights; dark as you could possibly be as Goethe in Schindler's List, and not exactly the hero in Quiz Show. Following Strange Days, I don't think the American audience will go to see Fiennes as a lead. You have to be a good guy. Otherwise you end up like Sam Neill, who is a tremendously nice person, but has played rotten roles for the past five years.'

Take Jeremy Northam, a young British actor who recently popped up in Los Angeles to suddenly find himself facing Sandra Bullock in a studio meeting. She liked his reading, and he was signed for The Net on the spot. It was, however, a negative 'bad guy' role. When he returned to the UK, he was advised to play a positive role, which he found in Emma.

'You have to remember that there's a paucity of leading American actors at present,' says one commentator. 'When young British actors get off the plane in LA – many of whom are good looking and very well trained – then bang! They're in the films. They are relatively inexpensive and they are second-rank stars. Above all, they work.'

## What can be done?

While British and English-language speaking actors have access to the Hollywood system, and France continues to service its own industry but not much else, the rest of Europe finds itself marginalized in its quest for stars. Some heavyweight European film figures have suggested, with a hint of irony, that a pan-European fund should be set up to invest exclusively in the marketing of European film-acting talent. Publicists, meanwhile, continue to point to the conspicuous dearth of European stars who interest the international press. 'It's hard to get the British and French press excited about each other's new hopefuls,' says Mayfair International's Zakiya Powell, an experienced former film publicist and now a sales agent.

> **'I think you need to take the press out to the films
> to write about new talent, because we need to raise the level of
> recognition of potential stars.
> And that goes for the American press as well as the Europeans.
> We need to budget for this kind of marketing of stars.'**
>
> Zakiya Powell, Mayfair International

Other areas of the fragmented European industry have a considerable impact on the cultivation of stars. All too often, European films dribble out in a number of countries over a period of months (and sometimes years), by which time that cast's members are busy on their next projects and are unavailable to help with promotional campaigns.

Certainly more sophisticated links with the international press are required, especially in developing some kind of faithfulness to Europe's cinematic star power. But above all, a major change in perceptions has to take place. Somehow we don't support our cinema talent in the same way we do our theatre and television talent. Europe's film industry needs to use more imagination and commercial verve when it comes to exploiting its considerable talent. After all, it's not as though that talent doesn't exist: Europe produces genuinely skilled, creative actors every year. The task is to make them worth something on the big screen.

It is this area of discussion that forms the basis of the European Film Academy's debate on the future of Europe's film stars, 'The Actor's Value: Does Europe need a star system?' In addition to looking at promotional and marketing strategies, the Academy points out the scant opportunities for specialized training of screen actors in Europe. Held during the London Film Festival, in November 1996, at the same time as this book was launched, the Academy hopes that concrete proposals and new initiatives can be pioneered to help Europe's cinematic cheerleaders do precisely that.

## Notes

1 *A Dose of Reality: The State of European Cinema*, Angus Finney, Chapter 3, 1993.
2 Istvan Szabo's Ebeltoft Lecture is available in *Final Cut: The yearbook of European Film College 1995–6*, pp. 54–6.
3 See *Falling Stars, Sight & Sound*, Angus Finney, pp. 22–6, September 1994.
4 For further information and a report of the event, see the European Film Academy's *Felix* magazine, issue Winter 1995; and *Final Cut: The Yearbook of European Film College 1995–6*.
5 *Ibid, Falling Stars, Sight & Sound*.
6 *A Dose of Reality: The State of European Cinema*, Angus Finney, Chapter 3, 1993.

# 5

# Europe's Corporate Players

'Russian—Jewish immigrants came from the shtetls and ghettos
out to Hollywood . . .
In this magical place that had no relationship to any reality they
had seen before in their lives, or that anyone else had ever seen,
they decided to create their idea of an eastern artistocracy . . .
The American Dream – is a Jewish invention.'

Jill Robinson, from Neal Gabler's
*An Empire of Their Own: How the Jews Invented Hollywood*[1]

'The real global films will be those ones that are totally able to
adapt to local culture.
Worldwide culture does exist in music, movies like Apollo 13 and
TV series like Baywatch, but thriving on that alone you will never
get a worldwide entertainment company.'

Alain Levy, president and chief executive of PolyGram

THE LONGSTANDING DEBATE about the state of Europe's cinema has tended to focus, somewhat unhealthily, on state and public support over the past decade. Propping up our film-makers and protecting national cultures has dominated discussion, while commercial imperatives and their blue-chip carriers have been largely laid to one side. The danger of such protective and essentially defensive obsessions has been to ignore the qualities that commercial entities can bring to Europe's film-making practices.

Over the past three years, Europe has nevertheless witnessed the emergence of certain key corporate players, some of whom are beginning to carve out a dominant position not just within Europe but across the international film market. For the purposes of this chapter, the analysis is divided into two distinct sections: physical studios, such as Pinewood, Barrandov and Babelsberg; and corporate players such as PolyGram Filmed Entertainment, which fit closer to the Hollywood model of a vertically integrated 'Major' film company, with co-ordinated development, production and distribution interests.

## The Hollywood heritage

The contemporary film-world's peculiarly lop-sided shape points all interested observers back to the roots of Hollywood. The seeds of uprooted European immigrants growing up under the Californian sunshine certainly played their respective roles in the building of the Hollywood studio system, but above all, the Jews who invented Hollywood succeeded through their 'sustained attempt to live a fiction, and to cast its spell over the minds of others'. Louis B Mayer, Adolph Zukor, Benjamin Warner, Carl Laemmle and William Fox came from Central and Eastern Europe, and shared poor and emotionally alienating childhoods. They may not have easily shared the same language, but they held a common determination to re-invent themselves in a new country. What author Neal Gabler and other historians have pondered is the extraordinary extent to which these people managed to champion their fiction across the world. Indeed, 'the Hollywood Jews created a powerful cluster of images and ideas – so powerful that, in a sense, they colonized the American imagination. No one could think about [America] without thinking about the movies.'[2]

When most people from around the world choose to consider Europe's defining world, images of art, architecture, literature and theatre spring to mind. And, ironically, these elements conspire to suggest one overriding contemporary image – one of chocolate-box tourist attractions. Individuals may also focus on one country, where they have previously visited or have family – reflecting Europe's historical fragmentation – but they will not instantly pipe-up about Europe's cinema unless, by some slim chance, they are in love with the medium to begin with.

## Approaching risk

That Europe's cultural relationship to cinema is different to Hollywood's is fundamental to understanding the European film industry's plight today. Hollywood's origins and the subsequent development of a corporate studio system has had enormous implications on the way the international film business operates today.

The Hollywood studio approach is relatively successful for a number of key reasons. Bearing in mind that nothing is certain in the film business, studios always aim to reduce risk. Hollywood does this in two key ways. First, to combat the lack of certainty, the US studios make a slate of films all aimed at the commercial market-place, and spread their investment risk. The so-called slate strategy assumes that for every 25 or so films they make a year, perhaps four or five will be profitable, one or two hit blockbuster status, and the rest will make a loss. None of the studios know which films will be successful, so the wider they spread their possible chances, the more options they have for winning.

Secondly, through vertically integrated distribution networks, including video, new licensing rights and television output deals, the US studios can shorten the period of recoupment, and edge closer to the 'profit-head'. They are also able to limit their exposure by off-loading some of the risk prior to production, by pre-selling certain rights. As David Puttnam and others have often pointed out, the US film industry is underpinned by pay-cable and video. 'All the major studios and the largest independent production entities have output deals with ancillary distributors that guarantee them a return of a third or even a half of the physical costs of their movies. We have no similar arrangement in place in Europe.'

Other considerations that point to the strength of critical mass help the studios limit risk. The strength and size of the studio libraries – basically large banks of film licence rights that the studio owns – gives them the opportunity to sell poor-performing films to ancillary distribution while driving those sales with blockbuster hits. Such clout in the secondary market-place helps secure loans from the banking community at favourably low rates of interest.

'Warners have probably dealt with the same bank for years when it comes to the movie division's cash loans,' explained Puttnam. 'The terms for anything from $500 million to $1 billion are really low, at around 2.75 per cent annual interest, compared to a British company, which is probably paying around 8 to 9 per cent a year. Both the lower cash expense and the hidden assets mean that you can't analyse the success or failure of the American studios on the same basis as any European outfit.'

The final major advantage Hollywood has over Europe is its concentration of film-making activity in one place: Los Angeles. The ramifications of a centre for talent, technicians and money to gravitate towards should not be underestimated. The seven or eight Major film studios stuck within a few miles of one another have always helped Hollywood's actions and impact be greater than the sum of its parts. Far from being a United States-run industrial centre, Hollywood is a magnet for all film-making talent, wherever it was born, or whatever the colour of its money. Even the smaller independent companies benefit from the talent cluster and level of activity in one place, picking up pieces left over from the Majors, and discovering new talent that then moves up the ladder.

Europe has never been able to offer such a focused centre for film activity. Neither does it ever look likely to do so.

## European barriers

While the Hollywood studios seek to minimize risk, the present European structures of subsidy finance and pre-sales to television have all but snuffed out market-driven entrepreneurialism. As film consultant and author Martin Dale points out: 'There are no Majors that pool risks, and few individual film producers have a consistent record of financial success ... Lack of risk makes it possible to produce a sub-standard product, because it doesn't make any difference – it's pre-sold anyway.'[3]

Financing films from Europe's private sector is very difficult, however, mainly due to the lack of an integrated infrastructure, which would help reduce the inherent risks of production. Even those independent producers who try to hold on to their rights and build up libraries still find that bank financiers (as opposed to private investors) will not be interested in bankrolling their slates. The problem is the lack of leverage that comes from critical mass – as any professional financier will want to know that there is at least twice as much money available in the underlying rights as the loan the producer is asking for.

According to Dale and other film industry analysts, the long-term basis for lifting the performance of the European film industry is to 'improve the way in which it is "published" and "commercialized".' Dale argues that this requires a two-tiered approach. On one level, producers need to operate more like 'labels' – co-ordinating their marketing and distribution strategies, and developing vertical integration in exhibition, distribution and production. On a second level, there is a need for media groups which can bring several such 'labels' together under a single umbrella to achieve greater critical mass. However, rather than suggest that Europe needs to create monolithic studios, Dale argues that multi-publishing houses could attract creative talent and develop sophisticated marketing and distribution strategies which would make the best use of such talent.

## THE STUDIOS

Europe's traditional 'studios' – as distinct from corporate multi-publishing concerns – are mere shadows of their former powerhouses of pre- and post-war production. The only real exceptions are found in the UK and Ireland, which have both enjoyed recent buoyant production booms. Nevertheless, industry commentators constantly fail to make the distinction between a studio as a production-service entity and a fully integrated 'studio' in the vertically integrated Hollywood sense. The latter may include a studio production lot, but this is just one component of a multi-layered series of creative and business investments.

European studio lots tend to be acting as petrol stations for Hollywood juggernauts, rather then generating their own development and production material. As producer Stephen Woolley explained to *Screen International* while shooting Neil Jordan's Michael Collins, 'The problem with England is that the studios feel a bit like hospitals. They're stuck in time around the 1950s. There's no consistency of film production to provide that US studio feel.'[4]

### The British situation

While consistent business may be lacking, the UK studios have been experiencing a boom period during 1994 and 1996, boosted by a considerable re-birth in domestic film production. Back in 1985 some 47 British films were made, including films such as Stephen Frears' My Beautiful Laundrette and Peter Greenaway's A Zed and Two Naughts. Unfortunately, the figure soon dropped to a desperate 27 films by 1989, which should be compared to recent levels of 73 films a year for 1994 and 1995 respectively. And while fewer than half of the recent films were 100 per cent UK-financed, the overall up-swing is significant in terms of finance, employment activity and the positive atmosphere that currently buzzes around the UK film studios.

Both Pinewood and Shepperton were bursting with business during the summer of 1996, housing blockbusters such as Luc Besson's $75 million The Fifth Element, Philip Noyce's The Saint and putting the final editing touches on Disney's live version of *101 Dalmatians*. Meanwhile, Elstree – long written off as dead and buried – re-opened under new owners during June 1996 in time to service Stanley Kubrick's first film for a decade, Eyes Wide Shut, to star Tom Cruise and Nicole Kidman.

## Europe's production houses

Typical of the French knee-jerk recourse to subsidy, France's flailing studio structures were bailed out by the former minister of culture, Jacques Toubon, who launched a programme under which films shooting in France were entitled to a larger share of the country's automatic aid system. The move won back Jean-Pierre Jeunet and Marc Caro's The City of the Lost Children to Arpajon Studios, having orginally been planned to be shot at Germany's Babelsberg. Meanwhile, Studios La Victorine in Nice hasn't handled a major film for a decade, and still requires major investment to bring its sound stages up to standard. Boulogne-Billancourt, the twin studios on the banks of the Seine, have suffered from political and financial confusion over recent years. Property group Compagnie Immobilière de Phenix (CIP) is to re-develop Billancourt, while the Boulogne studios are still running, and recently serviced Poly-Gram's French Kiss.

Italy's Cinecitta has witnessed an upturn, housing Cliffhanger, The Godfather Part III, and Sylvester Stallone's recent Daylight. Huge areas of space and lower costs have helped the studio keep its head above water, after going through a dance with potential bankruptcy at the start of the 1990s. Meanwhile, Spain has no significant studio capable of housing a serious-size film.

The Central and Eastern European studios have started to provide some significant competition since political and economic changes have begun to take proper hold. Koliba Film Studios in the Slovak Republic; Hungary's Mafilm and Prague's Barrandov Studios have all serviced major productions since 1994, and their international marketing operations make much of their lower prices, especially compared to the UK and Germany.

## The Barrandov experience

AB Barrandov represents an extraordinary turnaround from the situation in early 1991, the point when Czech Republic State subsidies were turned off and the complex had to become self-financing. The studio had 2,700 employees, a huge debt, no marketing plan and no domestic market. As Vaclav Marhoul, the managing director of AB Barrandov (sacked by his board and then re-instated during 1994), said, 'it was a crazy situation'.

His immediate response was to cut daily expenditure drastically, reduce the number of domestic films being shot at the studio, increase foreign productions and lay off hundreds of members of staff. He also restructured the studio into separate companies, dividing the studio's facilities into 18 separate profit divisions, and instigating a cost-saving incentive scheme for each divisional manager. Marhoul built on the studio's strong history of American, German and French productions, quickly attracting Hollywood Pictures' Swingkids, and gradually getting the number of foreign serviced and co-produced films up to ten per year by 1995. Rather than just looking West, Marhoul also discovered that Russian productions were an excellent potential market. Producers were complaining about the high costs of Russian studios, including problems like poor film development facilities, poor (and manipulated) dollar-rate exchanges and instant video piracy of any completed films. His efforts were also helped by a steadying Krone and a reasonable inflation rate which had settled at around 10 per cent by the end of 1995.

Quite separate from the studio operation, Marhoul is also running a film production and distribution operation, and controls the sales rights of the 800-title studio library. Development of screenplays is high up Marhoul's list of priorities, with a special Barrandov screenwriting foundation and at least 20 projects in development by 1996. The production wing of the studio produces just two domestic films a year, but has become pro-active in co-producing foreign films in return for Czech Republic and sometimes wider territorial rights. And now that AB Barrandov is making an operating profit, Marhoul is also prepared to invest equity in international productions, whether they are shooting at his studios or not. And he has adjusted to recent state privatization of television by building two state-of-the-art TV sound stages in 1994 to 1995. Moreover, his acquisition of Czech communications company Metropolitan Information Systems (MIS) has given Barrandov access to 400 kilometres of fibre-optic cable systems that will make the studio a major player in cable TV, information systems and other new technologies.

Many producers who have recently worked at the studio have been impressed, but not all. However, the problems experienced by the

Mission Impossible crew were to do with local government officials hedging for higher payments and the city's fluctuating prices rather than the studio itself. Marhoul bluntly asked Tom Cruise's company if his public complaints were to do with Barrandov, and the reply was a firm 'No'. Prices may be stable in Prague, but foreigners are expected to pay 60 per cent more for normal goods than locals, which has a significant impact on food and hotel costs.

But the studio also has some way to go before it can be happy with its international servicing. One recent potential client felt that the price list was not flexible enough, and was worried about the standard of the film processing facilities. Marhoul is acutely aware of the need to continue to develop the new technical facilities, but intimates that many 'bad news' stories have been put around by the studio's biggest rival, Babelsberg in Berlin.

Marhoul points to the difference between the German studio's French owners, with deep pockets and an over-riding obsession with real estate, and Barrandov's 'self-made' entrepreneurial private ownership model. 'At Babelsberg they have the money for investment and huge subsidies [nearly $100 million to date] from the Brandenburg region, while Barrandov has no state support, so we have to be more flexible and efficient.'

## The Babelsberg disappointment

So what of the German competition? Back in the autumn of 1993, Volker Schloendorff was at the centre of one of Europe's real hopes, heading up both the Babelsberg Studios at Potsdam, and its production company attached to the privatized site. While conceding that the 'mere existence of one company would not be able to answer how to make successful European films', Schloendorff suggested that he had an opportunity 'to develop scripts in a similar way to the American approach. We can hire writers, and work with teams of them from different European countries, and try to push scripts through a range of different stages towards production.'

Specifically, Schloendorff argued that there are enough small European pictures going into production every year. 'What Europe needs to develop are more large movies. I think we can create this through strategy. The only European films that have been truly successful throughout the whole of Europe over the last ten years or so were Cyrano De Bergerac, The Name of the Rose, The Lover, and earlier,

The Tin Drum. They all happened to be bigger-budget movies at $10 million or more, and unfortunately, they are all period pictures, but at least they united European audiences.' The Babelsberg head's dream was to build a German-based 'European Hollywood' media capital, blazing with productions and attracting a multi-dimensional level of work around the studio complex.

So far, the dream of growing into a production powerhouse has not materialized. By the autumn of 1995, Schloendorff conceded in a long interview in *Die Zeit*,[5] that while the physical re-structuring and modernizing of the former UFA and DEFA studio site has gone well, production – 'an area I thought I could handle with my eyes shut – I misjudged. We've taken part in 17 films of which none was a success. That's quite a record after having previously produced 17 films within a 20-year period, all of which were at least consistent. I've really had a raw deal. I believe that I can choose projects for myself, lead a team and win through, but I can't choose projects for others. I can't recognize whether material will be a success or not. Other people can do that better.'

Schloendorff readily accepts that he under-estimated, back in 1992 when he took over the challenge of running Babelsberg, how quickly his dream could be realized. Trapped between low Eastern European prices and the close British relationship with the Hollywood studios, Babelsberg was too slow to develop its television services and was left picking up the pieces when it came to housing larger international productions. High-profile projects that the studio won over – including PolyGram's La Machine and UGC's Une Femme Française – were dwarfed by mediocre co-productions like Mesmer, Victory and A Couch in New York, or films like The House of the Spirits or The City of Lost Children that eventually ended up shooting elsewhere in Europe.

Despite the very public problems, Schloendorff pointed out that Babelsberg's investors are content to see that production is growing and that there is a turnover rise by the end of 1995 of 10 per cent. 'The project is running as estimated, but . . . I do have doubts about why we don't make better German films. Why is there no exciting entertainment cinema in Europe?' Figures for 1995 were actually more positive, showing that revenue for the studio was up 40 per cent, to around $30 million, but that productions had fallen by 5 to 15 feature and TV projects.

While the interview resulted in a subsequent clarification about the relation between the Berlin Brandenburg Filmboard and Babelsberg, the damage was done. German producers and film-makers who had become sceptical about the high Babelsberg prices pointed to the interview as proof that Schloendorff had lost his and the studio's way. As one producer put it: 'The real danger is that the development and production opportunity has been missed, and that the studios ultimately end up becoming yet another German television production service. We've already got plenty of them. What we need is a strong multi-layered studio that helps feature film-makers and chooses the right material to put into production.' Others are even blunter, and suggest that Schloendorff should hand over the reins to a less high-profile film-maker, but someone with more experience of running a large enterprise with an eye on the bottom line.

## THE 'MAJOR' INDUSTRIALISTS

When examining the above problems, it becomes apparent that a production studio in its broadest sense is far from consisting of a physical 'monolithic' building and production lot.

> **'The studio actually represents an industrial system, because a good one contains all the elements that you need to not just make one film, but a package of films, many times over. Once an independent producer is supported by that structure, they will expand because there are more people around them to take on ideas, share information and blend art and business. This is something you can only dream about as a producer in Denmark today.'**
>
> Danish producer Mads Christian Egmont

Such institutions, however, are multi-layered and require huge sums of investment either through straight acquisition or by a gradual development and expansion plan. Traditionally, smaller European companies have not enjoyed a promising track record when trying to run ambitious production, international sales and distribution outfits. As one US analyst puts it: 'Even if they do well, they usually end up being taken over by somebody or going bust.'

Taking Martin Dale's point about larger publishers or corporations that develop critical mass further, there are positive signs over the past three years of larger companies gradually emerging in Europe. These include France's Canal Plus, the Bouygues-owned CiBy 2000 and Chargeurs;

Germany's Bertelsmann; the Spanish group Grupo PRISA; and the Dutch-owned, London-HQ'd PolyGram Filmed Entertainment. All of these corporations have singularly different approaches to the film and television industry, partly depending on their other activities and their varied enthusiasm for getting involved in film development and production itself. One of the oft-cited disappointments in the UK is the lack of interest shown by the Rank Organisation to invest in production, preferring to handle sales, distribution and its Odeon cinema chain. However, in May 1996, Rank announced its intention to start fully financing pictures for the first time through its film distribution arm, Rank Film Distributors. The films would be in the $5 to $6 million range, but this would increase if A-list talent were involved.[6] While the announcement was met positively by the UK production community, the jury will remain out until Rank invests at a consistent and creatively constructive level.

Overall, most of the above corporations concentrate on rights ownership and control of distribution. Their activities as a whole have come to play a leading role in film sales, financing and distribution activity and give rise to a potentially dynamic new look to the European film industry.

## Cautious Bertelsmann

Talking about making major investments and acquisitions and making decisions are two completely different areas. The Bertelsmann Group, for example, has been assessing Hollywood studios since the early 1990s, and has repeatedly claimed that it has a billion-dollar war chest. However, when it considered picking up US independents Castle Rock and New Line, Ted Turner beat it to both purchases. According to consultants and accountants KPMG, 'Some Hollywood observers say that after baulking at prices paid by the Japanese, Bertelsmann may have missed the boat now that Hollywood studios have increased in value post-Paramount', when Viacom paid more than $11 billion for the studio.

Nevertheless, Bertelsmann is the leading communications group in Europe today, and has a higher turnover than Time Warner Entertainment. It has virtually no debt, and has huge publishing and music interests that generate a high level of cash flow. But rather than concentrate on development and production, the Group's film interests have veered towards the ancillary end of the market and, above all, controlling rights wherever possible. During 1995/96 BMG International talked to several UK independent distributors about joint acquisition ventures after deciding not to take a stake in the UK's First Independent. Its policy is to set up rights-buying alliances with distributors across Europe on the same terms as its existing deal with Filmax in Spain. Films recently co-financed in this manner include First Independent's pick-up of Ridley Scott's White Squall and Larry Bishop's Trigger Happy.

The group's interests in private television, notably RTL2, a joint channel launched with CLT, and Premiere, the pay-TV channel that has now broken even, should have led the company into a long-term co-operation agreement with Canal Plus in the development of future pay-TV markets. However, by mid 1996 the two groups had clashed badly over differences in policy, and the collaboration was abruptly terminated. Instead, Bertelsmann merged its TV interests with CLT in August 1996, making the groups in control of the most powerful broadcaster in Europe. Rupert Murdoch subsequently abandoned his digital TV plans with Canal Plus and Bertelsmann, and allied with Kirch, although the different factions are on talking terms again.

It is also focusing heavily on the multi-media market, concentrating on pay-per-view, video-on-demand, Home Shopping and interactive television services. With the exception of German television and film production outfit Ufa, in which it has a controlling interest (although it merged with CLT, the international media group in July 1996), Bertelsmann has yet to make the huge leap into development and production of movies. Those who have worked inside the company argue that it's unlikely to do so. The tight accounting restrictions and short-term targets that are inherent to Bertelsmann's corporate practices will always, it is argued, throw up more obstacles than pluses when it comes to spending billions of dollars on a major studio. It's not the money but the mentality that is holding the group back from making a vertically integrated commitment right the way along the line.

## Grupo PRISA's rising star

Spain's largest media conglomeration has recently made significant inroads into feature film production as part of its strategy to broaden its audiovisual activities beyond the Spanish market. The group's principal interests include stakes in Canal Plus Spain; Sogecable, a domestic cable and satellite operation, Sogetel, the film and TV production arm, and Sogepaq, the film and TV rights acquisition and distribution operation.

The company's recent big-scale English-language outing, Two Much, starring Antonio Banderas and Melanie Griffith, flopped badly in North

America in April 1996, but had already managed more than $25 million-worth of pre-sales and excellent takings in Latin countries on the European continent. The film, produced for PRISA by Andres Vicente Gomez – who has a 24-picture production deal with Sogetel – was the first step in a plan to move further into English-language production, while also trying to prise open the US market for Spanish-language films. Of the 16 or so films it produced in 1996, three were in English.

The group is planning on adding to its strong vertical integration by constructing cinemas in Spain and Latin America with a US partner, and recently launched its own Sogepaq Video label to handle all Sogepaq Distribution's product. According to Screen International's Benedict Carver, the appointment of Hollywood producer Arnon Milchan's fomer European chief, Fernando Bovaira, to head Sogetel will see the group further expand its production interests into television. The overall plan is one of a 'mini-studio' approach, with strong foundations for PRISA to build on.[7]

## The Canal Plus phenomenon

Canal Plus has not fared well in its Hollywood film production interests. In August 1991 the group bought a 10.9 per cent stake in the then leading independent production company, Carolco Pictures, which it later increased to 16 per cent. After considerable further costs and exposure, Carolco finally went into receivership in 1995. A large-scale deal with Arnon Milchan's Regency International Pictures signed in early 1991 resulted in a mixed bag of Hollywood hits and misses, while the company's own LA-based production outfit, Hexagon, failed to stay the distance. The company finally acquired Carolco's 22-strong film library for a $60 million payment in spring 1996, paying a high price for films it had already spent considerable resources bringing to the screen.

It also added the UGC 5,000-title film library to its growing collection of rights through a share-swap deal with UGC in June 1996. The deal, which gave Canal Plus access to the strong former Weintraub/Lumière library, also meant that the pay-TV operation would in the future control more than 2,000 hours of television programming in addition to the library.

On the other hand, Canal Plus looks much stronger on its home territory. Although not allowed by French law fully to produce its own material, Canal Plus is obliged to invest at least 12 per cent of its annual turnover in local production and pick-ups, which amounted to $237 million in 1996. In addition to its 'studio-like' system of equity stakes in Le

Studio Canal Plus, Ellipse, Alain Sarde and Chrysalis, along with a housekeeping deal with Flach Film, the company has recently set up its own development wing. Canal Plus Ecriture underwent a major expansion at the beginning of 1995.

A new brief allowed the development initiative to find new writing and directing talent that had tended to be marginalized by the current French system of production finance and subsidy. The new development team was headed up by Nicholas Boukhrief and Richard Grandpierre. Boukhrief is a former editor of *Starfix* magazine and Canal Plus' *Journal du Cinema*; and directed the feature Va Mourire. Grandpierre's background is in production, notably with Les Films de la Colline. He co-produced the hit comedy La Vengeance d'une Blonde. The reason for the change appeared to be due to the growing dissatisfaction at Canal Plus, particularly on the part of deputy managing director Alain de Greef, with current French films. They were neither adventurous nor spectacular enough for the broadcaster's requirements.

'Most French films we are obliged to buy have similar subjects, small theatrical audiences and go on to attract a low number of viewers when we broadcast them,' explained Grandpierre. 'We will be looking to support films that have merits that are different to those sought by the Avances Sur Recettes [France's premier discretionary subsidy body'], including for example projects that could have attracted Channel 4 or a producer like Roger Corman.

Projects are expected to come predominantly from inexperienced writers or directors, although the new team will welcome projects from more established talent who are keen to return to making smaller, more experimental films. The new-look Canal Plus Ecriture will differ from its predecessor in terms of the range of projects, and its ability to assist the development process far beyond just script re-writing. As Canal Plus is prevented by its licence from acting as a fully fledged feature-film producer, Ecriture is expected to take its projects to producers, but not before early drafts have been completed. 'That should not be taken to mean that we will let a writer go off into the wilderness for six months,' said Grandpierre. 'There will be a close follow-up of everything we do, and we will be very demanding on deadlines.'

Ecriture will 'where possible' try to break the *auteur* stranglehold, Grandpierre confirmed. 'That kind of film will be made in France anyway, and has no need for us. I think people are starting to understand that they need to work with other people and be open to criticism and suggestions. We are prepared to drop projects if someone becomes too demanding.'

On the broader front, Canal Plus has forged a link with Sony Pictures Entertainment to establish a London-based company to develop and produce films with European writers, directors and cast. The initial brief is to produce two English-language films within two years from mid 1996. Sony senior executives are keen to move the group into foreign-language pictures if the new company works out. The partners are understood to be sharing the decisions and the costs.

The deal marks a move towards European investments and market penetration by Sony Pictures Entertainment, which already has deals with the Hollywood wings of Jean-Jacques Annaud, Paul Verhoeven and Luc Besson. For Canal Plus, this looks a less expensive and risky way of accessing potentially commercial, US-backed films than its previous endeavours. However, the deal was mooted back in October 1995, and took more than six months before finally being nailed down. Quite what that implies for the speed of the joint creative decision-making operation remains to be seen.

## The Chargeurs group

The textile and communications group Chargeurs has built up an array of entertainment investment stakes, including stakes in French exhibition Major Pathe, BSkyB, UK and German distributors Guild and Tobis, Jake Eberts' company Allied Filmmakers, French satellite service Canal-satellite, and the former MGM cinema screens in the Netherlands.

In February 1996 group chairman Jerome Seydoux bought the remaining 50 per cent of Claude Berri's Renn Productions, effectively taking 100 per cent control of the company and also taking over full control of the French independent distributor AMLF. The move added to the Chargeurs library, as Renn's catalogue, built up over a 30-year period, includes the director's hits, such as Jean de Florette and Manon de Sources, as well as his productions, including Roman Polanski's Tess and Jean-Jacques Annaud's The Bear.

As for the group's UK-based development and production interest, headed up by experienced producer Timothy Burrill, finding the right projects that subsequently work for Pathe Guild Cinema's distribution and Seydoux has not been easy. As Burrill points out, 'an awful lot of the first-rate stuff which I would have supported as an independent producer goes out of the window. Unless I can get Guild excited about a screenplay or package, then I'm certainly not going to get Jerome doing his number for it.'

Burrill is looking for strong screenplays or books to option that could be packaged with a top director, like Alan Parker or Stephen Frears; but has also spent time examining the new, upcoming talent in the UK, including the likes of Danny Boyle (Trainspotting), Antonia Bird (Priest) and Michael Winterbottom (Butterfly Kiss, Jude). 'Part of the problem I keep facing is that many of these directors are making distinctly black subjects,' Burrill explains, suggesting that he sees the group's responsibility to harness new talent to projects which may have a better chance to travel, particularly in Europe.

Like Canal Plus, Chargeurs has fared less well in Hollywood than in Europe. Its minority stake in Savoy backfired when the relatively new US mini-major slammed the brakes on with huge cutbacks in 1995. It was also a heavy investor via its rights company, Pricel, in Paul Verhoeven's $40 million international bath, Showgirls. While much of Chargeurs' risk was offloaded by heavy pre-sales, the negative impact associated with high-profile flops will not sit easy with Seydoux.

## The CiBy 2000 boutique

In a move mirrored by all serious corporate investors in film, CiBy 2000 and its sales operation, CiBy Sales, are soon to be complemented with a gradually expanding international distribution outfit. Up to the start of 1996, most of the company's production exposure has been off-set by a very strong sales operation, CiBy Sales, run by Wendy Palmer in London. Now the group is looking to gain further control over the exploitation of its catalogue, both old and new.

Only a company with considerable financial pockets could have set up a feature production slate by cherry-picking the world's top *auteur* directors. Having built up a reputation for successfully working with the internationally famous, the Bouygues-controlled film operation decided to expand its annual slate of films by 1996–97. The international success of Jane Campion's The Piano and the ongoing support of Pedro Almodovar, David Lynch, Emir Kusturica, and others have attracted some new names to the CiBy roster. These include Robert Altman's Kansas City; Mike Leigh's Cannes-winning Secrets and Lies, and Paul J. Hogan's Muriel's Wedding. (See also Case Study on The Flower of My Secret, page 248].

CiBy's approach is strategically important. By showing confidence in certain perceived arthouse directors, such as Jane Campion and Mike

Leigh, it is helping European and specialist film-makers cross over to a wider audience. Actively pre-selling them into the market-place also tests their work against distributors and audiences, rather than forcing them to fall back on soft subsidy money. Hand-in-hand with that approach, the company has an extraordinary track record at the Cannes Film Festival, where The Piano, Secrets and Lies, and Underground have won the Palme d'Or in 1993, 1996 and 1995 respectively.

CiBy has close links with TF1, the French broadcaster also owned by the same parent company, Bouygues. TF1 recently announced plans to expand into film production, while CiBy simultaneously announced that it was setting up a TV production arm, CiBy Fiction, in autumn 1995.

The first project was expected to be a six-part series based on CiBy's Palme d'Or winner Underground, featuring additional footage not used in the film. The move by TF1 was partly to broaden its English-language fare and to fulfil its EU quota requirements – which demanded that it invest an extra $3 million in European production in 1995–96 for failing to hit 1994's target. It is also due to the fact that the broadcaster's activities are too concentrated in France.

## Pulling together the fragments

If European cinema is beginning to achieve a critical mass and regain its lost position at the box office, it is essential that successful corporate publishing models emerge. This is an area which, over the last five years, has started to turn a positive corner. The above companies are all not only developing vertical, integrated structures, but are often pulling up small-er companies and younger, new talent with them. Producers and public funders should take a careful look at the positive steps many of the above companies have taken, and concentrate on working with them rather than carping from the sidelines.

## Notes

1  Jill Robinson, quoted in *An Empire of Their Own: How the Jews Invented Hollywood*, Neal Gabler, p. 1, 1988.
2  *Ibid.* p. 7.
3  *Europa Europa: Developing the European Film Industry*, Martin Dale, p. 67, 1992.
4  *Screen International*, 14 July 1995, p. 12.
5  *Die Zeit*, 1 September 1995, Andreas Kilb and Christiane Peitz.
6  *Screen International*, 'UK's Rank to make move into 100 per cent film financing', Stuart Kemp, 10 May 1996, p. 1.
7  *Screen International*, 'Broken English (Analysis)', Benedict Carver, p. 13, 5 April 1996.

# POLYGRAM
# FILMED ENTERTAINMENT

## Case Study

While Europe clearly has numerous other emerging corporate powers with interests in television and film, no one entity shares quite the ambition and rate of growth that has defined PolyGram Filmed Entertainment. After a shaky re-entry in the early 1990s, PolyGram suddenly crept up on the industry when Four Weddings and a Funeral swept across the world and grossed a $260 million theatrical take. Over the following pages, Michael Kuhn talks to the author about what it is taking to create a new film studio from scratch.

### PolyGram's selected film acquisitions since 1990

| Date | Company | Stake (%) |
|------|---------|-----------|
| August 1991 | Really Useful Holdings | 30 |
| September 1991 | Propaganda Films | 100 |
| September 1991 | Working Title Films | 100 |
| August 1992 | Interscope | 100 |
| January 1995 | ITC Entertainment | 100 |
| December 1995 | Island Pictures | 100 |

### Other production interests

| | |
|---|---|
| US | Egg (Jodie Foster); Havoc Inc. (Tim Robbins) |
| France | R Films; Noe Productions; Cinea |
| The Netherlands | PFE Netherlands |

### Distribution interests (to 1997)

UK, France, Benelux, Spain, Australia, Canada, US, Germany.

When PolyGram announced that it was moving into the international film business, the news was greeted back in 1991 with scepticism. Given that the company had experienced a rough ride in the late 1970s, when its foray into film met with a stack of disappointments and the company was taken for a ride by Hollywood producers Jon Peters and Peter Guber, it seemed surprising to many that the company was returning to its celluloid graveside some 15 years later.

However, PolyGram, which is currently 75 per cent owned by the Dutch electronics giant Philips, had been growing at a tremendous rate during the 1980s – around 15 per cent at a revenue and result level – and although there was still years of growth in the record business, it was becoming harder and harder to keep up that pace without entering new businesses.

Michael Kuhn, president of PolyGram Filmed Entertainment, explained it this way: 'Obviously if you're an entertainment company, you're going to look to entertainment first. We'd had a disastrous entry into film in the late 1970s, but nonetheless, film is a $40 to $60 billion industry, which is a huge worldwide business. A lot of the skills that a company like PolyGram has on the music side – where you try to combine creative flexibility and trying to understand the creative process, but still maintain the financial disciplines of a large company – we felt could be transferred to the film industry.'

What had gone wrong in the late 1970s? Several things, explained Kuhn. 'First of all, there was some bad management on the behalf of the then management of PolyGram. Secondly, it was a terrible recession in the music industry, which coincided with a very expensive foray into film; and thirdly, the film industry was at the end of a cycle, when it had all the risk of high costs but really only two income streams – television, which wasn't very lucrative, and theatrical, which had been flat. Video and pay-TV hadn't developed properly until the early and mid 1980s, and they are two crucial components of film financing today.

'When I looked at the film industry, several things struck me. First of all, you needed a tremendous amount of capital. When you look back at Goldcrest, and consider how little capital it had then, it was ludicrous. Basically you need $1 to $2 billion to have a reasonable chance of succeeding in the film industry.

'If you just look at the operating profit of most film studios, you wouldn't invest, because the operating profits are somewhere between 8 to 12 per cent if you are lucky. That's a pathetic return for shareholders given the amount of money you're investing. But what makes it a viable investment is if you combine that with the capital asset growth of the negatives that you acquire and the distribution system that you've built over a period of time. Then the returns become extremely big. For example, Murdoch bought Fox in 1987 for some $600 million and it's probably worth $2 billion today, representing one of the best investments you could have made, and that's why people get into the business.

'I thought that PolyGram had a reasonable chance for the following reasons: We had a tremendous cashflow from the record business, which even if you took all the potential expansion monies that you would need for the core business, still left a huge free cashflow which would be sufficient to support a film activity. Secondly, we had a very strong international infrastructure, which was largely devoted to getting bits of plastic (CDs and tapes) out to the public. Fifty per cent of the film industry is about gettting video cassettes out to the public. I thought that we could use that distribution infra-structure for the film industry. Thirdly, I thought that our label system, which worked very well for both Warners and for us, could be adapted to the film industry.'

## The method of entry

Kuhn was fully aware of the difficulties inevitably linked with the ambition of building a studio. One of the key questions at this early point was whether PolyGram should build a studio presence by organic growth or by acquisition. The problem with any acquisi-tion at that time was that it would cost several billion dollars. In order to get that amount of money PolyGram would either have had to get its shareholders to put up the money by in effect issuing more shares, which would have meant diluting owner-ship of PolyGram, which Philips did not want; or taking on debt, which it was perfect-ly capable of doing, but which was anathema to PolyGram's corporate culture. The answer became pretty obvious: if PolyGram wanted to go into the film business, it had to do it through organic growth.

'While it's a very tough way of doing it, at least you know where all the skeletons are, because you've raised them,' Kuhn added. That was PFE's Plan One, which was pre-sented for approval in 1991.

A ceiling of a $200 million cash exposure was widely misunderstood among the trade press and areas of the industry, argued Kuhn. 'Cash and ultimate profitability are two different things. If you're projecting future profits, which you do in order to calculate the ultimate profitability of a film, it has nothing to do with cash. You can have ten very profitable movies on an ultimate basis, but still go out of business because you run out of cash. One is not related to the other. The $200 million was net cumulative cash, and it becomes fairly obvious to anyone that if you do 20 movies a year with an average budget of $10 million, and $10 million apiece releasing them, the gross cash needed is far in excess of $200 million. When you look at a bank account, you're not really interested in the gross amount coming in, you're looking at the net cash position. Am I within my overdraft? The $200m is basically the net cash positive. The gross out is of course much higher. The key is whether the difference between the two stays within or exceeds the $200 million marker.'

PFE's specific methods of financing are quite radically innovative. According to a report in *Corporate Finance* magazine,[1] the $200-million film lease arranged by Sumitomo Bank and ING Bank in November 1994 was worked in such a way that the group could 'raise cheap funds to finance future film productions while taking most of the risks off-balance sheet.' The system works by PolyGram selling a completed group of films to a

US-based trust set up specifically for the transaction by the two banks. PolyGram then redirects the $200 million back into future film productions. Meanwhile, the trust leases the films back to PolyGram for a monthly rental rate. While the trust earns a monthly return on its loan, PolyGram receives money for future films.

US studios like Walt Disney have been using leasing structures for many years, allowing the studios to raise production finance while taking most of the risk off-balance sheet. There are also tax and write-off advantages to be gained from the deal.

## The PolyGram green-light system

From Kuhn's point of view, the traditional Hollywood studio system has always relied on a very centralized approach, with one 'great green-lighter in the sky to green-light movies. To me, that always seemed a very unhealthy thing, because one person's taste can be right for a certain period of time, and then tastes change, and that person's taste is out of favour. A very good example in recent times was Disney in its live-action side. It went for high concept movies rather than big stars, and it worked brilliantly. Then people clicked on to the theory, and found the movies boring and predictable, and Disney's live action went dry for a couple of years. Then Joe Roth came in and revived it, but it's still driven by his taste, and I don't think that's good business.'

**The good thing about the label system is you back people, not projects, and you back a lot of people with different taste. You hope to cover most bases, but you still apply the slate system.'**

Michael Kuhn, PolyGram

'When you analyse the film business, what you find is that nobody makes money out of production. You only make money out of distribution, which is very similar to the record business. In an ideal world you wouldn't be in production – you'd be Warners' licencee around the world in perpetuity. Unfortunately the world isn't like that. And you can't rely on the spot market to buy movies, because you cannot ensure a reliable product stream. So you have to get into production first. That's the really tricky time, and then you have to very slowly get into distribution, recognizing that there's no such thing as a free lunch, and that every time you get into distribution, and give up pre-selling rights, you are taking a risk. The process of building a studio means always looking over your shoulder and seeing whether the product flow is sufficient in quantity, and more importantly, in quality, to allow the company to forgo the safety of selling off a territory and taking over the distribution of the film in that territory and taking the up-side but also the down-side if it goes wrong. It's a necessary evil to be in production. And it always takes much longer to get movies into production than you think. Development takes a long time, and things fall out of bed.

'With the label approach, you are trying to spread your bets, so have some organically grown, and some that you acquire. Working Title and Propaganda are home-grown and we acquired some, like Interscope, and some were in the middle, like Egg, and we'll continue doing that. The organic ones tend to always happen by chance: you come across someone, and you like them, and think they have a shot at building something. I don't think there's one of our creative ventures where people haven't had split-ups and rows, but that's inevitable when you deal with creative people. They change, their taste changes, their relationships change, and you have to be able to manage the fallings ins and outs of those people.'

When it comes to the kinds of films each PolyGram production label is producing, Kuhn draws a clear line between local-language and English-language movies. In English-language movies, he assumes that they are all in the game of Hollywood-type, international repertoire, and they have to live up to the expectations of those demands. In the case of local-language productions, he is looking for success in the national territory and any success beyond is a bonus.

'It's a similar mix to our record production. Having films by Maurice Pialat or Jaco van Dormael, next to Barry Levinson's Sleepers, makes us a much stronger company than just being an outpost of Hollywood. That's what being a European studio is all about. Hollywood studios have never been interested in doing this. Neither have they been particularly strong on distributing local-language films, but that's understandable when you look at all the enormous levels of product that companies like UIP, Warners and Buena Vista are already handling. They're not interested in European films. It's not part of their remit.'

Slowly but surely, PFE has been reaching a production level of around 15 to 18 films a year, with budgets averaging $15 to $20 million. When the company reaches more than 20, with budgets averaging around $20 million, the company will have reached Kuhn's and his president of international, Stewart Till's stated ambitions. Certainly Four Weddings and a Funeral's success helped the board reach an agreement in the summer of 1994 to support Kuhn's second phase, which was gradually to lift the number and range of movies going into production, while consolidating PFE's distribution infrastructure and worldwide network.

'We are not in the business of cultural missions, we are in the business of business. The reasons one does local production, for example, is because if you have French-language movies in France, you have a much better chance of selling all your films to Canal Plus and TF1 and getting good screens in the Gaumont theatres, and so on, than if you don't. It's a corporate point of view, not a cultural one,' Kuhn stresses, underlining that the importance of foreign-language films is not that they break out into the international market, but that they perform well in their domestic territory.

By the start of 1996, PolyGram assumed 100 per cent ownership of Gramercy Pictures, buying out Universal Pictures' 50 per cent stake and working towards a fully-fledged major distribution operation by the end of 1996. Kuhn explains that, at present, Gramercy could release any size of movie. 'It's perfectly capable of releasing Batman on 3,000 screens. What it cannot do is release Batman and Forest Gump within the same month, which is purely a function of its size. It concentrates on specialized releasing, meaning you're going out of the door with releases of under 1,000 prints once or twice a month. That's more a function of people than of skills. Gramercy employs about 40 people; an average studio distribution and marketing division employs between 150 and 200 people, let alone all the other associated functions.

'Going forwards, what we intend to do although have not yet decided upon, is to keep separate marketing for big movies and specialized movies, but make as much of the infrastructure as common as we can. With some things it's no problem, like computers and bean counters, while other areas may have to be more separate. For example, when it comes to booking theatres, does the person dealing with a specialized film have a different set of relationships to the person dealing with 3,000 screens every time they book a big movie? Art work, trailers and creative marketing may need to be separated. In principle, we will keep Gramercy on the marketing side as the specialized releasing arm, while we will develop a PolyGram releasing wing for the larger movies as we go along.'

PolyGram was one of the frontline bidders for MGM/UA in July 1996, but lost out to Frank Mancuso's $1.3 billion bid backed by billionaire Kirk Kerkorian and Australia's Seven Network. Although the acquisition would have given PolyGram's bigger US distribution ambitions a jump-start, many European players breathed a sigh of relief. As one top administrator put it: 'The fact that it didn't win MGM means that PolyGram will remain more European than dominated by its Hollywood interests.'

## Notes

1  *Corporate Finance*, September 1995; p. 34.

# 6

# Co-production and Co-financing strategies

**'A co-production has to be thought out thoroughly beforehand. You need to think very carefully about the choice of partner. I have seen co-producers go bankrupt because the partners had different views on the artistic and technical aspects of a project.'**

Ryclef Rienstra,
former chief executive of Eurimages, now head of the Dutch Film Fund

**'The US is the only territory in which a producer can recoup his [*sic*] costs from a film's domestic release.'**

Bernd Eichinger, producer and distributor

**D**URING THE LATE 1980S, co-production became a buzz-word on the tips of virtually every European independent producer's tongue. Glibly presented as the vehicle to make 'truly European films', the practical realities soon triumphed over the 'dream ticket' euphoria. Experience demonstrates that while partners are clearly a necessity for financing most films in the 1990s, the question comes down to two specifics: 'How much?'; and 'In return for what?'

At the crux of the equation is the issue of cultural specificity and creative integrity: how can these tenets be upheld when placed next to a project's financing demands and various partners' different needs? Too often the strength and vision of a project are forced to give way to wider compromises designed to suit the needs of different partners. As Ellepi Films' Leo Pescarolo noted at a Media Business School seminar, 'Financing and Selling Films in Europe', 'Authors want their own films to be shot, not a vague European notion.'[1] Warnings about the dangers of 'Euro-puddings' and complex co-production 'points systems' have abounded over the past decade, leading to a new emphasis on co-financing as opposed to creative/financial co-production.

This chapter examines the growth of co-production as a tool to boost independent production, and includes analysis of new, multilateral legislation and attempts to overcome the thorny issue of language.

## The increase in co-productions

That the demand for producing partners exists is upheld by the facts. The growth in co-produced films has risen from 12 per cent of the total number of films made in Europe in 1987, to 37 per cent in 1993. According to research by *Screen Digest*, co-productions made up more than one-third of all productions in Europe.[2] In the UK alone, co-production was worth more than £92 million ($138 million) in 1994, up 200 per cent on the comparable figure for 1993, and double the previous highest of the decade. UK partners raised an average of nearly 50 per cent of the 37 official and unofficial films' budgets, and the rise was deemed by *Screen Finance* to indicate 'just how important co-productions have been to the recent revival of the British film industry'.[3]

Much of the above activity emanates less from choice, and more from financial imperatives. The pressure on money available for film production throughout Europe over the last decade has, at best, been unsteady, and, at worst, has plummeted downwards. Part of the problem is rising costs and scarce resources. As David Puttnam has pointed out, 'There is a statistic that bedevils us, and it hasn't changed in the 25 years I've been producing. Fifty-five per cent of the cost of films made in 1970 was attributable to labour costs. That was money paid for work done by the labour-force making the movie. Forty-five per cent are hard costs – the physical costs of filmstock, of rental equipment and so on. It is almost impossible for a producer or anyone else attempting to mount a film to deal with those 45 per cent of hard costs, hence a lot of the issue of recoveries is impenetrable. We are dealing with costs like the price of film, which fluctuates with the price of silver.' Add inflation and recent currency fluctuations across Europe, and the fiscal obstacles are clear.

Beyond hard costs is the issue of recoupment. The vast majority of European film-producing territories are unlikely to enjoy a significant return from a domestic film's performance at the box office. As Bernd Eichinger, German producer and distributor puts it: 'The US is the only territory in which a producer can recoup his (*sic*) costs from the domestic territory.' Hence the necessity for European partners to help raise the money, spread the risk, and ensure the wider distribution of the product. The more theatrical opportunities, albeit of normally modest scale, the better the potential returns from ancillary distribution.

## Jigsaw puzzles

According to Dutch producer Kees Kasander, there are three main types of producer. The first is the national but successful one, such as Claude Berri in France; the second is the American-style, which is internationally orientated in terms of ideas; and the third is the guerilla producer – who raises small budgets from a range of different sources across Europe. All three have to deal with co-producing in some form or other, but it is the last one that faces arguably the toughest challenge.

Kasander, speaking at 'A Bag of Tricks', a European Film Academy Master School in Berlin, explained the guerilla approach. He breaks the film's budget down into percentages: with perhaps 30 per cent from a home territory such as Germany, or the UK, and other co-production input of maybe 20 per cent, depending on the director and project. 'If you ask for more up front, then most people turn you down. The rest is raised through pre-sales and equity. Yes, there are subsidies also, but they're very complicated and you have to get them to work with the budget and partners. The key is to get the right combination of investment.'

He always tries to avoid making a pre-sale to the US, arguing that there will be an inevitable conflict between the creative elements of the film and the distributor's desire to control the script. Instead, he tries to pick up a US deal after the film is completed. For all other territories, a sales company puts together a list of estimated values of each territory. From these different sales projections, Kasander works out if he's high, right or low in terms of the budget.

Nevertheless, the differences in Europe's range of cultures and communication methods pose real problems, warned Bo Christensen, speaking at the same School. 'We can talk to each other, but do we really understand each other? One of the problems when you are trying to put a complex package together is that although people say something, that may not mean the same to another person from a different country. And contracts are very different for France, the UK and Germany, for example.'

Christensen argued that one of the key strategies is to think of co-financing as the main objective, rather than a creatively more challenging (and difficult) co-production approach. Some stories do genuinely call for co-production partners; but stories that have been deliberately designed to work in different countries have invariably failed, said Christensen. In contrast, a co-financed project must depend on a good story first and last, and that in turn requires strong development.

Part of the problem is that national subsidy systems were mostly designed before co-production or co-financing became real necessities, explained Christensen. 'Some overhaul of these systems is needed, where you have a story but it doesn't need to fit into quotas and language requirements in order to be made on a multilateral basis.'

## The additional costs of co-production

Co-production on a bilateral basis (country-to-country) is not especially new to Europe as a mechanism to finance films. France and Germany made many films together in the 1960s, and activity was high in Europe (excluding the UK) 20 to 25 years ago. The machine appeared to work relatively well, but now that the European film industry itself is ailing, co-productions are giving way to a swelling bureaucracy, carrying civil servants, not film-makers. There exists an increasing set of rules that arguably get in the way of co-productions and the associated benefits of working with partners across borders.

Co-production as a tool to finance a project is sometimes also accused of being very expensive. For example, Danish director Henning Carlsen believes that co-production is inherently inflationary. As a lecture in Utrecht in 1991, he cited Lars von Trier's Europa, which had a budget of 25 million Danish Krone ($2.8 million), but an additional 3.5 millon DK ($395,000) had to be added on top for legal expenses and travelling costs. Another example is Gabriel Axel's Oscar-winning Babette's Feast, which, according to producer, Bo Christensen, was initially planned as a Danish/French co-production. 'We had a lot of meetings in France with different potential partners, but we couldn't synchronize' he says. The Danish and French co-production treaty rules that there has to be a minimum of 25 per cent from a partner to qualify. At this point the Danish producers only needed 2 million to 3 million Danish Krone ($225,000 to $338,000) more to reach the 14 million DK ($1.58 million) budget target.

'The strange thing was that when we were negotiating with the French we had to keep taking into account the high cost variables that kept pushing the project up exactly that 25 per cent we needed. So instead of 14 million DK with the French 'in', we kept finding the cost of French participation resulting in missing the budget. Their prices were so high it was impossible, and they all wanted to come in both creatively and financially, under the treaty's terms. In the end I suggested we should go back to Denmark for that extra money.'

The additional communications' costs, higher legal bills and the price of complying with the extra rules are expensive. However, while Ryclef Rienstra, the former head of Eurimages, put the additional costs at between 15 and 20 per cent of an overall budget, his successor, Barrie Ellis-Jones, argues that in most cases they amount to around 7 per cent of a budget. 'It depends on how well-organized and experienced the production's partners are, and the level of legal and bureaucratic demands made on the deal. But I think producers are getting better at working out these problems, and that is helping keep the costs down.'

Beyond the cost implications of co-producing is the key issue of finding the right partners. As a Festival Film School in Galway in July 1995 (backed by the Media Business School and produced by the MediaXchange), a seminar on co-producing partnerships brought to light the importance of human elements in any co-producing deals. Irish producer David Collins and UK producer Judy Counihan both stressed the importance of researching the background of the company you might be thinking of working with. 'You should find out who their former partners have been and talk to them; how their films have been financed; whether the company is solvent and what their reputation is on a personal as well as practical level,' explained Collins. 'Good research can save a lot of problems and money later down the line.'

Counihan, who produced (with other partners) Before the Rain and Antonia's Line, stressed how important the issue of trust is in any deal. 'It's also important to like the producer you're working with. After all, if they don't have a sense of humour then there's little point in going through all the agony that any film takes to get made!'

## The new trend towards co-development

In addition to co-production, there has been a recent trend towards co-development, a process where a producer structures a project's progression by sharing aspects of the development process with a third party. The concept is to try to reduce the 'seed money' risk level, and to share the materials developed – including the final product if it is realized.

Clearly co-development can be applied in a range of ways to feature films. It includes areas such as:

- the combination of a TV broadcaster with independent producer
- the joining of a distributor with an independent producer
- co-development between two independent (or more) producers in different European territories.

The reasons and advantages of co-developing material were explained in a Media Business School Master Class paper by producer and lawyer Diana Costes-Brook, *Legal Aspects of Development and Co-Production of Feature Films*.[4] Her key points for co-development were:

- A project is of a size that a producer needs a partner to share risk and costs.
- A project may benefit from the cultural input of a European partner.
- Where more partners are needed, it can be the only way to make a project work creatively and financially.

In addition, she warned that successful co-development requires:

- keeping good faith, and checking financial stability of partners
- a careful legal overview of all issues prior to signing a co-development deal.

In addition to the above, a checklist of work details in development was included, which is relevant to all development planning. It included:

- the acquisition of film adaptation rights to the underlining materials
- commissioning of the treatment and/or script
- hiring of a director
- drawing up of a budget and schedule
- attaching principal cast
- location recces
- 'due diligence' on script
- copyright searches.

### New models for partners

All lawyers working in Europe have their own standard forms for co-production deals. When an independent company enters a co-production it has to execute an official co-production contract which satisfies all the criteria of the Treaty it wants to qualify under. (This presupposes that the producers want to make an 'official' co-production. Any official co-production allows the film to become eligible for support systems under each territory's rules.)

Part of the problem facing recent efforts to streamline the complex bilateral and multilateral legal implications of co-producing is that the specific intricacies *are* different for each European territory. Most European entertainment law firms, however, have similar documents which are more or less the same, because there are certain headings a co-production has to hit.

Flying in the face of those who hammer co-production models as over-rated and costly, some lawyers suggest that there's no other option.

> **'All this talk of how difficult and expensive it is to co-produce is rubbish. The fact is, co-production simply has to be done. Forget whether it costs more. The point is you won't have a movie unless you do it.'**
>
> Cameron McCracken, a former lawyer and now producer.

The concept of European co-production, however, has inevitably tended to clash with the varying laws that cover them. Most countries have very different laws or bilateral legal frameworks that historically have hindered their fruition. For example, Germany has co-production treaties with 11 other European territories; France with 21; and the UK with more than 5. And they all have their own specific regulations. Part of the over-riding problem with these agreements is that they are one-to-one treaties. It is becoming less common for a film to be able to be funded by just two territories in today's climate.

The idea of eliminating bilateral treaties in favour of one pan-European or at least more general agreement is not new. Italian propositions for such an approach were initially suggested back in 1981. But it was the inception of Eurimages that really tackled the problem head on. By recognizing that a co-production was bound to have more than two partners (i.e. multilateral), and by more recently acknowledging the strength of pure financial partners, Eurimages has taken Europe's cross-border potential for film-making a huge leap forward (see Case Study at end of this chapter for further details).

Financial rather than creative co-operation addresses one of the key hitches blocking many co-productions; namely, reaching detailed agreements on casts, crews, scripts and other specifics. Many industry experts argue that a project is likely to be more smoothly accommodated through a 'co-financing' model than 'co-producing' one. And bilateral treaties invariably require that a producer's financial participation be matched by an equivalent artistic and technical participation. Fortunately, in certain cases this kind of requirement is starting to change. At a seminar in September 1993 at the Dinard Film Festival in France, the new UK–France co-production treaty was discussed. In an effort to support co-financing outside the traditional points system, certain amendments were made, including dropping the need for a minority partner to have to provide a certain number of actors, for example. Purely financial co-productions were allowed where the minority partner was purely financial, provided that the contribution is limited to between 20 and 30 per cent of the budget. Most influential of all, a condition that a balance on co-financing productions is maintained between the two countries was set. According to an annex to the treaty, 'A temporary imbalance may be accepted. If the imbalance reaches the level of two films to the advantage of either of the contracting parties, then, for the country which is in deficit, only a majority co-production may be allowed to benefit from this agreement.'

Unfortunately, the legislation (which was finally signed in November 1994 and ratified in February 1995) quickly encountered a significant problem of 'bottle-necking'. The 'financial-only' section of the treaty was far more user-friendly to UK producers than to their French counterparts, mainly because access to the French subsidy system is so much more lucrative than the UK's. By the summer of 1995, three majority UK financial co-productions were approved, compared to one majority-French film, leading to an immediate blocking of further co-financing projects under the treaty. Despite efforts to sort out the impasse, the system continued to create problems by the time the British and French met once again at the Dinard Film Festival in 1995. Neither the CNC nor British Screen had come up with real solutions to the problem.

### The multilateral approach

Unfortunately, it seems to take an impossibly lengthy phrase of European film-lingo to address a negative system currently blocking European film-making. For all its alleged benefits, it's easy to see why even the more dedicated film-maker drifts out of hearing when someone reels off the imminent advantages of the European Convention on Cinemato-graphic Co-productions.

Described by *Screen International* as a 'giant leap towards a truly pan-European film industry without closing the door to North American partnerships', the convention will allow the streamlining of co-productions to reflect better the economic realities of film production. Access to Europe's national funds and subsidy systems (both national and pan-European) will be more readily available to a wider range of co-produced projects.

The convention applies to co-productions where all of the producers are nationals of states that have signed the convention. If not, there must be at least three producers from three states who are providing at least 70 per cent of the production finance to still qualify. Signatories must be members of the Council of Europe, which includes the EC states, Scandinavia and Eastern European countries.

The new convention is aimed at multilateral *film*, not television co-productions, and existing bilateral agreements are expected to remain in place. The difference is that the convention acts as a kind of enabling umbrella, cancelling out the obstructive bilateral problems when a multilateral production fits the ticket. According to McCracken, this means that in the case of two co-productions between two producers from different states, one of the two following scenarios will occur: first-ly, if no bilateral treaty already exists, the convention may be applied as a bilateral agreement; or secondly, if a bilateral agreement already exists, it will remain applicable.

On the other hand, if the co-production is between producers from more than two states, the convention will apply and will over-ride (where in conflict) any bilateral agreement between any of the states.

So how much does a qualifying producer have to put into the project? That sum cannot fall below 10 per cent or be higher than 70 per cent, compared to the 20 per cent to 80 per cent in bilateral contributions. And what about creative control? Although the convention contains a general provision that each co-producer's technical and artistic contribution should roughly balance its financial contribution, between 10 per cent and 25 per cent can be purely financial, with no creative or technical input. However, for this to pass the test, there has to be a majority co-producer whose technical and artistic contribution satisfies the conditions for the film to be recognized as a national product in that producer's state. A 'majority' co-producer in this sense may mean as little as a 30 per cent contributor.

As a general point, the co-produced film needs to qualify as a 'European cinematographic work'. The definition is reached by a points system, whereby a production needs to score 15 out of 19 points to put the ball in the back of the net. For example, a director is worth three points, an art director one point, and so on. However, a lower score may still be able to pass, as long as the film 'reflects a European identity'. Amusingly, this debatable concept is not defined, but McCracken suggests that it 'would clearly enable a certain amount of flexibility'. Each co-producer has to apply for approval at least two months before shooting starts, from the relevant government body in their state (for example, the Department of Heritage for the UK). Signatories must be members of the Council of Europe. By early 1996, the UK, Germany, the Netherlands, Finland, Austria, Denmark, Latvia, Slovakia, Sweden, Switzerland and Russia have signed the convention. Key states still to ratify included France, Italy, Spain, Luxembourg and Portugal.

Multilateral co-productions that qualify are able to access national funds in the same way as official bilateral co-productions. McCracken uses an example: 'In theory, a 10 per cent financial contribution by a French co-producer would entitle them to claim French nationality and receive French national subsidies. However, it should be noted that Article 6.1 of the convention provides that when a minimum contribution is less than 20 per cent, the state concerned may take steps to reduce or bar access to national production support schemes.'

According to CNC's Elizabeth Fleury Herard, the scheme is not seen as particularly useful from the French point of view. Talking at Dinard, she indicated that the CNC will be prepared to block minimum French producer applications of below 20 per cent, and argued 'that the convention will change little in terms of more co-producing'.

## A single European market?

Perhaps the most radical and forward-thinking proposal on co-production has come from the European Producers' Club, a group of 23 top producers who hope to promote the development of European cinema, with its headquarters in Paris. The Club has called for the harmonization of co-production rules in Europe and the creation of a new production incentive scheme to help underwrite the initiative.

Unlike other schemes, including the precarious European Guarantee Fund (see Chapter 1), the Club's proposals – known as One Cinema For Europe – have been thoroughly researched and were well received in the spring of 1996 by many who had read the plan. An annual cost has not yet been estimated, but it could be met by MEDIA II and the EU money earmarked for the European Guarantee Fund.

According to Hachette Premiere chief and film producer Rene Cleitman, the aim is to remove Europe's existing internal borders and replace them with a single external border. 'This will be more symbolic than real, but would be based on the common definition of what constitutes a European film,' he told *Screen International*.[5]

A points system would be used along the lines of Eurimages' definition of a European film (see Case Study, page 108), based on the nationality of talent, crew and post-production, but excluding origins of financing and the language of the film. All productions that qualify would then have equal access to national automatic subsidy systems, which would mean France, Germany, Italy and Spain opening their systems to the new Club proposal, although the UK would be excluded, as it has no automatic system. Smaller countries would be able to access all national funds, but producers from larger countries would not be able to drain the funds from smaller countries. If the French system was drawn upon excessively, then a compensation fund would be set up. As the Club's Phyllis Mollet explained, 'We would hope that if successful, it would be an incentive to other countries to consider making their support systems automatic so that they would benefit from the effect.'

The net effect of the new system would be to create a stronger internal European market aimed at breaking down some of the national fragmentation. Such a system would help create a critical mass, and aid producers constantly frustrated by the conflicting rules and regulations between different territories. If the UK was to become a member of the scheme, then the overall budget might rise by at least 100 per cent, and considerable work would need to be done at a governmental level if such a positively pan-European scheme were to be embraced.

## New partnerships with North America

While plenty of rhetoric is flying around from Europeans against the Hollywood Majors (including 'unfair business practices' inquiries into distribution chains), European producers have also tended not to think of US independents as strong potential partners as much as they might. One of the overwhelming advantages of the convention is that non-Council of Europe countries – namely the US and Canada – are able to participate by investing up to 30 per cent in qualifying films. This brings to the European producers' table an array of new financial sources and potential partners. 'The convention is not about letting Hollywood through the back door. Instead, it's a fine way of encouraging US independent companies to link with European producers on projects,' argues McCracken. (However, the umbrella advantage will not stretch beyond 30 per cent for the Canadian co-producing partner, who would not be able to access their domestic subsidies because Canada isn't a member of the Council of Europe.)

The political will required to squeeze the convention through the Council has also tweaked the often obstructive bilateral system. According to McCracken, bilateral co-productions falling under the convention will be 'subject to a much less restrictive regime than that generally imposed by the existing bilateral treaties. The most likely beneficiaries under the convention are likely to be those states that are also members of Eurimages, because they will enjoy access to both national funds or benefits, and the Eurimages' fund.'

## Miramax's unique role

Of all the US independent companies that play a role in Europe's film industry, Miramax makes it the company's business to be the leader of the pack. By the summer of 1996, Miramax had nearly 30 films that it has owned distribution rights for in certain territories around the world. It also had a massive 50 films either completed, in production or in post-production, more than double a normal Hollywood studio.

Since co-chairmen Bob and Harvey Weinstein's $80 million deal with Disney in 1993,[6] Miramax has expanded rapidly, something that Harvey in particular is keen to put the brakes on. The pressure of numbers has inevitably led to delays, with some films being forced to wait for months before Miramax can find a release date for them.

**'Quite frankly this year [1996], I am cutting down on production. I've built a library, so that we have enough films and don't *have* to do this anymore.'**

Harvey Weinstein, Miramax

'The profits are there in the company,' Weinstein explained. 'I have done a tremendous amount of movies now, and my philosophy was to build a huge library of movies and classic films. There will be another usage. If there ever was a Miramax channel, based on the 400 or so films in our library, then we will have built the security to exist and experiment.' By May 1996, Bob and Harvey finally completed the signing of the original seven-year deal with Disney which sees them through to the next century with their benefactors.

In addition to an aggressive acquisition policy towards European films, Britain and Ireland are making happy hunting grounds for Miramax's production ambitions. In addition to backing Emma, The Last of the High Kings, Snakes and Ladders, Talk of Angels, The English Patient and B. Monkey, Miramax committed $13 million in mid 1996 to finance Wings of the Dove, the Henry James adaptation directed by Iain Softley (Backbeat, Hackers). Miramax has a reputation for being the first to know about hot new talent and screenplays across Europe. When British Screen announced a £50,000 ($75,000) deal with Miramax to share half of its development costs for screenplay loans in June 1995, some were horrified that the government-backed agency was getting into bed with Miramax.

Simon Perry, British Screen's chief executive, stresses that the deal is only for the body's new-writer loans of £5,000 ($7,500), which have to be repaid if the film based on that draft ever gets made. Miramax has no say in what is taken into development, and who gets those loans. Miramax's first-look is an opportunity, when the first screenplay draft is delivered, to look at it at the same time as British Screen, and to decide within 45 days whether it wishes to take that project into development, make a deal with the writer, and finance further development on it.

However, both David Aukin, head of drama at Channel 4, and Mark Shivas, head of BBC Films, contend that writers at this early stage of their careers often don't have agents to protect them, and that they need careful nurturing before being let loose on the market. Miramax's aggressive reputation is an odd match for first-time writers. Neither do they believe that it is the right time for Miramax to look at a screenplay. As one experienced German film-maker put it, 'I wouldn't expect to show something to Miramax until it was on its eighth draft at least!' Perry defends Miramax staunchly, arguing that the company 'is a major funder of British cinema, and has a very strong and extremely experienced team of people to develop these projects.' By May 1996, 16 of the 20 screenplays had been delivered, and Miramax was showing keen interest in two of them.

Channel 4 has also taken the plunge, recently teaming up with Miramax for Michael Winterbottom's Sarajevo and Mark Herman's Brassed Off. Both projects were developed with Aukin's department.

'I was always very nervous about making films with Miramax,' Aukin concedes, 'but the way the deal works gives us final cut and a chance to protect the film-maker.'

## Silence on language

Language, and the huge range of them across Europe, is often presented as a key barrier to successful co-productions (and, indeed, a successful pan-European film industry). Interestingly, the new convention ducks, perhaps deliberately, this thorny issue. Unlike Eurimages or bilateral treaties, which stipulate that the language in which a film is shot needs to be in one of the co-production partners', the convention is silent on this point. Consequently, subject to any national requirements, the choice of language is entirely discretionary.

It is often suggested that the US, through Hollywood's successful vertical integration and global expansion, has ensured that English is the universal language of cinema. Such a tendency has serious implications on the level of a film's budget and its ability to recoup. As Bernd Eichinger pointed out in his Ebeltoft Lecture of 1994, 'If you shoot a movie that is meant to be successful in a lot of territories, one of the rules that you have to understand is that you shoot in English – not to do so rules out two-thirds of the market. Also, you have to understand that 50 per cent of the market is the US market.'

Overall, continental Europe's cinema audiences embrace dubbing in the larger (or Latin) territories, and sub-titling in the smaller ones; while Ireland and the UK remain firmly resistant to both, and in particular, dubbing. The implications of language for co-producing, co-financing and the production of films able to travel across borders are very significant. But so too is the tendency towards a sweeping attitude to 'foreign-language' films. As a report on a British Screen Advisory Council/MBS seminar, 'The Challenge of Language in European Film', held in July 1992, points out, 'The hegemony of the English language in cinema is now so strongly established that all other films are destined to be consigned to a single, catch-all category, defined simply by language. Foreign-language films, difficult to pre-sell, often even more difficult to watch, have no chance in the foreign market, or so conventional wisdom would have it.

'In lumping all non-English product into a single category there is an inevitable tendency to assume that the failure of a film in the international market-place stems from the language it was shot in. But what emerged most strongly from the BSAC/MBS seminar was that although in certain cases the *handling* of language can most certainly damage a film's chances of commercial success, the choice of language alone need not be a barrier to reaching mass audiences.'

One obvious example is Cyrano De Bergerac, whose producers placed special emphasis on high-quality sub-titles written by author Anthony Burgess. While it's not possible to suggest that fine sub-titling *improved* the French-langauge film's performance in the UK, its figures were impressive. Cyrano grossed £2,458,175 ($3.68 million) in the UK in 1991, taking more than five times the revenue of its closest foreign-language competitor.

The report goes on to argue that while 'few would care to deny that most foreign-language films have a tough time outside their markets' many other factors can serve to inhibit the international success of foreign-language pictures. The lack of a European star system, the heritage of the *auteur* tradition with its generalized failure to acknowledge the demands of the audience, and the pacing of European films, all play their part in preventing the wider success of foreign-language films.

'The fact that audiences often stay away from dubbed or sub-titled foreign-language films does not mean that they are resistant to dubbing or sub-titling *per se*. After all, most US films in Europe are dubbed or sub-titled, a fact which has apparently failed to have a serious impact on their popularity with foreign audiences.'

More effort needs to be put into the practical aspects of dubbing. The BSAC/MBS seminar was particularly useful in throwing light on new dubbing and sub-titling techniques, many of which clearly European producers and distributors would do well to learn more about. Technical experts who presented papers at the seminar stressed that producers and their different national partners must address issues of translation, subtitling and dubbing 'right from the inception of the project if they want to give the completed film the best possible chance of attracting audiences from all over the world'.

In the case of the UK and Ireland, a change of attitude and much greater degree of reciprocity appear to be needed. 'There are no real language barriers throughout the rest of Europe,' says UK British Screen head Simon Perry. 'There is a real problem of achieving fairness between Ireland, the UK and the rest of Europe, because at present there is a block in terms of selling foreign-language films into the English-speaking territories (including the US).

> **'The stupid reaction from the British is to think that because**
> **they share a language with America, they will be all right.**
> **The fact is that while UK films travel into Germany and France**
> **via dubbing, those countries' films have**
> **very limited access to British screens or television deals.'**

Simon Perry, British Screen

'What the British need to acknowledge is that our natural partners, who are the French, Italians, Portuguese, Spanish and German etc., should enjoy the same kind of access to the UK film market as we do to their markets. Unless we cut the short-term approach, the UK partner simply isn't going to be welcome in the long run.'

Perry suggests that cinema distributors will need help if the challenge of dubbing is really to be tackled head-on in the UK and Ireland. 'This is an area where some state intervention is needed. It's crucial that UK audiences have better access and higher entertainment value from foreign-language films. It needs investment in techniques and some trial and error with selected films. There'll be failures and fingers pointed, but dubbing has to happen.' If English-language speaking co-producers really want to develop better relationships with European partners, dubbing is a crucial strategy that has to be taken seriously.

There are indications that despite a widespread resistance from the critics, certain key European and US companies are working on some dubbing experiments. Guild Entertainment, the Chargeurs-owned UK distributor; France's Unifrance export agency; Miramax in North America, and British Screen came together on Gazon Maudit (French Twist), the French comedy hit. The companies all worked on the special dubbing project from French into English during early 1996. Special attention was paid to the technical process, and the key 'arthouse' cinemas in London continued to play sub-titled versions so as not to alienate the core arthouse audience. Unfortunately, the sub-titled version far outgrossed the dubbed version during the first eight weeks of play.

The experiment, however, is extremely positive and despite the financial returns should be encouraged. Chargeurs' Timothy Burrill pointed out, 'The attention to detail and care required for proper dubbing is critical. You need excellent sound technicians, dialogue coaches and top actors to work on the re-voicing process.' A very good English dub would cost between £60,000 to £80,000 ($90,000 to $120,000), of which Unifrance might contribute up to one-third, and so might Miramax. Also key to the process, according to Perry, is the need for a British–English dub, rather than American voices. 'This allows the film to be comprehensible but still have a European flavour to it.' It would still have a tough time with the critics and the exhibitors, but over a period of time the experiment might work.

Overall, what is clear is that while the language is not going to be the decisive factor in determining the success of a film, the wrong choice of language, or poorly executed sub-titling or dubbing, will wreck its chances of international success no matter how good the product is. As Perry puts it: 'The contribution made by language to a film can never be a positive one, but it can be a profoundly negative one.'

## Notes

1  *A Dose of Reality: The State of European Cinema*, Angus Finney, Chapter 5, p. 50.
2  *Screen Digest* report on Eurimages, 'European Co-production and the Role of Eurimages', June 1995.
3  *Screen Finance*, 'UK co-prods finance trebles to £93m', 26 July 1995.
4  *Legal Aspects of Development and Co-Production of Feature Films*, Dinah Costes-Brook, November 1993, MBS.
5  *Screen International,* 'European producers call for single movie market', Patrick Frater, 31 May 1996, p. 2.
6  See *The Egos Have Landed: The Rise and Fall of Palace Pictures*, Angus Finney, p. 283 for details of the Disney deal, 1996.

# EURIMAGES

## Case Study

Eurimages is the pan-European fund for European multilateral co-productions. It also gives support to documentary, cinema exhibition and distribution marketing, but the focus in this case study is on the fund's production support.

The fund was established in 1989 by the Council of Europe in Strasbourg. Eurimages' member states pay an agreed sum into a central pool which is then administered by a central selection team. The basic arrangement is in the form of an interest-free loan, repayable from producers' net receipts. A qualifying co-production must involve at least three independent producers from the fund's member states (two for a documentary, although they must be primarily intended for a theatrical release) and be directed by a European film-maker. The majority co-producer originally could contribute up to 60 per cent of the budget, but this was increased to 70 per cent in 1994 to come into line with the European Convention of Cinematographic Co-production. The maximum Eurimages will lend any one co-production is 20 per cent of the budget, or FFr5 million ($955,000). The minority co-producer participation cannot be less than 10 per cent of the total production cost. Requests are considered eligible if the shooting has not yet started and will not have begun before the end of the period of settlement of the application.

In practical terms, any application needs support from the film's respective national Eurimages representatives, who need to be fully informed of the budget, creative and practical elements, and its partners. They are then in a position to answer queries when the project is discussed at the quarterly board meetings.

### A rapid growth

Membership of Eurimages has increased from 12 to 25 over its six years, with notable recruits including Ireland and the UK (until its abrupt withdrawal in November 1995, see below). Eurimages had an annual pool of around FFr160million by 1995 ($28.5 million), marking a large increase of $18.75 million from 1989's $9.75 million figure.

'It was a very well-thought-out fund, right from the beginning,' explained Barrie Ellis-Jones, who took over from Ryclef Rienstra as chief executive in early 1994, but was forced to resign by the summer of 1996 due to the UK's abandonment of the fund. 'It made sense both culturally, and in terms of developing the troubled European market by 1988. It was also very clever to make it "end money". What that cash does is compensate producers for the additional costs of co-production (translations, travel costs, legal fees, etc.). Just taken at that level, Eurimages is creating a level playing field across Europe.

'From the UK, we could feel what a huge disadvantage it was for our producers not being part of it [up to April 1993]. When you know it would make a huge difference to your film industry if you were to join, then Eurimages was clearly pretty good.'

## The problem areas

Nevertheless, criticism does not escape Eurimages. Some allege that Eurimages is literally an extension of the French system, which has given French producers an unfair advantage in accessing funds. Ellis-Jones suggests that Eurimages was a development of France's open willingness to co-produce with (most) partners, but more importantly, that 12 countries were involved right from the outset. 'It was of benefit to all of those members as well as the French. Naturally it's imbued with French thinking, but its very existence, along with the MEDIA programme, helped stimulate the European Co-production Fund in the UK. There's a ladder with a lot of rungs yet to be put in, which runs up to Eurimages.'

However, the internal structures at Eurimages have come under criticism. Ironically suffering from rapid growth (now at 24 members) and a massive over-demand of funds, Ellis-Jones had his work cut out. 'There was clearly an administrative problem when I first arrived,' he conceded. 'There were 73 projects funded in 1993. That's an enormous amount of work, and each application was far too big and cumbersome,' and totalled 35 copies per application. Ellis-Jones promptly sought a way of setting up an internal photocopying system, and drastically cut the producer's paperwork in the process.

Although the process is theoretically 'automatic' – meaning that if your project fills in the right boxes correctly, it should automatically qualify – the budget is too tight for such a system to pay every correct application. The committee process also attracts its critics. 'The decision-making process at Eurimages is a process for a committee of nearly 30 people, all of them deciding which films will be backed and which films won't,' Simon Perry commented in his Ebeltoft lecture at the European Film College on 8 October 1994. 'I am completely perplexed by this . . .

'Eurimages should be run by one person. It should not be run by a committee. It should not be too "democratic". Money should be in the hands of people who can work fast and flexibly, and if they are no good – get rid of them.'

Nevertheless, Perry later went on record following the UK's move to withdraw, explaining that, for all its faults, 'there's little one can do about a fund if you are no longer a member. It's a disaster that the government pulled out, just as the UK's policy towards Europe was beginning to take shape.'

Nearly a third of all films made in the UK in 1994 and 1995 received assistance from Eurimages. Up until the government's withdrawal, the UK had benefited from funding for 56 feature films and documentaries in which UK companies were involved as co-producers. In return, the government was paying just over $3 million a year to the fund.[1] The Department of National Heritage responded to the widespread criticisms that met the decision by arguing that National Lottery contributions towards the film industry, estimated at potentially more than $120 million from 1996 to 2001, would fill the gap. Unfortunately, even by July 1996, the Lottery money's precise mechanisms were still under debate (see Chapter 7). However, the Labour Party announced in April that it will take the UK back into Eurimages if it wins power at the next election.[2]

## Spreading the finance

If administration is pressurized, then Eurimages' overall budget and loan system has also been heavily over-subscribed, and will become increasingly so now that the UK is out. The pressure on Eurimages' funds meant that they were being spread increasingly thinly. In 1993, the average loan was 12 per cent of each film's budget. By the third board meeting of 1994, it fell to just 7.5 per cent. In an effort to acknowledge the difficulties this presented to producers, the board of management agreed a new selection procedure at the start of 1995. Projects under FFr35 million ($6.7 million) were not to receive less than 10 per cent of their realistic budget, and those above that figure should not receive less than FFr3.5 million ($670,000).

'Any fund that has exactly enough money for every application that comes in, almost by definition, is a bad fund. A good fund doing a good job is going to create a lot of demand. It gives us a lot of choice, and a chance to refine what we're doing, and to select those with strong potential for the market,' said Ellis-Jones, adding that the tighter rules also correspond to the budgets themselves. One of the problems for applicants is that although they might apply for a 20 per cent contribution, the award is almost always considerably lower. Critics argue that this system simply encourages European producers to submit false, and in most cases, inflated budgets. In response, Ellis-Jones has insisted that Eurimages now takes a much more penetrating look at budgets. 'There are tight budgets, which have little realistic room for manoeuvre, fair budgets and loose budgets, and it's the loose ones that we are most keen to re-examine with care.'

Critics also became increasingly vocal about Eurimages' pitifully low recuperation levels, which, for example, are much lower when compared to an operation like the UK's British Screen Finance. 'Yes, it looks very poor,' agrees Ellis-Jones. 'But a very large proportion of the money has gone to co-productions coming out of smaller countries. They are inevitably the ones that struggle in the market-place and are unlikely to recoup quickly. We are operating in the pan-European culture and environment, where most producers expect to make their films via public funds, and not do well in the market.'

## Recoupment questions

Ellis-Jones argues that British Screen, for example, operates under very different guidelines. 'Recoupment is not in itself a measure of success for Eurimages, although at a certain level it is a loan, it is public money and it has a duty to get the returns that it can given a difficult environment.' Nevertheless, Ellis-Jones has taken recoupment seriously, and within a few months of his arrival he had encouraged the Board to introduce two new measures. Firstly, no application from a co-producer who had received assistance from Eurimages but had failed to meet their contractual obligations in respect of repayment could be considered by the Board. The second decision was that the repayment rate had to rise in line with the fund's contribution to a budget.

By April 1995, the fund had started publishing top-ten repayment tables,[3] and announced that a new system of monitoring had been installed to assist recoupment. The total amount paid back to that day was just FFr3.5 million ($670,000), representing an adjusted rate of nearly 2 per cent. But the figures are improving, and in 1994 the fund was repaid seven times the amount from the previous year.

Greatly in favour of recoupment, Ellis-Jones draws a clear line between the role of the European producer and the funder of those films. 'It's seldom understood that funding and the policies behind it are actually very different from making the thing. Expertise in funding is hard to come by and very useful. The operation's mission is not necessarily the same as the people it funds. Merely meeting the complete needs of the funded is not what it's all about.'

Ellis-Jones emphasizes the role of co-production in relation to the effect on pan-European distribution. As the table below demonstrates, 88 per cent of Eurimages-backed films are released in two of the producing territories, and 56 per cent in three.

### Distribution of Eurimages films

| | |
|---|---|
| Number of films released | 161 |
| Number in sample | 80 |
| **Release in producer countries** | |
| 3 countries | 48 |
| 2 countries | 18 |
| 1 country | 13 |
| 0 country | 1 |

*Source:* Eurimages

By the end of 1995, Ellis-Jones had started to consider ways of raising new funds designed for larger-budgeted films. Like other public funders, Eurimages is concerned to have an effect on the market-place, and is seeking new ways of participating in pro-jects which perform well at an international level. Although at an early stage, Ellis-Jones is exploring ways of supporting films with budgets in excess of $8 million by a new, separate fund. This would possibly involve contributions from Eurimages' five largest countries (UK, France, Germany, Spain and Italy) as they would be expected to be the main producers and beneficiaries of such a fund. Again, the plan had to be halted due to the UK's withdrawal. Just two Eurimages members would be required to apply, as long as distribution deals were apparent in further territories. At present, the fund's maximum and minimum rules make it hard for smaller territories to join larger co-productions. On the other hand, the 19 remaining members might be happy for an additional fund for larger projects, as it would add to their chances of being successful from the existing fund.

By the summer of 1996, the Council of Europe appointed Mireille Paulus-Levy as the new executive secretary of Eurimages. Paulus-Levy was born in Luxembourg, and has worked with the Council of Europe since 1974. She was involved in the formation of Eurimages, and has worked in the private office of the Secretary of the Council of Europe. Over the last two years, however, she has co-ordinated a 'plan of action' against racism, xenophobia, anti-Semitism and intolerance'; a role that may well place her in a good position when it comes to dealing with complexities of the European film industry.

## Notes

1  See *Screen International*, 'A further affront', Paddy Barrett, 8 December 1995, p. 14, for further analysis and the Irish reaction.
2  See *Screen Finance*, 'Labour says it will re-join Eurimages', 2 May 1996, pp. 3–4.
3  Top repaying films included, in order:

1  Toto le Heros
2  Bleu
3  Germinal
4  The House of Spirits
5  El Rey Pasmado
6  Rosaril
7  The Last Dance
8  Blanc
9  Le Pas Suspendu de al Cigogne
10  The Stolen Children

A selection of twenty recent films backed by Eurimages:

Le Huitieme Jour, directed by Jaco van Dormael (Belgium)
Breaking the Waves, directed by Lars von Trier (Denmark)

The Fifth Province, directed by Frank Stapleton (Ireland)

La Cible, Pierre Courrege (France)

Smilla's Sense of Snow, directed by Bille August (Denmark)

Antonia's Line, directed by Marleen Gorris (The Netherlands)

The Conspirators of Pleasure, directed by Jan Svankmajer (Czech Republic)

La Sicilia, directed by Luc Pien (Belgium)

Balkanisateur, directed by Sotiris Goritsas (Greece)

Armon Aika, Days of Grace, directed by Jaakko Pyhala (Finland)

Maria, directed by Einar Heimisson (Iceland)

My Mother's Courage, directed by Michael Verhoeven (Germany)

Brute, directed by Maciej Dejczer (Poland)

The Pillow Book, directed by Peter Greenaway (UK)

Beyond the Clouds, directed by Michelangelo Antonioni and Wim Wenders (Italy/Germany)

Guiltrip, directed by Gerry Stembridge (Ireland)

Farinelli, directed by Gerard Corbiau (France/Belgium)

Victory, directed by Mark Peploe (UK)

Land and Freedom, directed by Ken Loach (UK)

Lamerica, directed by Gianni Amelio (Italy).

# Support Mechanisms Across Europe

'Cinematographic production in Europe is in an extremely
critical position, and unless major efforts are made,
the twentieth century – i.e. the first century of the
existence of cinema – is going to end on
a near failure of the European cinema.'

The Treaty of Maastricht

'We can either become dinosaurs, locked in a cultural theme-
park of our own making, fed on a diet of pre-cooked subsidies –
or we can use our talents and imagination
to get back into the real game –
communicating or better still, delighting a viable audience.'

David Puttnam, film producer

MORE THAN $500 MILLION of national and European Union public
money is spent every year in propping up the production of European films. Some 600 films are produced in Europe annually, although
fewer than 250 actually find their way through distribution and successfully onto a cinema screen. A vast majority of the remaining 350 films
end up on televlsion, played late at night and never to see the light of day.

The $500-million investment constitutes regional and national sup-
port systems, and pan-European support in the form of MEDIA II (albeit
not directly a production subsidy) and the Council of Europe's Eurimages fund. When public television, new technology and distribution support is added to the production subsidy, the figure rises well beyond $1
billion. It should be stressed, however, that Europe's film industry is not
necessarily receiving special treatment. Other European-based industries, including manufacturing, transport, telecommunications and ncw

technologies, receive huge European subsidies on a regular basis. So too has Hollywood been protected by Washington legislation for a considerable number of years. Effective lobbying encouraged the American Congress to support producers and allow for tax-break incentives from 1976 to 1986 that were the envy of other sectors of American industry.[1] Anyone who suggests that Hollywood's strength has been built up without government support should reconsider the true links between Washington and Los Angeles. On the other hand, only $4 million exists in the US in the form of cultural-orientated subsidy finance for film-makers. As one LA-based independent lawyer put it: 'Don't even waste time thinking about it, It's zilch in comparison to what Europe has.'

This chapter examines the different approaches to film support in Europe, and analyses how effective different public-subsidy systems are at encouraging a competitive and vibrant film industry. It also considers the new MEDIA programme and certain tax incentives that are available to film-makers in Europe.

## Illusions of subsidy support

Typically, few European professionals can even agree on the precise wording and interpretation used to describe film support. When four key European film industry personalities were interviewed in 1993 for an analysis of European national subsidy systems, they shared one common viewpoint: none of them liked the word 'subsidy'. Producer David Puttnam called subsidies 'production investment credits'; administrator Dieter Kosslick preferred 'conditionally repayable loans'; British Screen's Simon Perry argued that he operates an 'intervention mechanism'; and the French producer Rene Cleitman insisted that France has no straight subsidies: 'The system is audience-driven and the French producer is totally free.'

The growing antipathy to the word 'subsidy' is a result of it too often being equated with 'free money'. In turn, this artificially protects feature films from the demands and commercial realities of the international market-place. As film expert Terry Ilott argues, 'It may be a useful and even essential thing to subsidize local production. But subsidies provide the film-maker with a phantom audience, whose "attendance" can boost the revenues of a film as if by magic. Far from addressing the needs of this "audience", the European film-maker, naturally, treats it with contempt.'

The point is that television and straight subsidy money is not at risk, and hence recoupment of it is not a requirement. Ilott concludes that 'If Europe is to raise the average level of success and reduce the incidence of failure, it must restore the link between production and performance. Far from eliminating risk, Europe should place it as the keystone of its audiovisual production system.'[2]

Other critics of Europe's subsidy structures argue that there are inherent problems that stem from the establishment of culturally-orientated funds. These in turn became dominated by the director, who in turn produced his or her own work or used a producer simply to fill in forms for public finance. No real links are created with sales companies or distributors, the tough areas of the market which take into consideration whether a film has an intended audience or not. 'We can't talk about a film industry in Europe,' says Danish producer Mads Egmont. 'This is partly because state support emphasized the creation of art over an industrial product, and did away with the producer. The challenge of the entertainment business has always been to fuse culture and industry together, and create an industrial package that keeps the audience in mind.'

There is an argument to suggest that Europe and its member states have been operating a defensive support strategy over the past two decades. Film-makers have been brought up either unconcerned about losses or profits, or one step better – attempting not to lose money when making films. The meticulous filling in of forms and applications, rather than concentration on where a potentially profitable market lies for their film, has presided over a subsidy-fed mentality. As such, films have consistently gone into production when they would have been better off not made at all. Others have been made at the wrong budget level, mainly because the producer, encouraged by soft subsidy money, has never been forced to look beyond the public cheque-book.

## A heated subject

The level of debate over European subsidy support has certainly grown more heated over the past three years, on both a domestic and pan-European scale. Europe's national and regional subsidy systems have come under increasing scrutiny and attack, as efforts to create a single market for European films have clashed with local rules, criteria and local funding bodies. Meanwhile, the MEDIA II programme has had a spectacularly uncertain start, caught between bureaucratic mismanagement and policy squabbles between the member states.

On the other hand, the ensuing debate has grown slightly more open and hence more healthy when compared to the protective slanging matches during the early 1990s. As a special working paper for the 100 Years of Cinema colloquium in Strasbourg (October 1995) stressed 'How can intervention be made most effective in ensuring that the films supported are able to be taken out of the cupboard and shown to the audience?'

The paper went on to criticize grants organized and selected by committees: 'However good the committee, it takes no risks and hardly bears any responsibility for its decisions. Unfortunately, the decision to make a film nowadays depends less on the producer's willingness than on a committee's view. Producers sometimes spend their time chasing public funds. There is a complex web of procedures open only to the few in the know. Ought they not be reorganized, or perhaps new thought given to them, with a view to a pan-European cinema policy?'

True to form, the Strasbourg colloquium did nothing of the kind. Instead, a muddled, rambling conference highlighted how little politicians understand of the workings of the international film industry. The most common thread in any argument was a call for more money for marketing European films to combat Hollywood's muscle, with little thought for development strategy, constructive subsidy structures, or why we should be making the films in the first place. As discussed in the following chapter on distribution, marketing support for prints and advertising is an extremely risky and unstructured approach. Unless the films are intended to reach a genuine public audience, one might as well throw the money down a well as spend it on a poster.

On a more positive note, the planned 'Subsidy On Trial: The Best Strategies For European Film?' conference at the European Film College, Denmark, hopes to bring together Europe's top public film fund executives in a mock-trial setting. The concept behind the court exercise is to ask if subsidy monies – which in many instances are designed to support national culture rather than a film industry – could be made to complement certain commercial aspects of the film industry. Should public support systems be considering some market incentives in addition to straight, non-repayable funding? On the other hand, are regional economic funds (as found in the German Laenders) acting simply to attract healthy rates-of-return into their region's pockets, rather than realistically stimulate strong film-making talent? The trial is planned to take place in 1997, and information is available from the European Film College.[3]

## The different approaches

Mechanisms for raising and distributing money for film vary greatly across Europe. National and regional governments set aside sums of money for film which are raised either through a levy, such as in France, or a tax, as in the German Laender system. The terms on which the money is passed to the producer determines the subsidy's 'weight'. For example, the more a producer returns on an investment, the closer the subsidy comes to being a commercial investment. At present, Europe's national systems can be crudely broken down into seven or so different mechanisms, five for production support[4] and two (selective and automatic) for distribution (see Chapter 9). The five production types are as follows:

1 Soft, culture-orientated subsidy systems. This money is rarely recouped, and normally applies to smaller countries where their minority language and size of market makes commercial recoupment almost impossible. Most national film 'institutes' tend to work on a culture-driven basis, alongside national broadcasters. However, this kind of funding is critical for the discovery and development of new writing and directing talent. There are many examples of directors who started their careers with 'soft' support, including Ridley Scott, Peter Greenaway, Bille August and Lasse Halstrom. Territories that have soft, culture-orientated funding systems include smaller territories like the Nordic territories, Benelux, Portugal and Greece. Germany's federal sources of public funding, including Federal Ministry of the Interior (BMI) and the Federal Subsidy Fund (FFA), also follow soft grant systems. For example, between 6 and 7 per cent was repaid to FFA on average between 1985 and 1992.

2 Regional, economic loans. This system drives the main German 'economic' Laenders, where interest-free loans are awarded in return for a production obligation to spend about 50 per cent of that loan in the relevant region. The system is flexible, with sometimes two Laender or more supporting the same production although the return is mainly to one region. Their recoupment level is just 10 per cent, but as Nordrhein-Westfalen Filmstiftung's (NRWF) Dieter Kosslick points out, the key aim is to build and establish successful film activity in the region, so the funds should not just be judged on recoupment alone. Other systems have copied the economic model, including most

recently, the Rotterdam Film Fund, managed by former SOURCES head, Dick Willemsen.

3 The 'tough' repayable-loan mechanism, which more closely matches an equity investment than a subsidy loan. This is the system championed by British Screen Finance and the European Co-Production Fund, and imitated in part by Scotland's regional funds and the Irish Film Board. The approach is not easy to balance, as it requires both a cultural remit to support new talent and projects that otherwise would not reach the market-place, and to take a tough enough position to see some of its funds recouped on a regular basis. It is this model that the pan-Scandinavian fund, the Nordic Film and TV Fund, run by Dag Alveberg, has taken a keen interest in examining. However, while the system looks attractive to professionals concerned about the new breed of 'overhead' producers, who do little more than fill in forms and cover their costs; culture and language are sometimes raised as obstacles to such a strident, commercial approach.

4 One of the leading kinds of production support, known as 'automatic' aid, is best explained by the French system. Producers registered with the Centre National de la Cinématographie (CNC) can apply for CNC funds annually. The level of annual subsidy is calculated as a percentage of a CNC levy on the gross theatrical receipts on all films (including imports) released during the year. Receipts from films made by each French producer and released in the previous year are added up and the producer gets a share of the levy in proportion to those receipts. The subsidy is only paid if it is to go straight back into film – either to pay off debts on former projects, or the more likely case of re-investment in new productions. A bonus is paid for the latter. The 'automatic' system has been heralded as constructive 'recycling' of profits from the industry back into domestic production. Spain has recently introduced an automatic system to its industry with striking results (see below).

5 The last system, known as 'selective' aid, is also best represented by the French system, and is applied in a strictly cultural sense. Selective aid in France is mainly distributed by a system known as the Advances on Receipts. Grants are handed out to projects normally on the basis of a screenplay, and are deliberately given to first-time or new directors, and to challenging or interesting cultural work. (This is much closer to the culturally soft system described in 1). While the above descriptions are useful for explaining the basic premises of the two types of

aid, it should be noted that the French system is currently under review. See the analysis later in this chapter for further details.

6 Tax incentives, as introduced by the Irish and French governments, have been used to attract private finance for production. The Italian government is now considering such an approach.

## What kinds of films are we making?

Before examining in further detail the UK, German, Spanish and French systems, it is important to establish the relative scale and market that European films are aimed at, if aimed is indeed the operative word. Film expert Neil Watson carried out a study to assist with the setting up of ACE, the Paris-based European Film Studio. He broke European film production down into three broad types:

1 Films that are expected to recoup in a single national market; embracing low-budget (under $4 million to $5 million) arthouse pictures usually financed, at least in part, through national film subsidy mechanisms. This sector tends to perpetuate the need for 'subsidy' rather than forming a springboard for broader commercial acceptance. It also includes domestically orientated comedies (such as Germany's 'Otto' series, or Belgium's 'Hector'), characteristic of almost every European territory, that have substantial popular appeal but only within national borders. Indeed, Germany has recently produced a string of successful comedies which have performed very well at the domestic box office but failed to travel.

2 Films, shot in any European language, which are expected to recoup across Europe as a whole. The industry consensus is that the current budgetary ceiling for such pictures is in the region of between $5 million and $6 million, although Farinelli (see page 183), showed that a $13 million film can recoup from Europe. This category includes higher-budget national productions, but largely comprises projects co-produced or co-financed with at least one European partner. A North American distribution deal is an attractive bonus but is not essential to the financing of such films.

3 Films expected to recoup from the worldwide market. A North American distribution deal is essential to the financing of movies of this scale. Such films are usually shot in English – with obvious recent examples including 1492: Conquest of Paradise, and The House of the

Spirits – but occasionally a large-scale foreign-language film can succeed in recouping. The example Watson cites is Cyrano De Bergerac, whose 'excellence' managed to 'transcend linguistic barriers'.[5]

Given that only around 10 per cent of Europe's films are currently ever shown in cinema theatres in another country, it is quite clear that our national and regional subsidies are mainly used up in the effort to keep heads above water rather than crossing borders. Part of the problem that compounds this trend is that historically, many European subsidy systems were organized with the aim of supporting national, and only national production. Hence these systems don't fit into the co-production models discussed in Chapter 6. Internal rules, points systems and the protectiveness of national language inhibits multilateral support.

## The Spanish upswing

The current upswing of Spanish film production and a turnaround in the fortunes of Spanish films at the local box office during 1995 is partly due to recent changes in the industry's financing infrastructure. The new incentives were announced by the Spanish government at the San Sebastian Film Festival in September 1994 and introduced at the start of 1995.

The key piece of legislation is an automatic subsidy scheme. The Spanish Film Institute (ICAA) now awards a grant of 33 per cent of a film's budget to any Spanish film that takes more than pta30 million ($230,000) at the box office, up to a maximum value of pta100 million ($773,000) per film. The strategy is to encourage producers to make more commercial films. According to top Spanish producer Andres Vicente Gomez, in practice it means that 'producers can also start their own films without having to go through committees', a major burden to speedy and sensible decisions under the old selective system. The former system was an advance subsidy on a project-by-project basis, where theoretically producers were supposed to use the advances for cashflow purposes or to 'top-up' a film's budget which should have already been raised from distributors and broadcasters. In practice this was rarely the case, and many producers became dependent on the state 'hand-outs' to an alarming degree. According to *Screen International*'s Benedict Carver, 'this not only led to distortion of the market but also encouraged production of the sort of films that in reality had little chance of recouping their budget at the box office.'

The ICAA still continues to grant a total of pta700 million ($5.4 million) per annum, in two separate up-front production subsidies, but only to new directors, those who have directed no more than three films, or to experimental films by more accomplished film-makers. The trend since 1994 has been to emphasize directorial debuts with more established names often finding themselves left out.

The new subsidy mechanism has coincided with some supportive co-operation between Spain's private bankers and its major broadcasters. The Federation of Spanish Producers' Associations (FAPAE) has been building on the landmark deal that it struck with the Official Credit Institute (ICO) and state broadcaster RTVE in late 1994. Under the deal, ICO agreed to loan pta2 billion ($16 million – increased to pta4 billion ($32 million) in May 1995) per annum over four years to RTVE for feature film production. During 1996 RTVE said that it would invest a total of pta3 billion in film acquisition and production, giving a welcome boost to the industry after the fallow early 1990s, when RTVE was in a financial mess. A similar deal worth pta1.5 billion ($11 million) per annum has been struck between ICO and private terrestrial network Antena 3.

Meanwhile, in January 1995 the Banco Exterior de Espana (BFX) renewed its agreement with the Spanish Ministry of Culture, increasing its credit lines for feature film production to pta4.5 million ($36 million) per annum. FAPAE is working on another film financing agreement that would see terrestrial pay-TV operator Canal Plus Spain link up with ICO or Spain's Banco Central.

In addition to public, broadcasting and banking support, it is important to note how Spain's private sector has become far more active in film financing since 1994. The main player is GRUPO Prisa, which has considerable media assets and production ambitions (See Chapter 5).

## The German scenario

Over the past five years, and despite recent high-level domestic success stories, national films have continued to take between 8–12 per cent of the German box office. The entire German support system has risen since 1993 from around DM200 million ($115 million) to DM250 million ($160 million), partly due to the arrival of the Berlin-Brandenburg Filmboard and also due to a restructured Hamburg Filmfund and new Baden-Wuerttemberg fund.[6]

As a 1994 report by London Economics stressed (and further expanded upon in the February 1995 report),[7] regional support from the Laenders has become so numerous as to have been described as 'a jungle of subsidies'. There has been a certain amount of leap-frogging by the government to provide more and more attractive aid packages for producers willing to locate production in a Laender. Indeed, according to one senior source, German producers would encourage writer-directors to 'become gypsies, and write road movies all over Germany so that they could access each fund accordingly!'

To limit these and other alarming tendencies, the Laenders decided in 1994 onwards to pool some part of their funds. However, calls for even further centralization have been consistently rejected by the regions.

> **'If there was no regional competition and effort to build up infrastructures in different areas, then the money would not be there for film-makers to use. It's crazy to suggest that the regional fund system should "go national" when effectively that would destroy much of the help available now.'**
>
> Dieter Kosslick, head of the NordRhine-Westfalen Filmstiftung (NRWF)

Rather than centralize, the main Laenders have tried to co-operate with one another. Since the arrival of Alfred Hurmer at the newly reconstructed Hamburg Film Fund, Kosslick, Klaus Keil and Hurmer have held a series of meetings in an attempt to collaborate more constructively. For example, monies offered by one board to be spent in a different region will be returned in kind over a period of three years.

## Berlin-Brandenburg Filmboard

When Keil joined the Berlin-Brandenburg Filmboard in October 1994, his plans surprised large sectors of the industry. Not only were his plans hugely ambitious – including the aim to 'double the German theatrical market share from 8 per cent to 16 per cent within ten years' – but he also wanted to achieve that goal by doing away with the 'watering can' approach of other regional funds and following a more market-orientated direction. He has placed a strong emphasis on development and packaging, telling *Screen International*: 'In Germany, the screenplay equals literature, which is a piece of art and may only be altered by the creator. This is a scandalous attitude. All the millions piled up in the film funds are a waste of money if the script isn't up to scratch.'[8] In addition, Berlin-Brandenburg's selection mechanism differs from the other funds by not working by committee, and Keil is himself free to green-light projects. And it operates as a private company, not a government-run bureaucracy.

'Part of the Berlin-Brandenburg application form is a recoupment plan, which was an unknown word in Germany,' Keil explains. 'Money is growing more precious, although we are just starting to apply this approach. We don't expect more than the money we have invested, and we won't become an equity investor until perhaps three or four years down the line. But I want German films to have a quality label once again.'

One of the areas which Keil has toughened up on is the requirement to have a domestic theatrical distribution agreement in place before any project receives production monies. While this approach makes sense in theory, in practice many German distributors already have production interests, and are far less interested in backing other, rival producers' projects for support. 'It's a major problem, because most of the distributors simply aren't interested in giving productions a pre-sale minimum guarantee, especially when they are competing for funds,' says one Berlin-based producer.

The other two problems that face Keil are the amount of time it takes to service applicants and get decisions made; and the budget difficulties he has faced between late 1995 and 1996. The second is not his fault, but lies with the complex politics and funding policies of the region. The first is less easy to side-step. After coming into the fund with a strong set of ideas and goals, the reality of running such a politically and administratively over-burdened system has caught up with his well-intentioned rhetoric. Local producers are almost all critical of the time it has taken to move projects forward with Berlin-Brandenburg. As one put it: 'Sometimes it's better to have a fast "No" than simply not hear anything for months.'

For a fund to function well, first-class staff and a smooth and prompt decision-making process are essential. If Keil is to make the most of the $30 million or so funds – albeit that the sums are under increasing pressure – then he will need to streamline some of his ambitious plans over the coming months.

The production support available from the NordRhine-Westfalen Filmstiftung (NRWF) is second to France's CNC in terms of size and power. Established in 1991, NRWF operates as a limited company, two-thirds owned by the regional broadcaster WDR, and one-third owned by the local Laender government. Consequently, two separate funds are operated – one fully funded by the region, and one 50 per cent financed by WDR and 50 per cent from the regions. Conditionally repayable loans are paid into a special account which can then be used for the producer's next project with the Filmstiftung, a system that Kosslick describes as 'recycling success', and one that made the fund initially very attractive to producers.

Kosslick has a difficult balancing act between the local government's demands and the broadcaster's interests in the fund-backed projects. For example, films backed by NRWF can seem less attractive to distributors if the monies have originated from the WDR-shared fund. WDR automatically takes domestic television rights on such a project. It was for this reason that producer Bernd Eichinger returned a DM1.25 million ($820,000) conditionally repayable loan which had been awarded to Der Bewegte Mann. Eichinger insisted on being able to choose where he sold the film, and did not want monies being controlled by a NRWF account that would only be accessed if and when he made a further film with the Filmstiftung.

While NRWF's track record of successful films has been distinctly varied, and has come in for strident criticism over the past three years, the level of regional support towards the film industry appears to be working. Figures produced by the fund and the region back claims that production houses, facilities and media activity have all increased considerably since 1991. Kosslick has also proved himself a skilled administrator, keeping both his political and television partners closely informed and abreast of NRWF's developments. Other German fund managers would do well to examine how Kosslick operates, especially given his lengthy experience in the field.

He is also quite clear in his own mind about the term 'subsidy'. 'We give conditional, repayable loans,' he explained recently. 'After five years if a film isn't successful, then it may be written off. Then it's a subsidy. But if a movie recoups, we then ask that they pay us back.' He also introduced a new incentive funding-style initiative in the summer of 1996. NRWF granted guarantees of $5.8 million to 11 production companies in North Rhine-Westphalia to develop projects as part of a development pilot project. Kosslick stressed that the money was not granted as a soft loan, but would have to be paid back.

## What is wrong with Germany?

Ask most German film producers about the state of their industry, and they will normally point to the subsidy system as a key problem. However, having slammed it, when it is actually suggested that the system is removed completely, they throw their hands up in horror. 'It may not work, but it's the only thing we've got,' says one defensive and very senior producer. 'Without it we'd have nothing.'

More specifically, criticisms claim that, firstly, more time and energy is put into applications for funding than the projects themselves; and secondly, projects lose their focus by trying to please committees and public broadcasters, rather than considering audiences.

## The new UK film world

Although Britain has very little direct government intervention towards film production, those bodies that do have money are surprisingly competitive and effective. The main sources of film finance via subsidized/government sources are British Screen Finance, which incorporates the European Co-Production Fund; and the British Film Institute.

The key definition when discussing UK film support is the difference between 'financial intervention' and 'subsidy finance'. Even the BFI invests money as a 'leverage' to attract either other public support and/or private money. BFI Production exists both to back new talent and partly to compensate for the market's structural inadequacies and difficulties, and unlike many softer funds has a very active sales operation.

The production department had a production budget of around £650,000 ($975,000) for 1993, which was expanded in 1994/95 to support three films per year at a maximum budget level of £450,000 ($675,000). BFI finance is designed to encourage creative talent to make films with the freedom to experiment with new ideas rather than those aimed at the market. Many of the crews, directors and producers involved in these productions enter the wider market following their induction with BFI films. For example, Stephen Frears, Karel Reisz, Lindsay Anderson, Peter Greenaway, Terence Davies and Derek Jarman all benefited from BFI support in the making of their first films.

British Screen Finance and the European Co-Production Fund (which is administered by BSF) are the most important sources of government intervention to stimulating production in the UK. It should be noted that recent commercially and culturally successful films, including Land and Freedom, Jack and Sarah, Before the Rain, The Crying Game, Orlando, Tom and Viv, and Damage have made British Screen's financial position relatively healthy as a result of its tough position on its investments. In 1994 and 1995, British Screen had £2 million ($3 million) in the form of direct government grant, and £2 million for the European Co-Production Fund (ECF). In addition, it had returns from its investments at healthy rates, plus an additional £2m from a BSkyB satellite TV output deal. According to British Screen chief executive Simon Perry, British Screen makes good returns on its investments by European 'subsidy' standards. This is mainly because it puts in the minimum investment required to help a UK film get made, and its loans are not soft. 'Our economic and cultural strategy is to put into the market films that would not otherwise be there. If enough of those films work, then the example will stimulate the making of more such films, with and without the support of British Screen,' Perry explained.

The other key factor behind British Screen and the BFI is the clear growth of genuine co-production finance for UK films. Most of this rise in activity stems less from choice, and more from financial imperatives. The fact is that in a relatively small country like Britain, which enjoys a low level of government support, co-finance is the *only* means of getting films made. Given that more than 70 films are now being made per year in the UK, in contrast to the lows of the early 1990s (with fewer than 30 films being made in 1989), production has improved considerably. However, of the 73 films made during 1994 and 1995 respectively, fewer than half were totally British financed, reflecting the difficult market-place.

Ironically, after many years of complaining about lack of government support, the British industry has recently received an unexpected shot in the arm. This new 'drug' package originates from the National Lottery, and is worth around £30 million ($45 million) per annum for all film-related activities, including film production (and development), exhibition, training, and distribution support in the form of prints and advertising support. Of that figure, the Producers Alliance for Cinema and Television anticipates that about £24.5 million ($36.75 million) will be available for production investment during the years up to 2000.

While on one level the support looks miraculous in terms of its size when compared to pre-existing funds for UK film support, the Lottery money has not come without its drawbacks. The Arts Council of England

(ACE), the largest body dispersing the funds alongside its regional partners, has tended to fall into the trap of running film-production funding decisions by committee. Single applications have suffered from some of the idiosyncrasies that go hand-in-hand with such a system. Indeed, one BFI project on Francis Bacon was rejected by, among others, Lord Gowrie, who complained that Bacon was a close friend of his, and it was far too soon to be making films about the artist.

One of the new strategies is the Greenlight Fund, administered by British Screen and aimed at halting the move to Hollywood by so many UK directors after they have completed their first feature film. The plan is to invest about £5 million ($7.5 million) a year in bigger-budgeted films on commercial terms, and a pilot year was carried out as this book was published. The Greenlight Fund also raised the problem inherent with its adminstration. Simon Perry, BSF's chief executive, already has considerable executive control over funding decisions at BSF and the European Co-Production Fund. If the Greenlight Fund is successful in its bid to continue, then a third fund run under his aegis may be too much for some to handle. That's not to suggest that his track record has been poor. On the contrary, BSF has not only enjoyed notable successes, but has over the last six years managed to reorientate UK producers towards Europe. Nevertheless, such power and individual taste concentrated in the hands of one public executive would be resisted by certain quarters of the industry.

What both the UK industry and the government are now searching for is a new model that could help attract private investment and 'enhance the quality, number and range of British films produced'. The Middleton Committee, appointed by the DNH and made up of film industry and city financiers, argued for a range of incentives. Its big idea was that Lottery money should be used to create one 'national' film studio, which would finance and release up to twenty British films a year. Many questions remained unclear about the proposal, including who would run such an all-conquering entity.

Unfortunately, the studio idea got in the way of Middleton's other more reasonable recommendations, including a package of tax cuts and incentives. But the damage was done. The report noticeably failed to win endorsement from the National Heritage Secretary Virginia Bottomley, prompting critics to wonder how its members could have been so incompetent. As Simon Relph, a top UK producer and BAFTA vice-chairman put it: 'The report was off-target – a poor and weak effort. They really didn't get to grips with the market and how it operates. On the other hand, even a modest tax concession would be a tremendous help.'

'Getting to grips with the market' was also supposed to be the guiding principle behind the Arts Council's own lottery plans for film. The Arts Council is hoping to use Lottery funds to back eight or nine companies (called 'franchises') made up of groups of film-makers and distributors who will work together to each make two or three films a year. Over time, it is hoped that these companies will build up good track records and become attractive to City and international investors. The concept was far better received than the Middleton studio plan, and an announcement by the Arts Council on its future was expected before Christmas 1996.

Overall, there are considerable problems as well as pluses that come with the Lottery money. For a start, the money was never actually expected by an industry that has long canvassed for tax incentives rather than straight subsidy support. The key will be to hold on to what the government *already* invests in British film, rather than allowing Lottery money to sweep all previous support from the British film industry's door.

## The Irish rejuvenation

In contrast to Germany and France, which have both enjoyed considerable levels of government support for many years, Ireland provides a different, and considerably stronger example of where state intervention can constructively stimulate both commerce and culture.

In 1993, the former Irish Film Board (abolished in 1987) was reconstituted. Coupled with Ireland's continuing membership of Eurimages, increased independent access to Irish public broadcaster RTE, and the Irish Government's Section 35 tax scheme (recently revised), Ireland has enjoyed a dramatic upswing in production between 1994 and 1996. From an average of just three films a year prior to the new Board, 16 Irish films with lead Irish producer involvement were completed in 1995.

According to Ireland's minister for arts, culture and the Gaeltacht, Michael D. Higgins – in words that are anathema to a UK government – culture is a vitalizing force in the life of any nation. Hence, he argued, it was very important to invest in culture at a time of economic stagnation. He wanted a five-year commitment to the Irish Film Board rather than leaving the body hanging from a string, like the last one.[9] The precise workings of the Film Board are not dissimilar to those of British Screen Finance, in that the Board looks to recoup its loans on relatively tough terms, while remaining flexible on projects that it especially wants to see reach the market-place. (See Case Study on Guiltrip, page 230.)

Higgins was also keen to refine Ireland's tax incentives for film-making. Tax incentives form part of a set of measures designed by certain states to try to combat some of Europe's cinematic weaknesses. Unlike direct subsidies, tax concessions are based on the principle of attracting risk-investors in an otherwise under-financed industry. National treasuries forgo immediate tax returns and hope that the increased film-making activity generated by the tax relief will later bring more revenue in the shape of invisible earnings, income tax on fees earned by crews and artists, corporation tax, and so on.

While some countries – chief among them the UK – remain unconvinced to date by this equation, others have attempted to revive or sustain the fortunes of their film industries with such schemes. Ireland provides the most recent example of a film industry which has been partly revived by the introduction of a generous tax shelter scheme. Under Section 35 of the tax law, investors in qualifying Irish companies set up exclusively for the purpose of making qualifying Irish films and whose directors are Irish residents, can write off their investment against tax. Ireland's higher-earning tax band is currently 48 per cent.

In order for the investments to qualify for an 80 per cent tax relief on money invested, not more than 60 per cent of the production budget may be raised by the qualifying company from investments benefiting from the tax relief. The tax relief investment element must be spent in cash on Irish goods and services. No less than 75 per cent of the work on the film must take place in Ireland. This is generally calculated in staff hours, but under special circumstances this condition may be relaxed and a lower requirement applied.

Officially, the investors are only allowed to put up risk investment and cannot exit the scheme before a period of one year. This means that no guarantee should be given up front that they can recoup their initial outlay out of pre-sales. Recoupment can only occur from net receipts after the sales agent's or distributor's commission has been paid. The maximum claimable allowance for any company is Ir£2 million ($3.12 million) per annum, while individual investors can invest Ir£25,000 ($39,000). The changes were also introduced in an effort to block speculative fundraising through the setting up of funds to accumulate finance for a range of pictures without actually putting any films into production.[10]

The recent revisions made in early 1996 stopped development relief and targeted the relief towards local and smaller budget pictures over large Hollywood productions. In practice, a late amendment was made over the summer to the new Bill. Following pressure by the producers' representative body Filmmakers Ireland, and some subtle steering from the Irish Film Board, the key revision allowed the retention of 100 per cent tax relief for smaller Irish films made for up to Ir£4 million ($6.24 million).

To place the Irish rejuvenation in some perspective, much attention was paid to the collapse of Divine Rapture in the summer of 1995. Not only was the film subject to considerable mismanagement, but the spectacle also highlighted the degree to which Ireland's industry had become 'overheated'. Crewing was becoming tougher, facilities under increasing pressure and the positive feeling of 1994 had turned into a frenetic, chaotic mess by the middle of 1995. Now that the government has included the sensible revisions to the Section 35 Bill, contrary to the notion that expansion is all good, Ireland will actually benefit from a slight slow-down in activity.

## The French tax system

While the Irish tax system has clearly benefited the indigenous industry, France's tax shelter investment scheme, SOFICAs (Sociétés pour le Financement du Cinéma et de l'Audiovisuel) provide the best-documented example of the opportunities and problems generated by tax initiatives in the European film industry.

The SOFICA attracts mostly higher earning individual tax payers looking to limit the amount of their income tax liability in France's higher income bracket of 56.8 per cent. These individuals may write off the whole of their investment in a SOFICA share capital, providing they do not sell those shares for five years (formerly eight years).

Under similar conditions, there is no tax owing on capital gain after the investor's exit from the SOFICA. For companies, the corporation tax relief is significantly less attractive, with a write off of just 50 per cent.

The SOFICAs were first launched in 1985–86, amid great hopes that they would provide a significant boost to the financing of independent films in France. By 1991 however, it had become apparent that the tax shelter investment provided a marginally better yield than straightforward bank loans. Over eight years, SOFICAs were able to return between 75 per cent and 80 per cent of their nominal capital sum to investors. For FFr100 ($19) invested, the immediate relief was FFr56.8 ($10.84). After deduction of the capital sum not recovered however – around FFr25 – the total yield was only about 4.5 per cent tax free per annum.

In 1992 the law was changed to accommodate pressures by SOFICAs to improve the return to investors. The banks managing the SOFICAs were allowed to offer investors a guarantee that they would buy back the entirety of their initial capital sum after eight years. Overnight, those SOFICAs were therefore able to offer a risk-free investment which – after the minimum duration of the investment was brought down to five years – offered an impressive tax-free return on investment of around 15 per cent.

The measure has fostered concentrations in the SOFICA market, which is now threatening to make access by independents increasingly difficult. In order to cover their risk, those SOFICAs offering to purchase the entirety of the initial capital put in by investors tend to work exclusively with the French 'Majors' such as Gaumont or UGC.

While the SOFICA guarantees its shareholders that it will re-purchase 100 per cent of what they put in, the Major to which the SOFICA is associated guarantees the SOFICA that it will reimburse all of those sums. As a condition of providing such a guarantee however, the Major will insist that the SOFICA funds, and only SOFICA funds, be used exclusively as production finance. In doing so, the Major has effectively access to an interest-free credit system.

The SOFICAs that are unable to align themselves with a powerful production studio, by contrast, are finding it increasingly difficult to survive. Independents are concerned that they will find access to SOFICA finance increasingly arduous. In an attempt to prevent a lockout, the government amended the rules, making it obligatory for SOFICAs to dedicate at least 35 per cent of their funds to film projects that do not emanate from the group with which they are aligned.

### The problem with tax breaks

According to Bertrand Moullier, PACT's head of European affairs, the disadvantage of current tax incentives in Europe is that they are exclusively national in character and are very cumbersome to use. The much-publicized Irish Section 35 relief, for instance, is prescriptive about the amount of cash raised through the tax-shelter Irish company which should be spent on Irish goods and services.

Tax incentives are primarily entered into by domestic governments as a means of generating value for the local economy. These conditions force European producers to enter into complex compromises which may range from the impractical to the downright counter-productive, in order to ensure that they make use of the statutory proportion of local craft and skills.

The conversion of all these national schemes into a single European Union tax relief mechanism is not for the European Commission to propose, as fiscal issues have been clearly identified by the Treaty as a national responsibility. Even if it were legally possible to unify such measures, no member state would see the benefit of it, as the principal attraction is precisely to be able to offer more attractive conditions than your neighbours.

## MEDIA II's new wave

On a wider, pan-European level, the European Community implemented an ambitious programme for Europe's audiovisual industry. Since a pilot phase from 1986 to a five-year run from 1991 to 1995, the original MEDIA programme spawned a wide-ranging gaggle of projects, described as an 'economic support mechanism for cultural activities'. Each project was co-financed by local authorities and the EC, with much politicking taking place over new schemes and projects designed sometimes as much to keep certain countries happy than anything to do with audiovisual strategy.

When Jacques Delmoly replaced Holde Lhoest as head of the MEDIA programme in February 1995, critics wondered whether his experience of the audiovisual arena was sufficient for the considerable task in hand. His task was to see out MEDIA I and usher in the new MEDIA II programme. A lawyer by training, Delmoly's task was to 'manage the negotiations for MEDIA II and ultimately to manage the programme itself'. Neither he nor the industry knew just how problematic that task was to prove to be.

The MEDIA II budget was requested at ECU400 million ($490 million), but that was subsequently cut to ECU310 million ($380 million), with ECU90 million ($110 million) put aside for what was referred to as the 'European Guarantee Fund' (see Chapter 8 on distribution). ECU45 million ($82.3 million) was set aside for training, and ECU265 million ($325 million) for development and distribution.

In an effort to centralize what had become a widespread and highly devolved system of management under MEDIA I, Delmoly opted for four Intermediary Organisations to administer the new programme. Their responsibilities include Development, Distribution, Training and a Management body which would administer the payments to professionals. The first three IOs have juries of professionals of up to 15 people. The IO gives both the jury and the Commission (which has the final decision over all awards) technical assistance on each area. Basically, the IOs preselect the applicants, which the jury subsequently approves and the Commission ultimately sanctions. The money, mostly in the form of repayable loans, is then paid by the Management IO.

In addition to the four IOs, there are three industrial platforms, each charged with responsibility for certain key audiovisual areas. These are animation (to be run by the same team as MEDIA I's CARTOON), New Technology (Media Investments Club) and Audiovisual Heritage (MAP TV). Each industrial platform is expected to work closely with the relevant IO where there are natural cross-overs, such as Development and Animation. (The key details on Distribution, Training and Development are to be found in Chapters 8, 3 and 2 respectively.)

Overall, MEDIA II purports to be a more economically-geared, and less culture-orientated programme. Delmoly argues that 'a lot of thought has been put into the structural weakness of the European audiovisual industry. There are two tremendous gaps – one of which is development, the other is in distribution. I would have personally preferred more overall monies for development, but we have a tremendous budget for training – at ECU9 million ($11.05 million) a year, a doubling of its budget under MEDIA I. But overall the emphasis will be on business skills and economic structures. We are much more interested in financing companies than individuals.'

When challenged about the lopsided nature of the funding that will go towards distribution (some ECU200 million), Delmoly answered that it is 'the story of the chicken and the egg. The producers and directors complain that the big problem in Europe is the absence of major distributors. But PolyGram are everywhere – they have production companies, a distribution network, high investment in training and development. The Think-Tank claimed that it was mostly a matter of distribution. I don't think that's true, and I'm sure that training and development are crucial to the problem.'

Nevertheless, MEDIA II is massively skewed towards distribution, something that Delmoly puts down to the professionals at the large European conference of the summer of 1994: 'I wasn't there, so I cannot comment. That, and reports by the MBS and others have stressed the importance of distribution and the current market imbalance.'

## Critics of MEDIA II

Wherever there are considerable sums of public money, there is inevitably consternation and carping. Critics of Delmoly and MEDIA II are widespread and became increasingly vocal by early 1996, as they witnessed a cumbersome bureaucracy fail to cope with the desirable 'smooth transition' into a new programme.

Under the original MEDIA pilot programme and initial five-year phase, the industry's professionals were allowed a considerable amount of control over the running and releasing of funds. Delmoly was concerned about conflicts of interest and empire building, and came up with a system that ultimately gives the Commission much more centralized power than in the previous system.

As this slowly started to sink in with professionals – already irritated by the inaccurate and beguiling calls for tender during early 1996 – some of them snapped. Thomas Frickel, a documentary producer/director, argued in a scathing *Screen International* comment article, that 'no other institution has matched the audacity and arrogance of the MEDIA programme . . . while the old MEDIA programme allowed industry representatives a say in its various projects, Brussels now treats movie professionals like lepers.

'Delmoly's declared goal is to smash the existing structures and break the influence of the professionals . . . the plan to decide market access anew each year is going in the same direction.'[11]

Frickel makes some strong points, including the abandonment of experienced administrators, the concentration of power almost exclusively in Brussels and, arguably, Delmoly's predisposition towards the French industry's concerns.

Other critics are angry about the abandonment of smaller, individual creative people in favour of companies and combines. The Association of Danish Film, TV and Video Directors even published an eight-page document that described the new MEDIA programme as a 'Zoo Story' that did little more than support Europe's largest countries and bigger, already advantaged companies.

The Americans have watched the endless squabbling and bureacratic mismanagement with detached amusement. On the one hand they are impressed at the political will to come behind such an ambitious programme; on the other hand they remain eternally suspicious of any subsidy that bucks the free market. As Michael Bartholomew, the Motion

Picture Association's director of European Union affairs pointed out back at the start of 1995, 'The way MEDIA II is structured at the moment it's going to run into big budgetary problems. Our concern is that the market stays open, keeping private investment attractive in Europe.'[12]

> 'We support anything that the Europeans are doing to develop their audiovisual industry, but it's not going to be done through massive aid funds.'
>
> Michael Bartholomew, MPA

Certainly, MEDIA II has a long road to climb if it is to prove in practical terms that its new structures can work effectively. Most serious of all, Europe's industry could look back at the 1990s with dismay in years to come. Here was an opportunity to pull together, to concentrate on Europe's diverse creative talents, and to focus on fast and effective forms of stimulation. The jury remains out on MEDIA II, and will stay that way for at least two years to come.

## The great debate

'Aesthetics and economics are intertwined when it comes to film-making,' stated Hal Hartley at the EFA's conference in Berlin. Unfortunately, neither factors have triumphed under numerous European support systems. Basic questions such as the following have rarely been asked: When is subsidy given out just for cultural reasons, and what result does that approach have for the mid- to longer-term health of the film industry? Do public funders and committees ask themselves about a film's ability to find a place in the market, or are they too often more concerned with political, social and employment effects? Which national incentive mechanisms could stimulate a stronger European industry if applied on a wider and longer-term scale? And are they practical on such a level?

Unfortunately, all these questions have failed to be constructively debated, let alone answered over the last decade. That failure could have a long-reaching effect on what Europeans see on their screens in the early part of the next century. It is possible to argue that European film has nothing to do with business. However, such a segmented approach denies the reality that the film industry – in addition to having a significant cultural and industrial impact – also has a political role to play in Europe's future. As Michael Kuhn of PolyGram puts it: 'If you don't have control of two things – sport and movies – then you will not be in control of broadcasting in Europe. These are the two software content-related distribution elements that drive all new kinds of broadcast, using that term in its loosest sense.

'You can see that with what Murdoch is concentrating on – sport and movies – sewing up all movies and sport until the year 2002 in the UK, then governments can do what they want, but he will dictate pay, service and so on, and yet they won't control it. To my mind, there is a strategic need which wasn't there previously for British and other European governments to get control of the content of movies and sport. They may not be the most profitable, but they are the most noticeable. If governments want to do something, then they should concentrate on those two areas. The first thing that has to be addressed is capital. It's not often realized that less than ten years ago, the American government actually did give Hollywood producers tremendous financial incentives, because they allowed them to write off the cost of movies and television production programmes against tax in a very advantageous way and it was open to no other corporate tax payer. When Hollywood became strong, it was stopped, but it was given as a chance to get going. It attracted tons of capital and got people interested in the movie business, so Europe has to find the equivalent here.

'What PolyGram has tried to do is come up with an idea for a scheme that would give that kind of capital on a massive scale to big players in Europe without being a drain on EU institutions or national institutions, and that's what our Guarantee Fund is all about.'

PolyGram has closely followed the European Commission's troubled plans for a European Guarantee Fund, but the chances of such a fund coming into existence still remained limited by the autumn of 1996. The objective of a ECU90 million ($110 million) Guarantee Fund – which needs to attract matching monies before it starts operations – is to attract more private sources of financing to the European film industry. It is a commercially-driven rather than culturally-driven concept, which is aimed at private investors and financiers (normally banks). At its simplest, the idea is that a Guarantee Fund would issue part-guarantees to help limit the downside risk to financiers and investors, and hence make more money available to the film industry for both production and distribution.

One of the obstacles in the way of the Commission was the vagueness of its own reports. The original feasibility study, published in June 1995 was unclear about how such a Fund would attract matching finance, and how it would be structured. More than a year later, the same questions remained unanswered. There are no financial incentives to attract private sources to provide matching finance. Meanwhile, Screen Partners, the UK-based deficit financier, put together a group of international insurers in a proposal to underwrite an equivalent sum to whatever the EC finally decides to put into the Fund.[13]

As of the end of August 1996, the most likely way forward for the European Guarantee Fund was that a pilot programme would be agreed by the Commission, but the overall chances of success look grim.

## Notes

1  See 'Establishing a competitive European film industry', *London Economics*, February 1995, p. 14 for further details of the 1976 US Tax Reform Act, which made films eligible for tax investment credit.
2  Media Business File, MBS, Summer 1996, p. 15.
3  Write to The European Film College, Ebeltoft, Denmark 8400 for details.
4  For much more detailed information and contact numbers of the national funding systems, see *Developing Films In Europe: A Practical Guide*, Routledge/MBS, Angus Finney (ed.), 1996. Also see *Sources of European Feature Film Funding*, PACT booklet, September 1995.
5  *European Film Studio Feasibility Study*, MBS, Neil Watson, 1992, p. 10.
6  Contact as 4 above.
7  'Film subsidies in Germany', *London Economics*, September 1994; see 1 above, pp. 29–35.
8  *Screen International*, 5 April 1996, p. 12.
9  National Film Theatre discussion, October 1995. Transcripts available from the NFT, South Bank, London SE1.
10  See INDECON report, *A Strategy for Success Based on Economic Realities: The Next Stage of Development for the Film Industry in Ireland*, December 1995.
11  *Screen International*, 5 April 1996, p. 12.
12  Moving Pictures International, 'Programme for Change', pp. 8–9, January 1995.
13  *Screen Finance*, EGF could get backing from Screen Partners, pp. 5–6, 25 July 1996.

# 8

# Feeding the Distribution Pipelines

'Film funding which cuts itself off from the market is condemned
to fail. The distributor as the middle-man [*sic*] between
production and the cinema must be already incorporated in the
pre-production and production stage.'

The German Distributor's Association (VdF) June 1994

'Having heard complaints about UIP and the US majors for years,
it was a ministerial recommendation that European distributors
adopt some common strategies.
What we are finding is that some may not be ready to do so.'

Jacques Delmoly, head of MEDIA II

ONE OF THE RECURRING industry debates over the past decade has
been focused on the distribution and marketing of European films.
There are many who argue that one of the key problems facing the European film industry is that it operates on all levels as a series of discrete,
fragmented national markets. This chapter looks at three of Europe's key
territories – the UK, Germany and France – and examines the debate
around pan-European distribution initiatives.

The strategic and competitive advantage of Hollywood is that it has a
home market of sufficient size to provide substantial returns from successful films. Although 'foreign' revenues have become increasingly
important to the American Majors, they benefit considerably from the
fact that their films stand a good chance of recouping from their domestic territory. Larger and/or successful films also benefit from the 'lift off'
the US home territory provides into the international market. Some
argue that if only Europe could treat the entire continent as a unified

home market, such economies of scale could be achieved, and European films would romp home at the box office.

The facts stacked against such a simplistic analysis remain ominous. Europe currently is producing more than 600 films a year, of which some 500 are produced in a wide range of languages other than English. Europeans go on average to the cinema just 1.6 times a year, compared to the Americans' four times a year. According to ACE research by London Economics, in 1992 Europeans managed to spend as much as ECU2.7 billion ($3.32 billion) at the box office, although this was spread throughout 3,381 film releases. By contrast, US box-office receipts of ECU3.7 billion ($4.55 billion) was confined to 414 releases. The five largest national markets in the EU – UK, Germany, France, Italy and Spain – account for nearly 80 per cent of the total spend within Europe, highlighting the significant problems encountered by smaller EU territories in keeping any kind of market share.[1]

With the exception of PolyGram's growing distribution network,[2] no European-owned 'major' company exists, let alone one that can be sensibly compared to UIP, Twentieth Century–Fox, Columbia TriStar, Warner Bros and the most recent and highly effective arrival, Buena Vista International. Armed with the fact that nearly 60 per cent of Hollywood's box office now comes from international grosses, compared to 40 per cent 'domestic' (in other words, the US), the Hollywood Majors are taking an increasingly competitive and exacting position in every territory they release films in.

As Michael Williams-Jones, the retiring president and CEO of UIP put it in his Ebeltoft lecture in 1995, 'Entertainment is big business and it is time for Europe to come to terms with the reality that Hollywood is not a bogeyman. The citizens of Europe have earned their democratic freedoms, including their right to choose their entertainment – regardless of what part of the world it comes from.'

Such strident words fall on deaf French ears. It is no accident that the French film industry's cheerleaders are constantly obsessed with what they view as a pressing need for a distribution system on a pan-European scale for European (and specifically French-language) films. As Sylvain Bursztein, president of the French Producers' Association, speaking at the European Film Academy's 'Strategies for Survival' conference in Berlin in June 1996 explained: 'The real problem facing the French industry is the recent collapse of its market share across the rest of Europe.' The figures support such a blunt analysis. In 1985, French films had 6.3 per cent of the Italian market, but this had dropped to 2.5 per cent by 1994; while in Germany they took 7.5 per cent in 1986, which dropped to 1.5 per cent in 1994. Even France's Spanish share has dropped in the same period from 4 per cent to 3 per cent.[3]

Neither has the US held fast for French films. Geoff Gilmore, director of the Sundance Film Institute and Festival, noted with disappointment during the EFA's Berlin conference, that twenty years ago French films played a vital role in the specialist US arthouse circuit. Today, they struggle to find any distribution whatsoever. According to the CNC's figures for 1995, of the 320 films released in the US, just 14 French productions were distributed. The top-grossing film was the re-release of Belle de Jour, which placed at 172nd, with a gross of just over $4 million.

The implication of such a market loss is seen by the French to raise important cultural as well as industrial problems, given the key role that language, (and the preservation of French as a leading world language), plays in France's national audiovisual policy. Unlike the British Government, which has only belatedly (and somewhat marginally) woken up to the impact a thriving domestic film culture can play in terms of promoting the national identity, France has long understood film's ambassadorial role. It is for these reasons that it has been preoccupied about the dominant position the Hollywood industry finds itself in in Europe.

## Implications of dominancy

According to a consultancy research study, *The Distribution Game: Can Europe Even the Score?* executed by Coopers & Lybrand,[4] the implications of the US Majors' dominance over European territories include the following assertions:

- Overheads of the distribution process are spread over a large number of films.
- The distributor's profit margin is ultimately owned by the studio and thus contributes to the overall income earned by the producers.
- The large volume of advertising spend undertaken by the major distributors results in considerable leverage over the pricing of advertising space in the various media.
- Similarly, the large volume of releases results in considerable bargaining power over the exhibitors; possibly resulting in preferable release dates and terms of trade.
- Audience information can be gathered for a wide portfolio of films,

and can be fed back to the studios for consideration in developing
future commercially orientated products.

- A worldwide distribution network provides knowledge and insight
  into all significant territories; only the US Majors have such widespread access to world markets.
- The Majors have much greater versatility in release strategies in the
  theatrical markets around the world; a worldwide network affords the
  luxury of direct access to the world markets.

The Coopers report concludes that the 'logic' behind the US Majors' distribution networks should provide the reasoning for 'European film-
makers to attempt to replicate the structural elements of the US majors'
distribution networks.' The report also suggests that 'as the European
independents rely heavily on US independent product, we consider that
US independent producers should be involved in such a pan-European
network.'

Despite the so-called logic, some three years after publication both
Coopers and others have failed to describe a more detailed plan for such
a pan-European vehicle, an area that this chapter will return to later.


## Business or culture?

'If you want to be in the business of movies – which is different to being
in the movies as a cultural medium (and the lack of making that distinction causes a lot of problems when talking about movies in Europe) –
then you need huge amounts of capital,' argues Michael Kuhn, president
of PolyGram Filmed Entertainment.

'Whether Eurocrats like it or not, the business of movies is really the
business of Hollywood, English-language movies. That's what the 40 to
60 billion-dollar business is all about. The distinction should be made
between those movies, and films which are culturally necessary to maintain national identities and cultures and so on. They are two very different things. You don't make money out of producing films. You make
money out of distributing them, and unless you get the distribution right
you can't have a chance of making any money. Most people don't realize
how much capital you need, and therefore get into the situation where
however successful they are creatively, they are never successful financially.'

By way of contrast to Hollywood's international distribution arms, which are tailor-made to release large, heavily-marketed films to the general public, the vast majority of Europe's domestic films are handled by a fragmented, under-capitalized, disparate gaggle of independent distributors who are struggling to retain their box-office share of just 10 per cent of Europe's overall gross per annum.

Neither does the geography of Europe make for simple arythmatics. European markets each have different markets with different values for the distributors (and hence the producer and investors). Rental rates commanded by distributors vary. For example, in Italy the distributor takes nearly 60 per cent of the box-office gross, while in the UK the figure is nearer 40 per cent. Given that ticket prices are higher in Italy, box-office revenues are worth 70 per cent more to an Italian distributor than to his or her UK counterpart.[5] Between 1993 and 1995, only a handful of films outside the top 100 for the UK and Germany, for example, were handled by the Hollywood Majors – a clear indication that the marginal box-office regions are the domain of the independent distributor. The market-place, however, has changed considerably since the mid to late 1980s, when the independent market experienced a sales explosion. By the early 1990s numerous distributors in Europe failed to keep up, and their numbers have dropped as a consequence. Some of the exceptions, such as the UK's Entertainment Film Distributors, BAC Films in France, and Neue Constantin in Germany, are in a minority of thriving independent businesses.

### The tough end of the business

'Distribution is probably the toughest end of movie-making,' says Neue Constantin's Bernd Eichinger. 'Firstly, it's an organization that has to be fed all year. Secondly, if you're not successful with what you distribute, you're dead. There's no other way to explain it. If you don't make enough money with those movies, the organization will stop.'

There is a further factor that has hit the European independent distributor. Television companies have pulled away from picking up films at the same time as a distributor purchases them. The old model would go something like this: A distributor would see a film at a market or festival, and decide to buy the licence rights for their territory. Before deciding on an offer, they would check with a broadcaster if they would pick up the free television rights, and the distributor could down-scale their risk. 'It has become much tougher because of the broadcaster's attitude to specialized films,' explained Rainer Kolmel from Kinowelt, a Munich-based distributor. 'Now we are having to take the risks, and they are holding back. It is especially difficult for projects that we want to get involved in early. Unless you can offer a strong package, they're not normally interested. And if distributors cannot sell their films to television, they will be unable to survive.'

Over the past five years numerous independent distribution companies have either crashed or have chosen to find wealthy parent-partners. Romaine Hart, owner of UK's Mainline Films and owner of London's long-running Screen cinemas, decided in late 1995 to drop her distribution arm. 'I simply couldn't make the money work,' she explained. 'It's getting harder and harder to keep a screen and in the end you kill yourselves with films that the critics love, but which nobody goes to see.'

Hart is not alone in her contention that distribution is tough to make work. According to the findings of a report into the British film industry, there are certain structural difficulties that distort the UK's independent distribution market-place. The report, entitled *Factors influencing the production, supply and exhibition of independent films in the UK market*, and conducted by Terry Ilotts' consultancy, Bridge Media, was submitted in 1994 to the Monopolies and Mergers Commission as evidence for the recent inquiry into the supply of films in the UK. The report's overall conclusions argued that independent film producers face 'enormous hurdles in securing effective theatrical distribution in their home market'.

## The UK problem

A UK mainstream market that provides Hollywood and other big-budget fare has been greatly boosted over the last decade by the building of multiplex cinemas, nearly all with substantial US investment. This has stimulated audiences into returning to the cinema, and is seen as a generally positive development. But alongside that, there is a parallel market which plays arthouse, foreign-language and specialist films. These films don't sit so easily in multiplexes, which have cleverly replicated Americana's popcorn-crunching culture. It is the parallel sector that is under real pressure: 'It is clear that the UK market is overwhelmingly dominated by the US Majors, and that non-US films are being desperately squeezed as a result,' suggested Bridge Media. In addition, compared to the US and other European territories such as Spain and France, the UK is underscreened. Britain has only 32.2 screens per million people, compared to 80 screens per million in France and one-third of the level in the US.

Bridge Media cited examples of British films that are disadvantaged by the UK's structure and system, including Ken Loach's Riff Raff, which was pushed off cinema screens to make way for an American film Backdraft (which subsequently performed worse); while Louis Malle's Damage was pulled out of London's Empire 2 cinema after just one week to make way for a pre-booked US film – despite the fact that it had almost broken the screen's weekly record in box-office performance. Independent distributors interviewed for the report said that only 40 per cent of their film releases achieved their optimum theatrical runs, with 60 per cent being pulled while 'still attracting substantial audiences'.

While Hollywood products continue to dominate our cinema screens, the UK industry actually *suffers* from the shared language with Hollywood. The result is that Britain loses its directors and stars to Hollywood very quickly. This makes it harder for producers of low-budget films with first-time directors to raise enough money to make local films at all. No dubbing or sub-titling is required for American films to play in the UK; while UK broadcasters make it easy for US films to come into the market, anxious to buy packages of blockbuster-led movies. In return, the UK has hardly penetrated the US box-office market. And in a broad sense, the British film's over-riding problem in its own market is that it is neither perceived as mainstream, universally popular fare, nor is it seen as a sexy, exotic foreign-language film.

### A changing landscape

The net result has been for a series of mergers and contractural links between larger and smaller distributors in the UK. Specialist outfits Artificial Eye and Mayfair have merged; PolyGram has a deal with Electric Pictures, and many of Miramax's releases in the UK go through Buena Vista since the Disney–Miramax deal in 1993. 'There's no room for independents that aren't financed by large companies in the market anymore,' explained Electric's Liz Wrenn, adding that the advances for films are now beyond a reasonable sum for privately owned companies.[6]

Nearly half the 69 films involving a UK producer that were put into production in 1994 had yet to be screened at a UK cinema by May 1996. Of those unscreened films, two-thirds did not have release dates. According to *Screen Finance*, 'the figures confirm the general trend of the last few years, in which it has become increasingly difficult for UK films to secure [domestic] distribution'.[7] Others point out that the real problem is that British producers go into production on films with little idea how their title will be distributed, or what audience it is intended for. And British producers are certainly not alone in this area of complaint.

Fortunately, since the Bridge Media report, certain films such as Shallow Grave and Trainspotting have proved that there are British-produced films that can find a thriving national audience. Other relative, albeit more specialized successes include Mike Leigh's Secrets and Lies, and Ken Loach's Land and Freedom. The latter, however, gave rise to a very public row between the film's producers and its distributor, Artificial Eye. Following excellent reviews and press coverage, multiplex cinemas asked for the film to move into their theatres, but Artificial Eye refused on the grounds that the film would eventually reach its audience anyway through a more controlled and monitored distribution strategy. While the film was exceptional in terms of cross-over potential, the example does raise some structural problems unique to the UK. For example, according to analyst Peter Keighron, the film was released on 15 prints in the UK compared to 85 prints in circulation in France. 'The numbers illustrate the difference between two cinematic cultures. One where "art-house" and "mainstream" occupy different lands separated by heavily guarded borders, the crossing-over of which is an economically dangerous adventure, and another where the walls have come down, if they were ever up.'[8]

## The French approach

France, more than any other European nation, has managed to hold on to a respectable share of its national box office. Leaving aside a blip in 1994, French films held a 35 per cent share in 1993 and 1995. Taken together with European films (and most notably, British films), Europe represented 44 per cent of the the total box office in the same year.

However, the relative performance of French films in contrast to American films is still weak. According to the CNC, nearly three-quarters of the 371 first-run films distributed in France in 1995 were domestic or American productions. Of those, 47 per cent of the 134 American first-run films opened in more than 100 cinemas, compared with 16 per cent for French films. As the CNC conceded, 'all during the year, American films enjoyed better distribution than their French counterparts'.[9]

The French market is heavily dominated by the top ten distributors, who were responsible for nearly 90 per cent of total receipts. Only one true independent company, Lazennec Diffusion, made the top ten on the back of the hit movie, La Haine. The problems facing smaller independents is the higher prices being paid for films, and the higher marketing and release costs – factors that are similar for all independents across Europe. There has been a subsidy administered by the CNC since 1978 to distributors who handle French or co-produced films and who have paid a minimum guarantee to a certain level or made an investment. The automatic reimbursement (which is collected via ticket sales) amounts to about $9 million, far more than most other distributors manage to find in recycled help in other European territories.

Nevertheless, it can be argued that the automatic aid has simply prolonged the fragmenation of the market-place, with some 164 active distribution companies releasing films in 1995, and yet only 90 registered receipts of more than FFr100,000 ($19,000). In addition, the French distribution market has been carved up by the French and US Majors' recent mergers and alliances. Gaumont and Buena Vista locked together in 1993, and UGC and Fox grouped in July 1995. The two alliances together controlled nearly 30 per cent of the box-office market in 1995, and also own or control nearly 13 per cent of the total number of France's cinema screens.

There are those who argue that such collusion is working against the interests of a healthy, non-monopolistic market. Meanwhile the American partners remain happy because they have access to the best screens via the deal. On the other hand, the French partners in these relationships have the upper hand, as they continue to control the prime cinema screens across the country, along with Pathe. And as PACT's European adviser Bertrand Moullier points out, Gaumont in particular has retained a century-old traditional concept as a provider of French films to its own market. 'That's a fine concept. When has a British corporation ever had to any degree a concept of cultural responsibility?'

## The EFDO dead-end

There has been a lot of fashionable talk about pan-European distribution over the past two years. But when people talk about support for distribution, what does it really mean? Repayable loans for prints and advertising? Or contributing money that distributors are able to risk up front, and use to provide decent minimum guarantees to producers? Meanwhile, the larger and stronger independent distributors in each territory are in many cases moving closer to production in an effort to become more competitive and ensure that they acquire top products. 'If I simply wait for films to be made and then try to acquire them, someone else will have got there first,' explained Rainer Kolmel of Kinowelt. Distribution, the lopsided cornerstone of the new MEDIA II programme in terms of funding, has also generated the most heated debate over automatic and selective systems, alongside administrative issues. MEDIA's new distribution strategy was to throw out the selective approach carried out by the European Film Distribution Office (EFDO), based in Hamburg since 1988. EFDO worked by granting repayable loans of up to 50 per cent of the distribution costs and no more than ECU100,000 ($123,000) to a minimum of three distributors for three different countries, who agreed to release the film, where possible, at the same time. The aim was to support the smaller-budgeted European films that experience a difficult time finding screens, and to help more films cross borders.

MEDIA head Jacques Delmoly made his views clear in the run-up to MEDIA II during 1994, saying that although he believed that EFDO had succeeded in getting some films more widely distributed, he was not convinced that there exists a real network of distributors today any more than there was seven years ago. Others have privately conceded that EFDO has often not been required by distributors of the more successful films, and they have paid back the loan without even drawing it down.

Dieter Kosslick, the former president of EFDO, defended the organization's track record and system, but argued that he would alter the guidelines if the model were to ever be used again. 'I would make sure that EFDO did not automatically have to support films that we already know are a flop in the market-place, because under the old rules we couldn't turn down those films.' While it is the smallest players who have maybe benefited the most from EFDO, has that support only allowed these numerous smaller entities to simply stay alive, hanging on by the skin of their teeth? Perhaps EFDO has encouraged the latter, acting as a lifeboat that perpetuates fragmentation, rather than structural consolidation. As one leading European producer puts it: 'It's a pan-European health service that helps bandage the weak rather than encourage the strong.'

In addition to the above problems, support for prints and advertising for a wide number of European films should be questioned at a more basic level. Throwing money at small films which, more often than not, have been under-developed and then produced with no target audience in mind, is tantamount to throwing support down the drain. But it is rarely questioned whether most films backed by soft subsidy, advances against receipts and television money, should have been made in the first place, let alone if they will recoup in the market.

## The German standpoint

It is a point that the German Distributor's Association (VdF) made very clearly in June 1994 in a hope that the German funding structures could be restructured to support more market-orientated films: 'Film funding which cuts itself off from the market is condemned to fail. The distributor as the middle-man [sic] between production and the cinema must be already incorporated in the pre-production and production stage.'

The VdF later reacted strongly against a proposal by Alfred Hurmer, the head of Film Foederund Hamburg, that he was considering different models for producer participation in film revenues to the FFA guidelines. (The FFA rules allow for a producer to receive money only after the release costs and possible distribution guarantee payments have been covered by the box-office rental receipts and other revenues.) It went on to suggest that the regional funds' distribution support should include:

- production funding only on submission of a distribution contract
- streamlining of guidelines
- a commensurate proportion of funding in the budget for distribution support (15 per cent to 20 per cent)
- abandoning the strict regional effect for distribution support.

For the record, the VdF has supported EFDO's efforts on a pan-European basis, but has still been particularly damning about the structure of public support overall.

**'25 years of film funding in the Federal Republic and five years of MEDIA policy under the EC have not led to any major improvement in the production and distribution structure in the FRG and the EC ...'**

VdF, 1994

## The MEDIA II row

Ironcially, for all EFDO's limitations, when European distributors finally saw the Commission's guidelines for applications for MEDIA II distribution support, many – including a furious VdF – wished that the original EFDO programme had remained in place. The guidelines had been published despite the fact that the Commission had rejected all applications to run the Distribution IO. According to Delmoly, 'technical problems' had blocked the lead application, a group that included former EFDO, Greco and EVE officials and a representative body of the CNC to run the automatic side of the operation. The real problem was how such a broadly based group could keep its overheads down if operating from France, Germany and Brussels. In addition, relations between the French and German elements were particularly poor.

In the Commission's call for proposals in May 1996, the section that caused most consternation was the guideline for 'Support of transnational distribution of European films and the networking of European films'. The selective system is for groupings of at least three European distributors operating in different countries and preferably with different languages, 'which propose to distribute one or more recent European films. The film or films must be released within a year of granting the support.' An incentive for releasing two or three films, rather than just one, is worked into the procedure, with loans per distributor going from ECU100,000 to ECU120,00 to ECU130,000 ($123,000 to $147,000 to $160,000) respectively according to the number of films being handled. There was some concern about the stipulation that half of a distributor group's proposed films needed to have budgets of less than ECU5 million, which was felt to discriminate against larger distributors trying to compete with Hollywood Majors.

Most independent distributors were unimpressed by the guidelines, but what shocked the industry as a whole was the proposal that its distribution loans should be repaid pro rata from the first revenues recouped from the distribution of a film. This effectively meant that MEDIA II would have to be considered in the same category as an equity investor or bank. On the other hand, dubbing and sub-titling support will not have to be repaid at all, a considerable support given that EFDO spent nearly half of its budget on this area during MEDIA I.

Overall, the selective aid will amount to $15 million per year for theatrical support, in comparison to the $7.5 million available under EFDO. In addition, the CNC is now carrying out a one-year pilot project to see how an automatic system could be applied to Europe as a whole. Although strong in principle, once again the practicalities of dealing with different territories, languages and money, alongside different distribution revenue and collecting systems, may prove insurmountable. The horrible truth that stands in the way of such an ambitious system is the reliability of distributors' returns. One possible solution would be for each member state to certify their territory's figures. However, some states would be unable to do so, leaving the system stranded politically.

## MEDIA distribution's critics

In a stinging response to the EC, Johannes Klingsporn, managing director of the German Distributors' Association, argued that the Commission has learnt nothing about distribution since the original MEDIA programme. Writing in *Screen International*, Klingsporn described the new guidelines as a 'triumph for bureacracy'.[10] In particular, he argued that the departure from the 'project principle', where several distributors handled one film, to the 'grouping principle', where applications by distributors have to be jointly co-ordinated for several films, will fail to function in practice. 'It ignores the fact that co-operation among European distributors is typically temporary and linked to single titles.' He also hammered the linking of funding budgets to the number of films per grouping, rather than to the level of advertising budgets, a policy that confounds market logic and will merely support small films rather than allow potentially commercial cross-over films to reach a wider audience.

In response to his critics, Delmoly finally revealed some of the frustrations of trying to put into practice guidelines that suit Brussels but appear to suit nobody else. 'We are asking distributors to behave more like a European network. Having heard complaints about UIP and the US Majors for years, it was a ministerial recommendation that European distributors adopt some common strategies. What we are finding is that some may not be ready to do so,' he said after a meeting in Paris with distributors in June.[11] However, he also conceded some technical problems still remained, but he suggested that these related to individual contracts between producers and distributors rather than the MEDIA II repayment conditions on its loans.

By 11 July 1996, D&S Media, headed up by MEDIA I's John Dick (EVE) and Robert Strasser (GRECO), was awarded the contract to run the new MEDIA II distribution IO. Dick will run the head office in Brussels; Antoinette D'Esclaibes will head up theatrical distribution, also from Brussels; Strasser will manage TV distribution in Munich; and EVE's Norma Cairns will head up video distribution in Dublin.

Despite an initial outburst of further criticism, D&S Media was by far the best equipped for the job in hand. While the Commission's guidelines for video and television were relatively sensible, the new IO had already made it clear to the Commission that the theatrical guidelines needed considerable streamlining, notably with regards to the repayment specifications. While none of the IOs are in a position to change the Commission's policy, they can advise on their practical implementation. That is precisely what D&S Media set about doing. Practical modifications were presented to the MEDIA Committee. These still maintained the Commission's objective of creating distribution networks and fostering cross-border co-operation, but clarified key areas of practice. For example, repayment structures and the tracking of distributors' royalty statements are now simplified and more in line with the way the film industry operates.

There were even signs that Efdo was prepared to put aside differences and help from the sidelines. A list of distributors and organizations who, according to previous experience, were 'undesirable' to give public loans to was faxed by Efdo to Dick's office in Brussels in the late summer of 1996. Clearly not all has been lost in the MEDIA II carousel.

## The juggernaut approach

There have continued to be a number of floated notions and vague proposals for pan-European distribution systems since the first *Dose of Reality* report. Few have found their way even to the research and report stage, let alone into action. Part of the problem is that national governments remain suspicious of putting finance into a supra-national model, while the Commission has been more interested in putting forward its Guarantee Fund idea than developing Puttnam's *Submission to the European Commission Think Tank on Audiovisual Policy*,[12] or any other proposals for that matter.

Puttnam's new strategy was proposing to the Commission a publicly-funded soft-loan support to pan-European consortia. The key features of the scheme would be:

- A small number of consortia that would be chosen by competitive bid.
- Each consortium could be made up of existing distributors or new entrants to the field.
- They would have access to soft-loan finance in order to promote the Europe-wide distribution of European product and seek new markets outside Europe.

- They would be expected to raise the majority of their capital on the open market.
- The loan agreement would be for ten years.
- Non-European holdings might be limited to 20 per cent to 30 per cent of each consortium.

The Paper argued that the key requirements placed upon successful bidders would be: firstly, to promote and enhance genuinely Europe-wide distribution of films, television programmes and software; and secondly, to promote the more effective marketing and distribution of films and other audiovisual products in non-European markets.

Beyond these goals, the longer-term ambition behind the project was to see valuable library catalogues built up by each consortia, and that the distributors would have achieved enough critical mass to trade commercially without the benefit of further public loan support.

While ambitious in scope and size, the submission's distribution proposal fell on deaf ears both within the Commission and from Europe's largest potential consortia members. The problem, put at its most crude, is that companies like PolyGram, Bertelsmann and Chargeurs are interested in controlling licence rights outright. Their investment plans are built around such longer-term libraries, and hence they have little intention of sharing those rights across a range of territories with other partners. Even Puttnam privately agreed that the plan's ambition was unlikely to be matched by the practical ease of implementation.

The only grand-scale pan-European distribution plan left on the Commission's table is the French trial of the automatic system. However, leaving aside the practical problems raised earlier in this chapter, the real obstacle is political. Many territories outside France have no intention of getting behind the scheme. Furthermore, its high visibility makes it very vulnerable. As one commentator put it: 'If it flopped, it would flop big and publicly, and there's no way Brussels or the French would want to take the rap for that. There will be no place to hide.'

A pan-European distribution vehicle is never likely to answer all the dreams of the European industry. As Eichinger and others have warned, until Europe produces enough commercial films that are capable of recouping their budgets from a range of territories, such an organization will collapse. It is unfortunate, some argue, that the MEDIA programme has found itself obsessed with distribution, when the key questions both before – in the development and production stages; and after – in the marketing and exhibition strategies – have to be answered if the European distribution juggernaut is ever to roll out of the station. After all, huge engines need fuel to run on.

## Notes

1  *ACE Market Module, Theatrical: L'Exploitation*, Report by London Economics, November 1993.
2  For a more detailed analysis of PolyGram and other major European distribution operations, see Chapter 5.
3  CNC Info, *World Cinema* statistics, p. 71.
4  *The Distribution Game: Can Europe Even the Score?*, Coopers & Lybrand.
5  ACE Report, *Ibid*, p. 18.
6  *PACT* magazine, April 1996; 'Fighting their corner', Peter Keighron, pp. 12–15.
7  *Screen Finance*, 16 May 1996, pp. 10–13.
8  *PACT* magazine, *Ibid*, p. 12.
9  CNC Info, p. 24, see chart:

### The top ten French distributors in 1995

| Company | Market share (in % of gross receipts) |
| --- | --- |
| Gaumont/Buena Vista | 21.7 |
| AMLF | 15.8 |
| UIP | 11.7 |
| Columbia | 8.6 |
| Warner | 8.2 |
| UGC-Fox distribution | 8.0 |
| Pan Europeenne | 5.3 |
| BAC Films | 4.1 |
| Michel Gauchon | 3.0 |
| Lazennec Diffusion | 2.3 |

10  *Screen International*, 21 June 1996, p. 14.
11  *Screen International*, *Ibid*, p. 2.
12  David Puttnam, *A Submission to the European Commission Think Tank on Audiovisual Policy*, 1994

# 9

# The New Way Forward

'No matter how grand our quest to become global
entertainment giants or pioneers of revolutionary technologies,
we cannot forget that it is the story that lies at the root of
every successful form of entertainment.'

Peter Guber, film producer, chairman of Mandalay and
former chairman of Sony Pictures Entertainment

'The good news for producers is that undoubtedly there will be
new forms of financing, but it will not reflect anything like the
amount of extra cash value coming from the new pay systems.'

Paul Styles, head of the media practice, KPMG

FOR ALL THE RISING EXCITEMENT during the early 1990s concerning the multimedia revolution, by the mid 1990s it became clear that like most revolutions, the public remained a good few steps behind the leaders of the pack. Just as the VCR took ten years to penetrate 60 per cent of Europe's households during the 1980s, so too are the range of new formats finding it hard to take off in the 1990s. Indeed, the very range of different multimedia appliances – including CD-i, CD-Rom, the Digital Versatile Disc (DVD), Interactive TV, High Definition TV, Video-On-Demand and others – has probably confused the high-street consumer, and has more likely resulted in the buyer waiting to see how the market settles rather than instantly reaching for a credit card. There are also likely to be casualties in the methods of delivery between cable, digital satellite and other systems. As PolyGram's Alain Levy puts it: 'Cable is here now. But there is nothing to say it will be in the future. Direct satellite may well replace it.' All the discussions and activity concerning new delivery systems may yet prove redundant in Europe if satellite succeeds in dominating over cable. Meanwhile, the secondary markets could yet become lost in a sea of competing decoding boxes, all accepting exclusive smart cards for rival niche services, and effectively cancelling each other out. Above all, there is a strong argument that new technology's success at expanding consumer demand for delivery systems will ultimately depend on the excellence of the software. Audiences want to buy and watch entertainment programmes, not state-of-the-art hardware delivery systems.

This chapter looks at the impact of changing technological trends and new delivery systems. Following an examination of the potential European network and its inherent problems, the chapter focuses on how quickly new technology will arrive in force, and how it looks from the perspectives of the changing market and the film producer within that market. How can producers benefit from the changing markets and new technologies? Are they likely to increase their opportunities for raising production revenue? And how are the key rights-owners and corporate entities organizing themselves in the coming revolution? (Those wanting detailed analysis of new forms of hardware and carrier systems and the surrounding terminology should look to specialized trade and industry publications, where there have been ample in-depth surveys and analyses.)[1]

Before examining the political and production implications of the new technological era, the first point to establish is that communication technology is gradually moving from an analogue to a digital format. The price at present to implement fully or convert to digital systems is still too high for mainstream uses, but its cost is, like all technological innovations, coming downwards. The over-riding advantage of digitization is that it allows a vast array of transmission possibilities. Once an image is digitally composed, it can be sent down all sorts of pipelines, including fibre-optic lines, cable, digital satellite receivers or digital terrestrial airwaves. It can send pictures at such speed and density that an enormous increase in the number of services is anticipated. Digital technology lies behind the range of distribution and political debates that this chapter opens up.

While there are numerous exchanges, and in some cases, battles raging over network technology, standards, copyright laws and associated new highway finance, none of the key changes yet relate directly to the production of feature films in Europe. This is not to suggest that feature film production is unaffected by the current volatility. Hollywood producer Barry Spikings told the *Financial Times* Cable, Satellite and New Media Conference in February 1995, 'The initial programming of choice will most likely be filmed entertainment' on new channel and network systems. He pointed out that the $100 billion that North American corporations are set to invest in wiring that continent by the year 2000 would be difficult to justify unless 'the superhighway is carrying content that audiences are prepared to pay for and allocate their disposable time to'.[2]

While Spikings' argument that 'content is king' holds good, precisely how film fits into the new home-entertainment world is less clear. Sport, news and children's programming all have a major place in the software competition, and it is sport, not film, that has recently hit the headlines with huge, multi-million dollar deals. Films cannot deliver consistent quality, and all pay-TV systems are padded by B movies and less impressive fare. Blockbuster movies may drive the service, but they don't come wall-to-wall.

However, in an era of international deregulation, the world's corporate entities who are interested in tying up the future highways have decided that the key position to take up is of being a gatekeeper or 'mall operator'. They want to control who will be able to show what to whom, and will also aim to control the pricing of consumers' entry fees for access to each salami-slice of software. Hence, they have placed the emphasis on laying down distribution foot-prints in their effort to capture audiences. It is a highly competitive race: 'The industry-wide drive to lock-up distribution is, in sum, a strategy of running scared: media moguls everywhere are driven by a common fear that they will be frozen out', suggested a *Time* magazine article about Rupert Murdoch's empire.[3] Such paranoia was partly behind Disney's merger with Capital Cities/ABC, while other key players like John Malone's TCI have tied up 20-year access agreements for Disney and Turner programming. Other informed analysts see that a powerful telephone company such as British Telecom may make a dynamic move in the UK over the coming months. If a Labour government is elected in Britain, BT may well bid (via MCI) for Rupert Murdoch's News Corporation. It would probably keep Fox and sell off the newspapers, but the access to software and distribution would serve the giant nicely in the new bouts for control over the superhighway.

## Europe's information revolution

Europe's largest players, including Bertelsmann, Canal Plus and Poly-Gram, all have global distribution ambitions. In addition, one emerging company is interesting due to its unusual international links. The Dutch-based Nethold (Payco) was formed by an alliance between M-Net, the South African TV group and Richemont, the powerful international conglomerate with deep financial pockets. The two corporations are operating various fast-growing pay-TV assets and transferred their European and African broadcasting outlets to digital satellite in late 1995. The group already has 43 subscribing countries, and has signed substantial library deals, including an ongoing access deal with Twentieth Century–Fox. Bertelsmann is also spreading in various directions, and has shown a strong interest in areas such as interactive CD-Rom through its BMG multimedia subsidiary. It has stakes in various games producers, and has developed with Canal Plus a new 'Media Box' decoder which unscrambles encrypted signals for paying viewers.

Distribution and control of 'gates' is an expensive business, especially when combined with high programming costs. The way all these large combines aim to operate is by working on huge economies of scale and delivering a large number of services. Such activities require large resources and some clear notion of the technological environment they are being applied within. However, by mid 1996 Europe was still lacking an integrated fibre-optic network that would allow for a fully interactive digital media capacity. According to Roger Pye, a KPMG consultant who carried out a report for the European Commission, *Investing in Infra-structure for the European Information Society*,[4] the cost of providing such a network could amount to $412.5 billion. Key to such cost analysis is the concept of universal access, which is politically desirable but places a high cost-burden on investors. Such an approach would impose an infrastructure on Europe's technological development, rather than allow for an organic, market-driven expansion.

Adam Singer, president and chief operating officer of Tele-Communications Inc. International, responded to the KPMG report by arguing that an European superhighway will need to grow rather than be constructed: 'The information revolution can be encouraged, but it cannot be formulated or dictated or regulated. The moment you do that you kill the blind evolutionary force that is creating it.' He also argued that the key to providing the maximum number of services is to ensure the lowest possible distribution cost, pointing out that the fundamental reason why the US will 'streak ahead in this information revolution – *free local phone calls*. What Brussels should be calling for is a change in the telephone price structure.'[5] Pye's analysis did not examine the growth and dominancy of satellite delivery systems. Given their ascendancy as shown through the success of BSkyB, despite technical problems, it may be that in time to come the overall cost of 'cabling Europe' is simply too much to bear, and satellite will continue to dominate delivery.

National governments have traditionally tried to rein in satellite operators and control the speed of technological change. Indeed, media legislation when compared to telecoms legislation has tended to be piece-meal, local, restrictive and usually enforced with all kinds of boundaries attached to it. But despite government attempts to control their domestic markets, the entertainment market is going global. 'Everywhere you will find conflict between what the governments would like to see happen and what might happen,' says PolyGram's Alain Levy. 'What might happen is driven by two things: the five or six entertainment powers and the speed of technology. I think both of these are working against governments. It will be interesting to see who wins.'

## The copyright problem

It is also true that giant media players do require the government in Brussels to come to their aid. The new digital age is bringing with it a number of transnational issues, of which the most pressing is control and protection of copyright. Copyright, which protects the expression of intellectual creation, is not just a European issue, but an international phenomenon, and it is impossible to escape the fact that at the fundamental level, the ownership, control and exploitation of primary rights will need to be protected. The issue has been taken up with the EC by the European Film Companies Alliance (EFCA), which includes members such as PolyGram, Chargeurs, Bertelsmann and Rank. The body has put pressure on the Commission to ensure that a suitable legislative environment to protect copyright is established, and that global rules to enforce the rights of copyright owners are put in place.

'We believe that Europe's position in the entertainment and cultural sector will be determined by the level of copyright it grants to film companies', wrote Stewart Till, president of PolyGram Filmed Entertainment, in *Screen International*.[6] 'Historically, the US has always had powerful copyright laws, and this has contributed significantly to the strength of the US in the global entertainment market. We are concerned that when electronic transmission of music and films by digital means – across the Internet, for example – becomes more commonplace, copyright owners will be unable to enforce their rights for payment. If their investment is to be maintained, current legal definitions in relation to broadcasting, rental, distribution and reproduction will have to be updated to take account of new digital technologies and consumer habits.'

Till cites three key areas where rights' owners dealing with the electronic transmission of film and music should have protection: 'First, film companies should be guaranteed exclusive rights to authorize or prohibit distribution and reproduction of their material across electronic networks, enabling them to control the commercial usage of their productions. Second, these exclusive rights are essential if the industry is to avoid the damaging principle of compulsory licensing, whereby companies are forced to sell their product at predetermined rates. It is much better to leave such matters to the market. Third, copyright legislation can only be effective if it is enforced. Co-operation between the hardware and creative industries will be essential if technological standards for systems of production are to be devised.'

The subject of copyright is taken up with enthusiasm by Till's boss, Michael Kuhn: 'Everyone's eyes may glaze over when they hear that word, but the truth of the matter is that unless something is done to protect the product of this vast investment then people won't want to invest in it. If anyone can copy any record or film, then there wouldn't be a business. We've tried to find a new approach to this, which I call "Copygate", which will enforce a policy whereby chips are put into all black boxes (including video, TVs, computers and decoders) that allow intellectual property rights holders to switch off access to their programmes entirely, partially or freely or for pay. In other words, the system enforces the rights electronically through a very practical device.' A similar 'Copygate' protection system is in force in the audio industry. Every audio recorder has a chip in it which prevents the consumer copying a CD more than once, and Kuhn sees no reason why it shouldn't be expanded into the audiovisual industry.

The copyright question is growing extremely pressing, especially given the imminent distribution of films to living rooms via the Internet. US software company Narrative Communications announced a technological breakthrough in June 1996 which essentially speeds up Internet access to the film.[7] Up to now, the Net has lacked the bandwidth to handle animation, video and most audio traffic. A faster Internet would help both film distribution and CD-Roms, which will be looking to distribute their titles on line.

### How quickly will distribution outlets change?

The demise of the VHS video tape has been greatly exaggerated since the early 1990s. Video rental – worth some $2.2 billion in Europe in 1994 – has seen a small but steady decline since 1989, with an ever-increasing shift to a blockbuster-driven market. In the mid to late 1980s, features also dominated the sell-through (retail) market (worth $3.87 billion in Europe in 1994), but these now share the market with sports, children's, documentary, and other non-fiction areas. As John Dick, former head of MEDIA I's Espace Video European, explains: 'While independents have seen a decline in revenues, the major players still look to video to generate large chunks of revenue.' It's no accident that Blockbuster bought up CityVision in the UK, nor that Blockbuster has now merged with the giant Viacom-Paramount Studio. Non-theatrical revenues far outstrip box-office takings around the world, and video has, and still is, playing a key role in those revenue stakes. As Dick adds: 'The desire to keep up with new developments must be weighed up against the cannibalization of existing revenue streams.'[8]

But how quickly will the new ancillary industries develop? 'In business, you are either in general a believer in the substitutional theory, or in the incremental theory. I believe in the second,' Kuhn explains. 'In other words, a particular form of distribution might be hit for a short time very dramatically by new methods of distribution, but it will remain in some form or other, for a considerable period of time. It may well be that the rental of video will completely disappear, but the video business as such will remain a very strong business for years to come. All these new systems, all of which are becoming increasingly difficult to differentiate from one to another, will become incremental sources of income. That's not to say that video will remain as big a business as it is now, but it's hard to see how the rental on tape will survive if you get efficient pay-TV and Video-On-Demand (VOD), and the corresponding revenue sources will definitely be larger.'

The industry has not helped itself by loudly trumpeting new arrivals, such as the newly-styled digital versatile disc (DVD), only to meet delays and postponements. In the case of DVD, it was supposed to be launched in the summer of 1996, but has now been delayed due to problems, including copyright agreements, and is unlikely to arrive until mid 1997 at the earliest. DVD is an upgraded version of the digital video disc: a five-inch, CD-like disc capable of holding a full-length feature on a single side, and with three times the picture quality of a VHS tape, eight different language tracks and a Dolby digital sound system.[9]

## The technological snail: Video-On-Demand

While DVD's future will greatly depend on both the hardware and the software being readily available to the public, Video-On-Demand continues to hog the future limelight. However, the fact is that moving to full Video-On-Demand at the press of a consumer button is an extraordinary technological leap forward. Put simply, somewhere in the new system, there is a massive digital video process that is storing thousands of hours of compressed digital film and television information. When the consumer dials up their choice of movie, at any time they like, the library has to deliver down a line within seconds.

> **'Video-On-Demand is being solved, but it has taken longer than anticipated. To make it a mass-market product as opposed to something the guys in the white coats can do is another matter.'**
>
> Paul Styles, KPMG

KPMG's Paul Styles, who has studied and worked on the issues surrounding new technology in great depth, says 'We're predicting that meaningful VOD channels for the normal viewer will only occur as a phenomenon by around 2005. But they are still unlikely to be so sophisticated as to be able to call up the whole of a back catalogue of a particular cinema culture. Services like that may well be 20 years away, and may well be replaced by other phenomena which are more like on-line computer networks that will have the ability to transmit full motion video down telephone lines.'

Styles, like many other analysts, stresses the length of time these systems may take to enter the normal household. The individual consumer will have to choose whether to buy the new services through a digital cable box, a new 'intelligent' TV set, or a personal computer so powerful that it can do all the processing for the TV and cable sets. 'By the year 2000, the consumer is still likely to be expected to pay between $500 and $750 for this "lovely" capability, so it's a consumer decision of the same ilk as buying a first- or second-generation VCR. Besides the cost outlay, you will also still have to pay a subscription per week or month on top,' explains Styles.

## Household demographics

Research carried out in the US by IMR Research was not particularly encouraging about VOD. Given a choice between a $5 pay-per-view (PPV) movie and a $1 video store rental, 91 per cent of US consumers would choose the video rental, despite the home convenience of the PPV. Asked if $2 would be acceptable to charge for a telephone-line transmitted movie, 80 per cent said no, while just 6 per cent of the survey's respondents currently connect to an on-line service each week, although nearly 40 per cent expected to do so in the near future. When non-owners were asked which consumer electronics products they would like to own, digital satellite dishes came top (60 per cent), followed by camcorders (52 per cent), home CD-Rom drives (42 per cent), TV/VCR combination machines (42 per cent) and big-screen television sets (42 per cent).[10]

A similar survey in the UK released in spring 1996 showed that 72 per cent of the people interviewed would not use PPV, and that 66 per cent of cable and satellite homes would not use PPV.[11] It will clearly take some time for the concept of paying for hardware, then for the monthly services, and *then* for extra services per-view on top to take hold.

However, the above statistics were updated in the spring of 1996, when the results of Bell Atlantic's VOD trial in Virginia became public. According to a leader in *Screen International*,[12] while the latest home-video statistics pointed to a declining appetite for renting pre-recorded cassettes, Bell Atlantic's research showed that the trialists 'liked nothing better than to browse through all 655 titles on their changing monthly menus (nearly three-quarters of which were ordered up by at least one of the 100 trial users). Moreover, they were willing to pay five bucks a time for the convenience of never having to leave their couches.'

## How big will the cake be?

When the phenomenon of pay-television is finally added to the phenomenon of pay-based digital services, the final question is how big this ancillary cake will be. KPMG predicts that while there is definite growth in the cake, the level of growth beyond the move to pay-TV and the point when the average European household spend is around 30 dollars a month is much less clear. 'We think that hierarchies of payment systems will emerge which will be demographic and socially orientated,' Styles explains. But there will be demographic distortions. KPMG anticipates that middle-class families with children will consume the $30 norm; while the vast ageing European population above 55 will be less important. Others argue that the 'rich elderly' who are living longer than previously, will still constitute an important strand of the market, a demographic phenomenon referred to by advertisers as the 'grey panther' market. There is also the rise of the phenomenon of the 'poor young'. From the 1960s to the 1980s, young people living at home or in rented accommodation had a high percentage of their income available to consume leisure products, including audiovisual games, videos, CDs and CD-Roms. However, according to Styles, the full impact of the new 'poor young' in Europe is becoming demographically significant. 'I'm not talking about Generation X or Generation Y, nor about the underclass. But the fact is that we can no longer necessarily see young people as the driver of new entertainment services outside the family or mature social groups. This may be speculative, but it will have major ramifications in 10 to 20 years from now,' he warns.

## The producer's quandary

At its simplest level, most producers in Europe usually give up part or all of the copyright in return for the financing of their feature film. While the new forms of distribution add a new layer (or more) of rights to the product, the producer is still facing the quandary of how to realize the value of those rights, and hence raise more finance towards production. In addition, nobody is quite sure what the real value of future rights will be, so there is significant posturing and attempts by financiers to roll additional rights up with existing ones.

As Marc Devereux, a senior lawyer with Simon Olswang & Co. stressed at the MBS Television School in Lubeck in November 1994, the way a producer sets up deals at the development stage is very important, and can have major ramifications for the exploitation of rights at a later stage of a project. Multimedia rights, copyright positions and recent changes in the law need to be advised upon, with producers and broadcasters needing to be especially aware of clearance problems in the future. The new EC directive on copyright, which became law in July 1995, changed rights ownership, and contracts need to be checked with care.

Europe's pay markets are growing, albeit at different rates, and by the year 2002 to 2005, most pay-television services will be worth as much as the public and private sectors. However, a cynic could argue that a large percentage of the additional revenues from pay-TV will be spent on sports and film out-put deals, the two key drivers of pay-TV. (The third is children's programming.)

International rights acquisitions for events such as the Olympics, or Hollywood film library deals would appear to leave little for smaller film out-put deals at first glance. However, as the market matures, all television services will tend to become more domestic in content. There is a relentless trend all over the world that part of people's viewing is that they want to see things that relate to their own culture and values. Styles points to the example of BSkyB, which in its early years essentially ran re-run channels of Hollywood and Australian programming, backed up with some third-grade UK material and a lot of original factual sports material. By 1995 the programming mix was starting to change, with the commissioning of increasingly domestic (albeit mainstream) soaps, game shows, and telly-novellos and mini-series, alongside the British Screen output deal of domestic movies. The jewels in BSkyB's crown, however, remained its exclusive sports deals.

Given that an additional £2 billion ($3 billion) pay-TV revenue will be added by around 2002 to the public and private £4 billion spend, about one-third of that additional £2 billion will go into original UK/European programming, adding a fairly substantial revenue stream which is new to the UK market. In contrast, France, predictably, has been highly Francophile in its programming and production for cultural and political reasons. The German market never enjoyed a particularly healthy public service or commercial television system, and has tended to have a more American feel to its programming. And yet even in Germany domestic TV production is gaining momentum, while movie-of-the-week production is experiencing a boom at present.

While the traditional single or primary sources of film financing remain the dominant method of raising money for production, new hybrid and more complex deals will emerge as the pay-TV revenue share becomes more significant. Styles argues that this fragmentation of the market will lead to significant changes in the kinds of relationship that exist. Given that around two-thirds of viewers stay with the network in most given territories, and one-third switch to pay-TV, financing config-urations will gradually emerge that mirror that market share. In addition, as pay-TV operators and their parents become more wealthy, they start to buy up strategic rights.

### The start of niche and B-movie channels

As competition continues to increase, terrestrial networks will decide to spend the majority of their movie acquisition budgets on key blockbusters and the surrounding guff that the Hollywood studios insist on packaging with them. They will also be forced into pre-purchasing, co-financing or co-producing at an earlier stage, as the competition for top programming will be growing. There is an argument that this will leave room for the emergence of B-class and niche movie channels, as the networks have not had the cash left to sew them up. As the digitization of channels opens up the network, arthouse channels are also likely to emerge.

The competition for new products to drive pay systems will soon per-colate down to the production financing and co-financing areas, where split rights deals will be done by a primary financier – who will be either a pay-TV operator or a network. As such, traditional windows are likely to be mixed up in the future. In some cases the film will go straight to pay-TV and then the network, and in other cases, vice-versa, depending on the value the co-financiers judge the product to offer. And the area most likely to be squeezed in the short term is between video and pay-TV.

What is arguable over the next few years is that the new technological outlets will simply be repaying the extra press and advertising costs and extra production values that it will take to launch fresh films and kick-start new revenue streams for the technology. Marketeers will have to spend more to differentiate their production, and it's possible that the Hollywood studios will decide to cut down on the average number of films they make. At present the weekly competition is eating them all up, and eating into the marketing that drives all ancillary sales and markets. As one agent puts it: 'It won't be surprising to see one of the Hollywood studios buy another one, and reduce their numbers.'

The precise nature of the emerging *markets* across Europe will also differ in different countries. By 1996, it is clear that there are emerged pay markets in Germany and Benelux; emerging markets in the UK, France and Scandinavia, and developing markets in Spain, Portugal and Italy, and smaller territories in the EC. 'What is likely is that there will be an emergence of blocks, with strips of financial interest which spread across borders,' says Styles, adding that it will be difficult to say in the mid 1990s what these will look like. However, an example could be provided where a producer will do an upfront deal with a particular network or pay service that will entail the ceding of certain defined distribution rights at a part-European or pan-European level. And there lies the problem that Devereux and other entertainment lawyers are wary of: the distinction, delineation and protection of these different pay rights which cross borders and at present come under few pan-European or global agreements or controls.

## The effects on producers

Quite how the new media environment will operate from a producer's perspective is uncertain. 'There is good and bad news here for local producers. The good news is that undoubtedly there will be new forms of financing but it will not reflect anything like the amount of cash value coming from the new pay systems,' Styles explains. 'It will be a wise producer who thinks very carefully about their funding arrangements, and doesn't get themselves locked into a funding formula which would benefit the actual production of a movie but limit its distribution. The key for the producer is to work out what strings are attached to new forms of upfront financing, and also work out how much there is a cultural trade-off in terms of level of exposure between the growing market and the established networks.' For example, will it be better for a first- or second-time producer to gain network exposure with a lower budgeted movie, but with a wider audience? Or if the budget offered up by pay-TV is significant enough to help the product break through anyway?

## The production challenge

The irony of all this is that distribution in the new world is not going to be limited. As Strauss Zelnick of BMG Entertainment North America puts it: 'The common perception about the information superhighway is that a proliferation of creative output will flow through the networks once distribution barriers have been eliminated. The reality is just the opposite. Talent is limited; distribution is not. There is simply a shortage of highly creative talent capable of generating products with mass-market appeal.'

If there is a perceived creative limitation in North America, then it is acute when it comes to Europe. One of the challenges facing the European producer of drama and movies is to come up with the creative goods. Any channel-surfer across European channels will find Star Trek, The X-Files, Murder One and other top-rated fare. Where are the European equivalents of such shows? Just as the film producer needs to address his or her ability to reach an audience, so too does the pay-TV producer. The money will become available for considerable budgets – big enough to match the millions spent on US shows like NYPD Blue – but Europe's producers will need to come up with the goods.

One example in 1996 showed some promise on this front. The Channel 4-backed, NBC-financed adaptation of Jonathan Swift's Gulliver's Travels, produced by Duncan Kenworthy (Four Weddings and a Funeral), succeeded commercially where other classical adaptations have failed on a global scale. Armed with a $20 million marketing NBC war chest, Gulliver's Travels attracted an opening US share of 33 per cent and 57 million people, a performance that shows, with the right talent, development and ambition, that it can be done.

### Europe's Top 20 Audiovisual Companies*

| Rank | Company | Country | Activities |
|------|---------|---------|------------|
| 1 | ARD | Ger | Rad/TV/Prod |
| 2 | PolyGram | Neth | Mus/Cin/Video |
| 3 | KirchGruppe | Ger | Prod/Dis/TV/Sav |
| 4 | Bertelsmann | Ger | Rad/TV/Mus/Prod |
| 5 | Thorn EMI | UK | Mus |
| 6 | BBC* | UK | Rad/TV/Prod/Vid |
| 7 | RAI | Ital | Rad/TV/Prod/Vid/Mus |
| 8 | CLT | Lux | Rad/TV/Prod |
| 9 | Fininvest | Ital | TV/Cin/Prod |
| 10 | Carlton Com. plc | UK | Rad/TV/Prod |
| 11 | Canal Plus** | Fra | TV/Prod |
| 12 | TF1** | Fra | TV/Prod/Vid |

| 13 | RTL | Ger | TV/Prod |
| 14 | ZDF | Ger | TV/Prod |
| 15 | BSkyB | UK | TV |
| 16 | Rank | UK | Sav/Cin |
| 17 | SAT 1 | Ger | TV/Prod |
| 18 | ORF | Aus | Rad/TV/Prod |
| 19 | France 2 | Fra | TV/Prod |
| 20 | France 3 | Fra | TV/Prod |

* For country-by-country statistics, including video, satellite and cable penetration figures, see Appendix 2, p. 252.

** Ranking on consolidated turnover and results
(*Source:* European Audiovisual Observatory)

## Notes

1 See *Screen Digest*, October 1994: 'Superhighway state-of-play: the world-wide picture'. Also 'Multimedia New Technologies', *Denton Hall Bulletin*, Autumn 1994 for expansive glossary of terms; and KPMG's report: *The Emerging Digital Economy – A Field Guide to the Economics of New Media*, 1995. Also see *Screen International*, 7 June 1996, and EMAP's publication, *International Broadcasting* for further information.
2 *Screen International*, 'Highway-code breakers', Oscar Moore, p. 12, 10 March 1995.
3 *Time*, 12 February 1996, p. 14.
4 'Investing in Infrastructure for the European Information Society', KPMG, address, 27 April 1995, BAFTA.
5 *Screen International*, 5 May 1995, p. 14.
6 *Screen International*, 12 January 1996, p. 12.
7 *Screen International*, 7 June 1996, p. 9.
8 Media Business File, summer 1995, p. 30.
9 See *Screen International*, 7 June 1996, 'Small Revolution', Colin Brown, pp. 12–13 for full analysis.
10 *Screen Digest*, April 1995.
11 The *Observer*, 25 February 1996, 'A CIA MediLab/BMRB survey of 500 adult viewers in the UK'.
12 *Screen International*, 'Who pays the piper . . .', 5 April 1996, p. 12.

# Case Studies

# TRAINSPOTTING

## Case Study No. 1:
## The new team approach

*Producer:* Andrew Macdonald.
*Director:* Danny Boyle.
*Writer:* John Hodge.
A Figment Film in association with Noel Gay Motion Picture Company for Channel 4.
The principal members of the cast included Ewan McGregor, Ewen Bremner, Jonny Lee Miller, Kevin McKidd, Robert Carlyle and Kelly Macdonald.

### Outline

**Trainspotting is a £1.7 million ($2.5 million) film, adapted from Scottish author Irvine Welsh's novel about a group of young heroin users in Edinburgh. The film is one of the most successful British productions made over the last ten years, and is one of PolyGram's top performing UK films of 1996. Two weeks before the film's release, Macdonald, Hodge and Boyle talked to Angus Finney at the National Film Theatre during a PACT/BFI series of screenings and seminars, 'State of the Art', about the making of the film.**

### The team's origins

After studying medicine at Edinburgh University between 1982 and 1987, John Hodge worked as a doctor, but also started to explore screenwriting in the late 1980s when he began to work on the script for Shallow Grave. He showed the screenplay to his sister, who knew Andrew Macdonald. 'Andrew told me that he was a producer, and had been a script editor in Hollywood, none of which was exactly true!' Hodge joked. Macdonald was then working on Taggart, a TV production, when he read the screenplay. Macdonald liked the screenplay, but warned Hodge that he would have to rewrite it 'umpteen times, which is what happened over the next year and a half'.

Macdonald entered the film business in a more traditional way, leaving school and starting as a runner in Scotland then London, and then spending some time in the US from late 1985 as a script reader. He worked his way up, partly through commercial companies and then via location managing for Palace Pictures, working with producer Stephen Woolley and assisting on films like David Leland's The Big Man and Zelda Barron's Shag, the latter as the director's assistant. He also directed some documentaries and short films during this time.

'I wanted to produce a feature, and thought that the only way this would happen was by taking a chance – rather like the Coen Brothers and Blood Simple – rather than waiting for it to happen. I had done some directing, and had gone to the National Film School, but I didn't like that much,' Macdonald explained.

Danny Boyle started his career in the theatre, working for a touring company, the Joint Stock Theatre Company, and then moving with Max Stafford-Clark to the Royal Court Theatre, where he was deputy director from 1985 to 1987. By the late 1980s he switched tack, training to become a director: 'I always wanted to work on camera. You can work very hard in theatre but you never get much of a feeling back again. It's very much an actor's medium, and they push you away once you've done all the rehearsals.'

A producer's job at BBC Northern Ireland was advertised, and Boyle knew some people in Belfast. He got the job, and on arrival said that he was going to direct the films as well as produce. 'They were a bit startled, but as nobody else had applied for the job they gave way. There was a wonderful cameraman there, Phil Dawson, who taught me all the technicalities.'

He produced Alan Clark's controversial Elephant, and directed some episodes of Inspector Morse and Mr Wroe's Virgins, an acclaimed series for BBC2. Boyle then tried to get a feature film off the ground. He could not get anywhere, despite going for countless interviews and meetings. Finally he saw the screenplay for Shallow Grave, which he liked very much. 'A lot more directors turned up than producers had done for the Belfast job, but I got the job.'

## Moving on to Trainspotting

Well before Shallow Grave grew into one of Britain's most successful hits for a decade – taking £5 million ($7.5 million) at the UK box office and nearly $30 million around the world – the three film-makers had pledged to stick together on future projects. Collaboration was at the front of their minds, with people who'd worked on the production of Shallow Grave, and the film's backers, Channel 4.

While Shallow Grave's editing stage was being completed in the winter of 1993, Macdonald met a friend in the business who raved about Irvine Welsh's novel, Trainspotting. She gave him the book, saying that it might possibly be a film. Macdonald does not read many books, but he found the book 'extraordinary'. He tried to buy copies for Hodge and Boyle, but the first print-run had sold out.

'I thought that if we could convey the energy and excitement and the freshness of this book in cinematic terms, as it does in literary terms, then we would really have something. I had no idea about the narrative or story at that time.

'I've always been very anti-adaptations. I think that the best cinema work generally comes from original screenplays. Trainspotting was kind of different, because it wasn't really a novel. I finally gave it to John and Danny in early 1994, saying, "What do you think about this?"'

According to Hodge, the book is a vernacular read, and offers a very broad picture of many assets of society. In addition, there are fascinating characters with horrific lives, wrapped around with humour and caustic language. Hodge was initially horrified by his first reading although he found the book very good. When he went back a second time, he was struck by 'how much humanity was in it, but I was concerned about how to turn it into a film. It wasn't really conceived as a novel, and there really isn't much narrative structure. There are lots of different characters, with internal monologues going on. I really didn't think it could be a film, and if it was to stand a chance then the author should be approached to see if he could do it.'

After further discussions, Macdonald felt that there was a difficulty in going back to Welsh. 'Often there is a problem with authors, especially ones that don't write for cinema. I didn't want this to be just something that people who'd read the book might turn up to see. I certainly didn't want it to be something like Bonfire of the Vanities. I wanted it to be a piece of cinema that people who'd never heard of the book, and knew nothing of Scotland, might go and see. John had to find a way to make it work for cinema.'

Boyle never tired of the novel, and describes it as a 'real masterpiece, which is not meant as a throwaway comment. Initially I waddled along, trying to make sense of it, and then suddenly it blazed with truth. There's something there that I didn't know about, which was a big thing. I also went back to Clockwork Orange, and on re-reading it, I realized how little Kubrick did. The book is just the film, and it was adapted straight. All three of us went to see two versions of the stage play, one of which Ewen Bremner was in. But John managed to manipulate the book much more than either of the plays managed to, and I really admired that.'

## Channel 4's support

It still took a year to convince the team that the project was the right choice, and a lot of wrangling over adaptation rights continued during that time. The role played by Channel 4, starting with Shallow Grave and then moving straight on to backing Trainspotting well before Shallow Grave's successful release, was essential to the development of Trainspotting.

'Channel 4 had recognized John Hodge's screenplay for Shallow Grave without knowing him, and they recognized me as a potential producer, without knowing anything about me,' explained Macdonald. 'And at that time, Danny had been turned down for nearly every British film that had been made for four years by British producers.

'The key is that Channel 4 understands how to make this kind of scale of film. They've put together a team that works like a studio; nobody else in the UK can do that. Their films cost between £1 million and £2 million, and take roughly the same amount of time to shoot, and they understand that they should be British films and British stories, not co-productions. It's phenomenal to me why British Screen, the BBC and others cannot work like this.

'We could have gone for a genre movie after Shallow Grave's success, with American actors and more money, or gone for real broke with a Judge Dredd; or we could stay at home and do something more difficult like Trainspotting, which nobody would have wanted to back. But here was a chance to say, this is what we want to do.' Crucially, certain elements of the story – including a baby that dies and returns as a haunting image – were unlikely to survive any pre-investment from an American backer, something the entire team was wary of.

David Aukin, Channel 4's head of drama, asked Hodge what he wanted to write after Shallow Grave. When he replied Trainspotting, 'Aukin didn't even read it, he had so much faith . . . luckily. We also were working as a team well beyond the three of us, including the cameraman, the production designer and others, which saves a lot of time. The same applies to the financier, where we knew each other's strengths and weaknesses. We know certain things that Channel 4 asks for that we don't pay much attention to, and other things we really do. He [Aukin] trusts us and we trust him, and that's a very important and difficult relationship to establish.'

### Screenplay teamwork

Once it was agreed that Trainspotting was definitely the next project, the three team members spent the first two weeks meeting up and talking about the book. They discussed which characters they liked most, which chapters, incidents, pieces of imagery worked, and even which lines they felt were important. They also discussed which parts they could dispense with.

A shortlist of characters was drawn up, alongside bits of language and incidents that were priorities for inclusion. Hodge took the list away and tried to fit as much of it as possible into a very rough first draft of around 40 pages. 'Of course, a screenplay is a much shorter document than a novel, and there was hardly even room for our shortlist,' Hodge explained. 'A lot of it had to be eventually discarded [in the final screenplay] because there simply wasn't enough space. We didn't do any censoring on the grounds of what some people might call "taste and decency". We wanted to represent what was in the novel, and capture the very striking tone of the book. However, I didn't want to glamorize or attract people to drug use, but I hoped that the screenplay would be honest in the same way that the book is honest about the euphoric effects of taking heroin.

'Although I quite enjoy watching realist films, I can't write that way myself. I'm always looking for a way out of a realist situation. So when I came to write the scene in the toilet, the idea of seeing that in a totally realistic way was totally off-putting to me. So I just went with the flow.'

## Britain's television culture

Hodge completed his first rough draft in November 1994. Boyle recalled reading it going home on the tube: 'I just roared with laughter. The feel of the book is surrealistic and he'd captured the tone brilliantly.' The team share a common view about so-called 'realism' in British film-making, which Boyle argues stems from the UK's television culture.

'People working in television are always asking themselves: "What's the real solution to [any given] situation? What would really happen?" That's what television people depend on, and fall back on, and it defines the relationship between the viewers and the makers of television. It's a pact that I've tried to steer away from, firstly in my television work and certainly in Shallow Grave. People go to the cinema to see something bigger than yourself, larger than your own life. It can still be about life in some way, but the insane, huge films like Apocalypse Now, or Nic Roeg's films are the ones that I longed to be able do . . . taking people up the jungle and driving everyone insane!'

Channel 4 agreed to finance Trainspotting for £1.7 million, although as Macdonald stressed, that included 'absolutely everything: insurance, contingency etc. But we wanted to make it as tightly as possible, and we struck a bargain that we retained final cut in the theatrical release and that the Channel had television cut.'

## Research on the culture

The first point of contact for the research was the author Irvine Welsh. According to Macdonald, 'Irvine was the obvious man to ask about everything – dates, locations, drugs, and the truth of the piece – but he wasn't really available. His attitude was: "I like you guys, it's your film, get on with it. I can't believe this book sold 130,000 copies . . . I'm writing other books now."' So the team got stuck into their own field research. They went to Leith, the Edinburgh suburb where the novel is set. There they went to a lot of needle exchanges, met many 'on–off' junkies and talked to the drug squad. They also benefited from Hodge's own experience as a doctor. 'Most people don't know the difference between amphetamine drugs and opiates, and what's on all the lists, etc. John explained a lot of this to Danny and me on a five-hour train journey to Edinburgh, and that was quite an eye opener,' Macdonald said.

Boyle pointed out that while the book was 'amazing, we still somehow wanted to do the research to check it, to make sure that it was true. It was so depressing. You realize that it's not what the book is about in essence, and it's not what you'd want to make a film about. A junkie's life is eroding and debilitating, constantly descending. You realize that when reading the book, it's not taking that journey. It's something different – about the energy and the force that makes you want to take drugs at a certain stage in your life. It also shows the casualties involved, as we do in the film, but we wanted to capture that life. Nobody will go and see a film that has the usual Christiane F. elements. You know what's coming in that kind of film, and it's debilitating.

'When we met these people it was a bit of a confidence sapper about whether we could make the film. Then we met these guys from a drug rehabilitation centre called Calton Athletic in Glasgow. We were introduced to them by the mother of one of the girls who worked in the art department. They were incredible. They don't play any part in the methadone [or reduction] programme. It's almost fundamentalist in the Centre's approach, saying that if you join them you have to give up [drugs] now.

'The only drug you're allowed to take is tobacco, nothing else. And if you break that rule you're out. They use substitutes like sport, especially football, and also psychotherapy sessions, which sound incredibly wanky and Californian, but these are working-class, really heavy guys, who sit there around a table and pour out what they've done as a result of heroin. They've nicked clothes off their babies and sold them at the market, everything, and it all comes out. But they support each other.

'You can sense life from these guys, and they gave us all an incredible boost about how to make the film. We asked them if they'd help us during the film, and they were on set every day. When we were shooting the cooking-up scenes and things like that, we started to realize that what Irvine has written in the book is nothing in comparison to what the real junky goes through: the degradation. They were there to constantly remind us of it. It was an amazing presence, but it was difficult to acknowledge them and pay respect. We're vicarious, going in there for six months, taking what we want and then disappearing again. Every day they are still struggling, carrying on their lives knowing that they could slip back any time.'

Macdonald gave the Centre a small profit-share in the film by way of recompense for their dedicated time and support of the production.

## The actors

The team was keen to use actors from Shallow Grave, but for various reasons many of them couldn't work on Trainspotting. There was no obvious part for Kerry Fox, and Chris Ecclestone was acting in the BBC production, Our Friends in the North. 'We wanted to use Ewan [McGregor] but said that he could only play Alex [Renton] if he lost weight. It's ridiculous, because when you meet a lot of the real junkies, they're just like all of us, all shapes and sizes. But there's this fix that we have that someone on it is wafer thin, and Ewan lost two stone and shaved his hair. It was great to get that, but it was a condition of casting,' Boyle explained. Parts were also found for Keith Allen and

Peter Mullen, while cameo roles were given to Irvine Welsh and game-show host Dale Winton. Ewen Bremner (Spud) had played Mark Renton in the play, but was cast to play the 1970s throwback, a drug enthusiast who indulges in substances purely to avoid himself.

McGregor has pointed out in other interviews that working with Boyle 'makes you almost feel as though the film's already been made and we just have to find it.' Boyle builds up a scrap-book filled with images and photos, which he shows to his actors. 'You have a good idea of what quality and texture he wants the film to have, and how he's going to shoot it,' McGregor said.

## The studio space

According to Boyle, one of the problems with working in Britain as a film-maker is that many people live in very small houses and flats. After finding substantial space for the Shallow Grave flat, he was keen to retain that freedom for Trainspotting. 'When you work with a film crew, you automatically lose about a third of the space you're in because of the lights, the people and all the technical equipment. I wanted to have a bigger space so that we could try to give some sense of environment inside a house,' Boyle explained.

'Usually, the other side of the equation is that for a landscape, or geography, you go outside. Britain is so disappointing as a landscape, because we're fed on a diet of American or international landscapes which are massive. Britain feels slightly mundane by comparison. But when you work inside, you can have more freedom and create bigger spaces.'

A makeshift studio was discovered in the form of an empty Wills Cigarette Factory in Glasgow, which had two floors at one time filled with 5,000 people making cigars and cigarettes. Boyle decided to build a warren of rooms with holes knocked through walls to connect them. Ironically, when Boyle went back to check some details in Muirhouse, he found the drug ghetto had already done precisely that some time ago.

Most of the film was shot in Glasgow. Shooting started in May 1995 and lasted for seven weeks: four weeks on location and three weeks in the studio. Just two days were shot in London with a reduced crew. Boyle and Macdonald would spend the evenings watching the previous day's rushes on video. Both of them missed the voice-over, leaving scenes feeling incomplete. Boyle found that very hard: 'I realized how good a film like Martin Scorsese's Goodfellas is, in the way that it uses voice-over so effectively. I started off thinking it's a substitute for the visual, but actually you need to visualize a lot more because you need to create a lot of material to allow the voice-over to have its time.' Hodge spent about three days on set rewriting certain small elements, and reworking the structural aspects of the film's ending. He also later rewrote the voice-over to work with the editing of the film.

### Editing

Boyle explained that the team had taken a 'cruel, cold decision that the end film would be 90 minutes. This was partly due to the fact that there's a lack of narrative, and we wanted to restrict ourselves. Also, film-makers become attached to things that ultimately don't matter to an audience, and you kid yourself that they do. Your film ends up like Heat or Casino at three hours long. The first cut that we looked at was about 2 hours 20 minutes. It was quite interesting, and you felt that feeling: "Aw . . . this is quite interesting, let's leave it like this . . ." But we were really tough about it.'

The film was edited by a Japanese editor, Masahiro Hirakubo, who is a major element of Boyle–Macdonald–Hodge set up. According to Boyle, Hirakubo 'works in a kind of rhythm, and is very organized. We like to try to view the film as a whole at the end of each editing sequence. We'd watch it on a screen and get a lot of the rhythm of it. But John's writing is very cut, and we are given very little, and yet somehow you get a very clear picture of the film.'

There are 245 scenes on the pages of Hodge's script, prior to further edits in the cutting room. Macdonald pointed out that 'that's an incredible number of cuts, but it enables Danny and me to visualize the film without cutting backwards and forwards.'

The music was deliberately centred around Iggy Pop, Lou Reed, and David Bowie, but from there it took off into contemporary culture. 'We didn't want to make a period film set in the 1980s. If you look at the book very carefully you can trace it, because there are a lot of 1980s references there. We wanted to set it now, so that it felt completely contemporary. The music allows us to travel in time, which is why the arc of the music was from washed-up punk, to the King of Punk – Iggy Pop – right the way through dance music and a quick trip to London's dance culture, right the way through to Brit Pop, with Pulp and Blur.'

While the artists were all helpful and supportive, tying up the music rights was far more complex. 'Completing all the music contracts is like making three films all at the same time,' Macdonald warned. 'That's because you're dealing with individuals, all of whom have to give their permission – Lou Reed, his manager, his publishing company, and then the musicians. Each song has two contracts, one for publishing and one for recording, so there are 44 contracts some of which are 50 pages long. They were in American, Californian and Scottish law, you name it, it just went on and on.'

In addition to the music, Boyle explained that the production had to be crafty with its costumes: 'Our brilliant costume designer, Rachael Fleming, managed to do something that was accurate to period but that made you feel that there wasn't any barrier between the way we are now and the way the characters are on the screen.

## The marketing phase

Given the drug-related nature of the story, Trainspotting was always set for an 18 cer-
tificate in the UK, although Macdonald contends that this was hardly likely to stand in
the way of the target audience of 16- to 24-year-olds, the main cinema-going audience.
The CD album track and re-release of the book (both in orginal cover form and in a
cover redesigned along the lines of the film's poster) also linked directly into that audience. However, crucially, the film managed to cross over to an older, plus-35 audience
as well. Critical coverage and an interest in what 'young people are up to' helped, Macdonald suggested, but most important of all was very strong and sustained word of
mouth. He was also keen that the film avoided being labelled as an arthouse film, and
felt that the music was extremely important in the positioning of the film, telling Screen
International that 'British youth culture is fashionable at the moment, and the rise of
"Britpop" has been phenomenal. We want the film to tap into the same audiences.'
EMI released the soundtrack, and PolyGram collaborated closely with EMI on the marketing of the CD despite their normally competitive relationship.

PolyGram spent an initial £850,000 ($1.275 million) on advertising for the film's UK
launch on 23 February 1996, a sum that amazed many other distributors and industry
commentators. The film opened with a platform release, with 13 prints in London, 23
in Scotland and selected sites in Cambridge, Oxford and Dublin. By 8 March the film
widened to 175 prints.

A special teaser trailer was shot by Boyle with plenty of humour, and a photo shoot of
the key characters was used to form the basis of a poster that looked like a train ticket, with the catchline 'This train is expected to arrive . . . 23:02:96', with the words
below 'From the team that brought you Shallow Grave'.

In addition to strong critical word-of-mouth from advance screenings, the British press
ploughed into stories about the team, the controversial nature of the subject matter,
and revived the book. Welsh's novel was re-released and reprinted with a film tie-in
cover, while Faber released Hodge's screenplays for Shallow Grave and Trainspotting.

PolyGram's confidence in the film was fully justified. By June 1996, Trainspotting had
taken more than $17 million at the UK box office.

## Leaving Britain?

After Shallow Grave's success, Boyle was asked by Twentieth Century–Fox if he'd like
to read the screenplay for Alien 4. 'No, definitely not!' was his instant response. He
finally did read the screenplay, which he found very entertaining, as did Hodge.

However, the team decided in February 1996 not to take up an offer by Fox to direct,
produce and rewrite Alien 4, despite all three liking the project. Macdonald explained

that ultimately they felt that the film had to be shot in Britain if they were to keep control of the project.

'Hollywood is international,' Macdonald pointed out. 'Fox is owned by an Australian, and some of it is owned by Japanese, a Canadian and by British people. It is the international place for making big, internationally marketable films, Everywhere else will never be able to compete with Hollywood. If you want to make a certain scale of film then you have to go and make it there, and you have to understand what you're buying in to and what they want. If you understand the deal then you stand a chance.'

Overall, all three film-makers stressed the importance of working together as a team. 'You can forget it sometimes,' Boyle said. 'But for the moment it's really crucial to the success of the films.' On that note, the team decided to stay together for their new film, A Life Less Ordinary, a $12 million romantic story set in America and to star Ewan McGregor. A complex set of deals for the America side of the film's investment included healthy rewards to Figment Films, strategically requested so as to allow their company to remain independent and free to continue to develop new and interesting material.

# FARINELLI

## Case Study No. 2

*Producer:* Dominique Janne.
*Director and co-screenwriter:* Gerard Corbiau.
*Language:* French and Italian.
*Screenwriters:* Andrée Corbiau, Gerard Corbiau, Teff Erhat, Michel Fessler, Marcel Beaulieu.
*Production companies:* K2 S.A. (Belgium co-producer); Alinea Films S.A. (French co-producer); Stephan Films (French producer); UGC Images (French co-producer); Le Studio Canal Plus (French co-producer); France 2 Cinema (French co-producer); MG (Italian co-producer).

### Outline

**Farinelli is a $13 million feature film, developed over a period of three years and reaching production in early 1994. Producer Dominique Janne has a producing colleague, Nadine Borreman, who was on the EAVE producer's training course during 1993. Borreman continues to work with Janne's Brussels-based company, K2. Here Janne talks to Angus Finney about how he brought together a complex $13 million Belgium/ French/Italian co-production.**

### Dominque Janne's background

Janne originally worked in advertising and marketing, running a commercials and marketing company which he ultimately sold to help underwrite his independent production activities. His first major film production was The Music Teacher (Le Maître de Musique), a film directed by Gerard Corbiau and released in 1988 to considerable success. The next film the two men collaborated on was a feature called Coming of Age. It was an average success at the box office.

### The idea stage

After Coming of Age, Janne and Corbiau decided two things were needed for the next film: first, that they should try to find an event; and second, that they should make a movie that went back to the music.

'Because today people only go to the cinema if the movie is an event, there had to be a special reason beyond the acting that attracts people away from television and towards the cinema,' Janne explained. 'We wanted to go back to the music because there is an essential treasure of emotion in using it. More exactly, when you use music as an essential dramatic instrument of the movie (and not only as a sound background), you can access the whole emotion that relates to a public that has not always had the opportunity to discover its richness by him or herself. It is as if the "concretization" of the music in a story was helping the audience reach the full emotional richness of the music. In the case of Farinelli, it didn't take months of discussions to find the right idea beyond the concept of involving music, because we had always intended to make this subject for years.'

According to Janne, this period of work normally takes a long time, and many of his and other collaborators' ideas do not go beyond this stage. 'The first stage is to find an original idea. The second stage is to try to find a dramatic line in that idea. If something fits both, we then spend three weeks or so deliberately not speaking about the idea. Then we talk again, and if we share the same enthusiasm, then we decide to go further,' he explained.

Farinelli was a famous castrato of the eighteenth century, and his story was definitely an original, unusual and interesting idea, confirmed Janne. Why unusual? 'Because there was no film about this kind of monstrous character, or a similar one, to date. I say "monster" because a castrato is almost like a freak in a circus. It was sexually appealing because of its inherent ambiguity. But we still had to find a dramatic point of view. Without that, you would simply have a beautiful documentary but nothing more. The problem with most historical films is that they are documentaries – sometimes beautiful ones – but nothing more. So we began to work on the idea, and searched for the axis that would make the film work dramatically.'

## The musical content

In addition, a musical consultant was brought on board to research, interview experts and trace the kind of music relevant to the period. Most importantly, the researcher investigated whether a castrato's voice could be reproduced using a combination of a soprano and a contralto's voice. 'We tried to find a voice that could provide the same emotion as a castrato. We explored several ways of making this work, including using both kinds of voices.' New technology was used to bring the mix of the two voices together, but this 'joining' work was only completed just one month before the film's final mix, and some two years after the initial research stage.

## The dramatic axe

The second point was to find the 'dramatic axe' of the story. Here was the story of the most famous, but also frustrated castrato of the eighteenth century. Farinelli became a counsel to the King. 'It was impressive and brilliant, but it was not exciting.

Then one of our writers came up with the idea that it should be the brother of Farinelli who was responsible for castrating him, although Farinelli did not know that. At this point the idea moves away from documentary and towards a drama.'

Just as the music for the film needed research, so too did the story. Once Janne has decided on an area for a potential feature film, he hires researchers who are instructed to find all the books and documents published on that subject. The researchers make summaries of the books, basically a list of factually interesting material with some continuity of dates to plot a life. The most interesting books are also read by Janne himself.

'If you read carefully, reality has a dramatic richness, a tension that you can use. So you use historical facts, and between two historical parts, the work of fiction relates them. Because history never tells us what Farinelli did between so-and-so date and some other time. You have the main framework, and then you work it up, respecting it in line with the character.'

## The early writing stage

Janne makes sure that nothing is actually written at this point. 'Once you write, you are fixed with it. I think it's important to speak without fixing. The writer/director, co-writers and myself all read the research and then discuss what we have read.'

'We had nearly 20 sessions with the writers and myself, with reports made of each meeting. We don't discuss the screenplay's dialogue, but concentrate on facts about the initial idea and the initial dramatic point of view. We don't talk about the storyline in any detail at this stage. These meetings are all held before any treatment is written, although "soft" memory reports were made of each meeting without individual points of view. After this stage, you begin to see things and crystallize ideas. As a group, we begin to structure the elements of the project, and make some lines through that. Once this higher level, involving the facts and the dramatic axe, is reached, then it's possible to start to write.'

However, before actually writing any treatment or first draft screenplay, Janne insists on a phase he calls 'latence'. This allows his collaborators and himself to question the level of the film, and any key points they still feel unhappy or unresolved about.

## Full writing stage

By this stage, a list of around 25 main points exist on paper. They are not in sequence, or in some chronological order. They merely form an outline, which is gradually worked on, and it gradually moves up to 40, 60 and then 80 or so points. Gerard Corbiau, the director, was also the lead writer on Farinelli.

'Over a period of two years, from the idea to the first version we were satisfied with, we developed 11 very different versions of a script. By the fourth one we felt we had a strong script to work with. These editions were serious re-writes, not just polishes with the odd page changed,' Janne explained.

Janne deliberately 'postpones' sending out any drafts of the screenplay until he is confident that a really strong version has been achieved. Part of the reason behind this strategy is that few professionals ever read a script twice: they are too busy.

Secondly, Janne creates a sense of interest in the project by telling small stories about it, and setting up a 'rumour' about the project. When decision-makers next see the producer, they ask how the project is going. It is almost like building up word-of-mouth among financiers, so that when they finally see the script after maybe a year of rumours, their appetites are whetted. 'It's a very close film industry all over the world. If you have a good idea, good subject and you start the word, then it begins to go round . . .'

## The background of the writers

Gerard Corbiau started working at RTBF (Belgian Television) in 1968 and has directed more than 50 films for television. In 1987 he directed his first feature film, The Music Teacher (Le Maître de Musique), which was nominated for the Best Foreign Film Oscar in 1988. In 1990 he directed Coming of Age, an adaptation from Charles Juliet's autobiographical novel.

Andree Corbiau, a co-writer, worked at RTBF. She was also a co-writer on The Music Teacher and Coming of Age.

Michel Fessler, a co-writer, owns two arthouse cinemas in Lyon. He has been a producer and director at FR3 since 1983, and the director of numerous TV films.

Teff Erhart, a co-writer, works at RTBF as a director. He has directed several series and films, and has won several prizes.

Marcel Beaulieu, a co-writer, has worked on features and films for television.

## The development costs

The development process from idea to script involves considerable amounts of money if done properly. Janne proceeded to put together a rough estimate for a film of the size of Farinelli for the purposes of this case study. Rather than looking to cut costs, Janne made it deliberately realistic. It included:

    One director and two writers for 18 months: $225,000

    Four researchers at $5,000 each over one month: $20,000

    A producer, who charges a fee for 18 months: $75,000

    Overheads (office, travel, additional costs): $50,000

    Total: $370,000 (£250,000).

For Farinelli, the overall development budget put forward to the European Script Fund was ECU265,000 ($336,680), of which SCRIPT contributed a repayable loan of ECU30,000 ($38,100), or 12 per cent of the development budget. The Centre National de la Cinématographie (CNC) awarded the project ECU92,000 ($115,000) for the film's development and pre-production. 'The SCRIPT Fund application was very straightforward, and didn't present us with any difficulties, and the monies were repaid on the first day of production. We introduced our project to SCRIPT on 26 July 1991, and received an agreement on 22 October 1991. There was no script at this stage, just a detailed treatment.'

'The above budget represents a huge amount of work. If I was running a MEDIA development programme, then I would make a much larger commitment from the outset to a project's development. From the very beginning, I would say, "Okay, you will receive up to $400,000 in three phases, if everything goes well." Why this way? Because in this case I would then be able to phone a top writer, and tell this writer that I have the right amount of money to pay him properly. This way no time is wasted.'

Janne argues that the need for a project to grow quickly is often halted by the hunt for development finance. He also pointed out that while the difference between larger budgeted films and small films may be considerable in overall budget, the difference in respective development costs should not be so far apart. The length of a script and the time it should take to grow from idea to screenplay should be fairly similar. 'The trouble is that many producers do not really know what to do with development. They discuss detail, but not the dramatic importance of the project.'

## Budget and production finance

The FFr60 million ($13 million) budget was relatively high for a French-language project. Janne knew that the main finance would have to come from France. Canal Plus took pay-TV rights and invested a considerable sum of money via Le Studio Canal Plus, around one-quarter of the budget. Other investors included: UGC, which also handled worldwide sales on the film; North-Rhine Westphalia Filmstiftung; France 2; RTL/TV1; Eurimages; CNC; the Ministry of the French Community (Bel); and SOFICA. Discounting was arranged to cover the pre-sales, costing around FFr2 million ($395,000) in fees and interest. No pre-sale was made to North America, something that Janne explained is 'impossible to achieve if your film is in the French language'. However, Sony Picture Classics bought the film after having seen a trailer at the Cannes Film Festival. For a full breakdown of the investors and their respective contributions, see the chart below.

## Total budget for Farinelli (in French francs)

### France

*Producers*

| | |
|---|---|
| Stephan Films and Alinea Films | 2,460,000 |
| UGC Images | 3,840,000 |
| Studio Canal Plus | 4,000,000 |
| France 2 Cinema | 4,000,000 |

*French public (government) sources*

| | |
|---|---|
| CNC | 1,900,000 |
| CNC development | 600,000 |
| Eurimages | 4,200,000 |

*SOFICA tax shelter*

| | |
|---|---|
| Studio Image | 2,000,000 |

*Advance on pre-sales*

| | |
|---|---|
| UGC-DA | 3,000,000 |

*TV pre-sales*

| | |
|---|---|
| Canal Plus | 11,000,000 |
| France 2 | 5,000,000 |

### Finance outside France

| | |
|---|---|
| Belgium | 6,000,000 |
| Italy | 3,000,000 |
| Germany (NRW) | 5,400,000 |
| Spain (pre-sale) | 2,000,000 |
| **TOTAL:** | **58,400,000** |

*Source:* K2 S.A., Brussels

## Casting and director

There were two main options when it came to casting Farinelli: one way was to go for a well-known group of actors; the other was to cast unknown actors. Finding a famous actor to play such a sexually and personally challenging part as Farinelli was not going to be easy. Neither was it necessarily appropriate, in Janne's opinion. 'It soon became quite clear that we should cast relatively unknown actors, and the best options were from Italy.' The story of the two brothers' backgrounds from Naples fitted well into an Italian casting plan.

Gerard Corbiau's background didn't present Janne with any major problems with the financiers. The Music Teacher had been so successful that most of the backers were happy with the choice of director. Shooting began on 7 February 1994, and the film was shot mostly on location in Cologne, Germany. 'We were very satisfied with our experience there, and found interesting people and technicians to work with,' Janne confirmed.

## Marketing Farinelli

A short but very carefully produced two-and-a-half-minute promo-reel was taken to Cannes in May 1994. On the back of this marketing pitch the following territories were sold: North America (Sony Picture Classics), Japan, Canada (French speaking), Singapore, Turkey, Venezuela, Costa Rica, Argentina, Uruguay, Paraguay, Chile, Israel, Greece, Cyprus, Australia, Papua New Guinea, South Korea, Brazil, Switzerland, Mexico, Serbia, Montenegro, Macedonia, Poland, Croatia, Hong Kong, Morocco, and Spain (up to 31 December 1994). Guild Entertainment later picked up the UK rights for the film, and released it in September 1995.

The key sale was to Sony Picture Classics. The executives responsible for handling the film were the team, including Michael Barker, Marcie Bloom and their partners, that had handled Corbiau's The Music Teacher. 'Michael said to me right from the beginning, "Listen, I want this film to be put forward for the Oscar nominations and the Golden Globes,"' Janne explained. The film went on to be nominated for an Oscar in March 1995, and won a Golden Globe award in January 1995. Both nominations raised the film's profile in Europe as well as the US by a considerable margin.

However, Janne retained a great deal of control over the visual images associated with the film, something that was not delegated to the distributors. His previous experience in running an advertising agency gives him first-hand experience in this part of the business. 'The images for a film are extremely important – everything from the poster to the trailer, the advertising images, even the postcards and invites. The initial advertising campaign was produced under our control,' Janne explained.

The result was one strong image of Farinelli in full costume, with his feathered head-dress flying out above him. The Americans softened the image slightly, and certain elements were changed for the Italian market, but the overall image remained the same one.

This aspect of control over the images and their transfer to different mediums of the media is very unusual for a producer to maintain. 'I don't find it normal to complete a film and then give it to a distributor who knows less than us about the film, especially about its dramatic axes. But the point of view of the distributors is definitely important to take into consideration as they are in the best position to judge the need and the expectations of the public.'

Normally the distributor would pay for all marketing materials. But 'the power is where the money is,' so Janne feels that a small section of the production budget should have included a sum for the original concept work done on marketing.

### The festival circuit

Janne and the co-producers made a radical decision that Farinelli should not be played at any film festivals. 'My feeling about film festivals is that if you put your film in competition, you must be convinced that your film is the one which will win. Cannes is particularly dangerous because it's crazy there. So it is really important to estimate your film's needs in terms of the press and communication supports before delivering it to the festival critics.'

### The release

The film was released in France and Belgium at the start of December 1994. The reason behind this approach was 'because the classic family goes to see this kind of film – a period costume drama on location – plus it helped that Christmas was coming. (The Music Teacher was also released at the same time some seven years earlier.)

However, the French intellectual-newspaper critics received the film very badly. On the other hand, television, radio, women's magazines and journalists liked the film, indicating a strong divide between the two different sections of the press. Corbiau and the main actors made themselves available for interviews around Europe as the film was gradually released. With no major stars, the need to have support from the cast and director was very important. What Janne needed to do was to find a way of by-passing the critics and reach the main media publicity outlets.

### Mistakes on reflection

Janne identified on reflection a key mistake that he regrets: the film suffers from a structural weakness during the English part of the story. 'At a certain point we said, "Okay, we'll see later in the cutting what we can do about this." That was an error, because we ended up having a big problem with the structure during the cutting. Most people who see the film realize that something is slightly wrong, although very few people can actually identify what it is caused by.

'Of course, it's easier to cut something on paper than it is during the final edit, and a lot less expensive. And your options after the film is complete are limited. We couldn't consider a re-shoot, partly because it was simply too late, and too difficult finding new time with an actress.'

Janne also explained to a certain extent how the mistake over structure came about. 'At first you have this very large film which you are going to make. Then you narrow everything back down, into more and more angles. At a certain moment, if you discover a remaining big hitch, it is a real psychological problem to turn around two months into shooting and say, "Hold on, we still have a real outstanding problem". It often happens, because under the pressure of reality when you come to do the physical work, things can show up a remaining problem.'

Janne compiled extensive press and critics' reviews of the film from across Europe, and proceeded to go through many of them with Corbiau. 'There is always a reason why people say something is good, bad or whatever. It's interesting and it's important to think about these things when the film is completed. Okay, so why was it received in this way? Should we consider things we could have changed? What are the implications for our future work? It can be interesting to sit down and analyse everything properly.'

## The role of EAVE

Nadine Borreman was involved right from the start of Farinelli. However, when she attended EAVE, Janne had a slight problem because neither he nor Corbiau could be at the sessions, and certain elements of the work in progress were at sensitive stages during her EAVE year. 'It was not easy for her. But I firmly think it was a useful training programme, and these are very precious things to our industry.'

Dominique Janne is now working on a number of feature film projects, including Felix, by Benoit Mariage; and Bon Miguel de Manara, by Gerard Corbiau.

# ROB ROY

## Case Study No. 3

*Producers:* Peter Broughan, Richard Jackson.
*Director and executive producer:* Michael Caton-Jones.
The principal members of the cast included Liam Neeson, Jessica Lange, John Hurt, Tim Roth, Brian Cox and Eric Stoltz.

### Outline

**Rob Roy is a $30 million feature film about a historical Scottish hero, developed over a period of three years and reaching production in late 1994. Producer Peter Broughan was on the EAVE producer's training course during 1993. Here he talks about the film's journey through development and into production.**

### Peter Broughan's background

Peter Broughan's initial work was closely involved in film culture. He worked with the Scottish Film Council; ran Cinema City in Norwich when it became a full-time regional film theatre; and worked for Granada Television as a researcher. He moved on to join the British Film Institute in the production division, where he assisted BFI filmmakers as a kind of in-house producer. During that point Broughan worked on Peter Greenaway's The Draughtsman's Contract, an important film for both the Institute and the UK film industry's development during the early 1980s. He subsequently joined the BBC as a script editor, moving up to join BBC Scotland in Glasgow and moving into producing. He worked on Tutti Frutti, a major TV success; and originated a TV series called The Justice Game.

During these years, Broughan discovered that he really enjoyed working on the early development process. 'For me, the most exciting and rewarding phase of the producing process is when you have the idea yourself. You then engage a writer, and spend time bringing that idea into script reality. From my point of view, things become relatively less interesting after that stage is successfully completed and the project has moved into production.'

Broughan became a freelance producer in 1991, setting up an independent company, Bronco Films, based in Glasgow. After a year of developing film and television drama projects – including producing a documentary for Yorkshire TV – he decided to formalize an 'umbrella' arrangement with Talisman Films, a larger independent production company run by Richard Jackson. Broughan was paid a fee and a small overhead payment in return for Talisman taking a majority share in his projects in development. The deal helped shore up Broughan's chances of developing his slate of projects to a more advanced stage. He was also finding the financial implications of being an independent producer very harsh indeed.

## The idea for Rob Roy

In the summer of 1991, before his Talisman deal, Broughan was driving home from his Glasgow offices, worrying about his ability to survive. 'The thousand quid here, and the two thousand there that I was getting from broadcasters and so on towards projects simply wasn't stacking up. The producer's share of development deals simply isn't enough to run a business. That was how I found myself agreeing happily to the offer from Talisman.'

At one point along the road, some mountains came into view, and Broughan's heart lifted a little. 'I was having a debate with myself about ideas, and I was a little depressed and angry that things were not adding up. I felt there must be an idea that was right under my nose that I had missed – something very local and yet very international at the same time – that hadn't been done before.'

'A voice in my head said to me: "It's Rob Roy."'

'But I don't know who Rob Roy really is.' Broughan answered his own thoughts. 'All I knew was that he'd been a rustler and a cattle man around that area in the early eighteenth century, and a lot of the iconography of the area has been associated with his name. But he wasn't a main figure in Scottish or British history. So I stopped off at the library, and picked up a couple of books and began to read up about him.

'I was astonished at this character that was revealed, at how vivid and exciting his life was. Although not directly a major political player, Rob Roy was very closely involved with the politics of the time, particularly on the Jacobite side, intriguing for the return of the Stuart line as opposed to the Hanoverian line.'

From that germination of an idea, Broughan began to condense his research and reading on the character into a treatment. He'd found seven books on Rob Roy, which covered all the material written during the twentieth century on him. 'It wasn't a very creative treatment, more a description of the character's main life story – a distillation of the reading for a film idea.' It was around 20 pages of A4, and made the most of Rob Roy's epic, romantic, period strengths and 'real life' basis.

## Finding the right writer

In November 1991, on his way back from Movie Makars (a Scottish writing and producing course now held every year in Inverness), Broughan talked to a regular collab-
orator John Brown about Rob Roy. The two men often share thoughts on projects,
and the subject came round to who should write the screenplay for Rob Roy.

'We'll never get him, but it has to be Alan Sharp,' Broughan said.

'That's a wonderful idea,' Brown replied.

'Well, it's pretty obvious, but the question is: Will I be able to get him?'

Alan Sharp had been one of the most dominating figures in Scottish film-making over
the last two decades. 'He was the classic working-class guy from the shipyards who'd
written a novel and been projected to Hollywood on the back of two Westerns that
he'd written on spec,' Broughan explained. One of them, The Hired Hand, went on to
become Peter Fonda's directorial debut.' Sharp had also written about soccer, and was
something of a Scottish cultural hero for Broughan and many others. Broughan knew
that Sharp had been living in New Zealand, but spent around half his year in America
or in the UK.

His problem was how to best approach Sharp. Agents didn't seem appropriate, while
the distinctive 'Scottishness' of the project indicated a more personal, direct approach
would be the best. Daniel Boyle, a Greenock writing friend, helped Broughan to find
a phone number in New Zealand, but the producer 'steeled himself for a couple of
days' before finally plucking up the courage to make the cold-call.

Sharp took the call very well. He was interested in the project, but was worried about
the biographical element because he'd recently completed a difficult TV biography
which he was unhappy about. Broughan pushed to keep Sharp on board, saying: 'Well
can I still send you some information about the project?' Sharp agreed. A couple of the
best books plus the treatment were sent to New Zealand.

Within a week, Sharp called back, saying that he was interested in principle in following up what Broughan had outlined in the treatment. 'It was incredibly stimulating, and
yet very daunting at the same time,' Broughan recalled. He now had a very real project on his hands.

## Travelling to New Zealand

Broughan knew that he needed to go to New Zealand if the project was to move forward properly. In order to finance part of that expense, he applied to a fund called the
Scottish Export Assistance Scheme. Although they normally help Scottish industrial-
ists market their product outside the European Union, they decided that Broughan's

project and the need to 'market' it to Alan Sharp was a suitable use of their money (which Broughan had to match with his own 50 per cent contribution).

'Finding the money in itself was quite important. If a producer – especially one that is penniless – gets on a plane and goes to the other side of the world to see a writer, then he's probably serious.' Broughan had gone out with some friends the night before flying, and arrived with a hangover at Auckland airport. Sharp met him there, explaining that they would have to wait a few hours for the next boat to take them to the small island where he lived. They had breakfast, and then drove 40 miles north to Warkworth, a small town where the ferry left for Kawau, the island. Around 80 families live there, all of them in houses which hug the ocean.

Alan talked mostly about the Kennedy assassination during the breakfast, something the writer has long been obsessed with. Gradually the two men talked about other things, but not the Rob Roy project. 'By the time we were on the ferry, I was feeling very happy and relaxed. Harriet Hall, Sharp's partner, was waiting on the end of the jetty – which struck me as a very romantic way to arrive at a writer's home to start a project.'

Broughan spent the next two-and-a-half weeks in the family house, occasionally talking about Rob Roy, a lot about football and sometimes about nothing. It was at the time of the LA riots following the Rodney King trial (March 1992), which they watched on the television set next door. 'Five of Allan's family live in LA so there was a particular anxiety on their part for their safety.'

Ideas about the project were gently bounced around, but Broughan did not push any schematic notion on Sharp. 'The writer's creative process is largely mysterious, and the relationship between a writer and producer is equally mysterious – with lots of chatting in an oblique manner, knocking ideas backwards and forwards. You have to tune in to a writer's rhythm. Of course, we did go into a much more detailed, analytical phase later. But at that point it was about who the characters were, how many could be contained in the story, how much weight certain incidents should be given.' The setting-up stage was helped by the fact that Broughan left after two-and-a-half weeks, leaving Sharp to get on with the project.

'Right from the start it was apparent that we were taking on a big Scottish movie, and that really engaged Alan. But if we'd really focused on the chances of it being made, we'd have given up then. You have to ignore the "odds against" factor to do what we were doing. It had a deliberate ambitiousness built into it right from the start, and that was why I brought Alan Sharp in on the project. He was the only choice, given that I had deliberately set out to pull together and produce the biggest Scottish film ever made. There was no one else who had the quality, experience and, ultimately the potential confidence of a studio.'

## Development funding

Sharp made things fairly straightforward for Broughan when it came to financing this stage of development – the writing of the first draft. He agreed that Broughan could deal with his London agent, Anthony Jones of Peters Fraser and Dunlop, rather than his LA agency. Sharp spoke to Jones and stressed that he did not want the up-front fees to be too punitive on the project. Soon after Broughan returned, he found that his application to the Scottish Film Production Fund had been successful.

The Fund had 'very bravely' agreed to loan £15,000 ($22,500) towards the development of the project, to be repaid if the project went into production. At the time, this was the highest sum ever loaned by the Fund, but the subject matter and the involvement of Sharp convinced them that the loan was appropriate. The director Kate Swan, and board chairman Alan Schiach, were particularly supportive of the project. 'The pessimist part of me thought that they would never go for £15,000; but another part of me reckoned they might just go for the punt on Alan Sharp. After all, here was a chance to reclaim a brilliant Scottish screenwriter,' Broughan recalled.

Talisman's Richard Jackson then proceeded to underwrite the development of the project after the Scottish Film Production Fund had committed its loan. In May 1992, via British Screen, £5,000 ($7,500) was also raised which was intended to support the writing of a treatment. However, the treatment was only written after Sharp had completed the first draft, purely because that was the way he worked. 'It was a bit of a fudge, but we certainly used the money properly towards the development,' Broughan explained, although he was disappointed by the relatively small size of the award.

An application was made for 'Team' funding loan from the European Script Fund, repayable on the first day of principal photography. A sum of £12,000 ($35,100) was approved by the autumn of that year from SCRIPT, meaning that Broughan had raised £32,000 ($48,000) towards the development budget. That sum approximately covered Sharp's fee for a full first draft and a polish, although he was 'always very generous about the number of passes he did on each draft'.

Each development contribution made the next agency that much easier to lure into supporting the project. However, even the total only really covered the writer's fee. It didn't cover the overheads or the producer's fees, which were guaranteed – as was Sharp's initial fee – by Talisman. Without that crucial support from Jackson, Broughan would have found the development process very difficult. Jackson had been very supportive of the idea of Sharp as the writer of the project, and his respect for his earlier work had helped convince him of the value of underwriting the development process.

## The first draft

'The first draft was awful. Absolutely terrible,' Broughan recalled. Sharp had come over to Scotland in late 1992, and sat at Broughan's kitchen table, writing a first draft. 'We sat there and I read it, and it was a really critical point. What do I say to Alan Sharp, because this is not working? So we addressed it head-on. Every time I said, "This doesn't work," Alan would reply, "You're right, it's because of . . ." He wasn't at all defensive, but in retrospect, it was part of the process he probably had to go through. Taking on a historical subject, quite a large slice of history, a complicated political time, plus something that had battles in that version of the script, was a considerable task. He had eaten all the history up and then run it though his system. And then we turned around and asked what the story was. How do we compress all of this Rob Roy stuff into a two-hour screenplay?'

At that point, Sharp started to make decisions about what to keep in and what to keep out. At that point a key battle disappeared, and a more focused, personal story emerged. 'We called that phase, "draft zero". But by that time Alan and I had the kind of relationship where we could deal with it. It's always advisable to be honest – you can't start telling lies to your writer or yourself about what has to happen. He did say later, "If you'd said you'd liked that draft, I wouldn't have respected your judgement very much."'

The two men spent a long time working out what had to happen to 'draft zero' for things to work better. What were the main focal points of the story? Broughan's experience as a script editor certainly helped, and he also feels that he is more prescriptive now than when younger. But ultimately his suggestions still had to be dissected by the writer, who has the ultimate responsibility for writing the screenplay.

A deal over cattle became the initial plot focus; while Sharp decided to invent the character of Cunningham (played by Tim Roth in the film). 'When you're trying to compress a lot of real material, you have to take refuge in fictionalization. It can really help the narrative process.'

## EAVE 1993

Broughan decided to take the EAVE course during 1993. By the time the first session of EAVE came round at Leeds in February that year, Sharp had delivered 40 pages of a new draft. There were some shades of drafts in between those pages, but this particular draft was important to Broughan because he began to get an idea of whether the project was stepping back, or stepping forwards. 'I didn't really want to show the pages around, because it was a work in progress,' Broughan said. 'I'd worked a lot with scripts before, and I was a little paranoid about something being seen when it was still being formed, especially with a project that was so dear and important to me.'

Broughan had decided to take the EAVE course because he wanted to learn about Europe. 'I increased my knowledge about how the European film industry operated. Bernie [Stampfer] was very good at sketching out the whole map of Europe, and where all the connnections are. It was a nice group, and it was very helpful for me on the European level.'

While Rob Roy did become part of sessions at Ebeltoft and Amsterdam later that year, Broughan ultimately went a very different track. EAVE was excellent for his under-standing of the European market, but the direction his project was going had little in common with the programme. Meanwhile, Sharp completed the rest of the new draft by April 1993. 'It was good, although there was still some way to go. The relief was enormous for me, because I felt the engine was right back on the tracks. The script was beginning to have some narrative drive and a focus; and it was a real movie. It wasn't television. It was big, bonny, albeit a little mis-shapen, but you could see how the surgery had helped.'

### Finding a director

Some time back in Los Angeles Broughan had casually mentioned the idea of a film of Rob Roy to Michael Caton-Jones. He'd known the director slightly, while Caton-Jones' career was progressing in Hollywood at some pace. Two years later Caton-Jones and Broughan met up in Hollywood to discuss a different film about soccer, and the pro-ducer mentioned Rob Roy much more fully. Caton-Jones passed on the soccer pro-ject, but suggested that Broughan went to see Jay Maloney, his North American agent at CAA in Los Angeles.

'Michael seemed the ideal director for Rob Roy,' Broughan said later. 'He's young, he's Scottish and he's on the rise in Hollywood. What better could you ask for, as long as we could raise the money on his name.' Meanwhile, the director's London agent, Tim Corrie at Peters, Fraser and Dunlop, really liked the script, and felt that Caton-Jones would be perfect for the film. However, 'to all of our surprise, Michael didn't like that early draft,' Broughan recalled. Caton-Jones' This Boy's Life was just coming out, lead-ing him to say later that he hadn't focused on the script properly in that form.

Broughan and Sharp went off to make the script better, and put feelers out for ways of taking the project further. But it wasn't until August 1993 during the Edinburgh Film Festival that things began to happen. By this stage, Sharp had delivered a second draft, 'which had a really good smell about it. You knew the script was starting to shape up.' By then, Richard Jackson had paid for a second stage of development, including a sec-ond draft. Broughan bumped into Caton-Jones in the bar of the George Hotel on the last Friday of the film festival, and the start of the International Television Festival week-end. Caton-Jones was at the film festival for a celebrity interview alongside the presentation of This Boy's Life.

During an amiable conversation, Caton-Jones made it clear that he wanted to re-focus on Rob Roy. This was a surprise to Broughan, who thought the director was going to say that he was sorry he'd passed on the project. It was at that point that Caton-Jones started to engage in the project fully, and became very well disposed to potentially directing the film. 'It was a very exciting point for me, because by then I had what I thought to be the beginning of a very good script, and I had the involvement of the perfect director. I was convinced we could raise the money on Michael,' Broughan explained.

Early in 1996, Alan Sharp, Richard Jackson and Broughan went out to CAA in Los Angeles to talk about the project in a 'very serious way'. Sharp had revised the second draft, which Caton-Jones was very taken with. The 'team' had their first proper script conference at the house which Caton-Jones was renting. 'Michael made some very good comments on the script, many of them negative although well argued. He was interested but still not a hundred per cent committed to the project,' Broughan said.

Around that time, following a meeting at CAA, it was announced that Mel Gibson was definitely set to direct and star in Braveheart, also a Scottish period drama. 'We'd been kind of aware of Braveheart, but we weren't sure of its status. After half an hour of total depression from us all, suddenly Michael became very very pro-active. He absolutely committed to the project at that point. Everything that happened after the Braveheart announcement and Caton-Jones' commitment moved at an extraordinary pace.'

## Casting

'The next stage after having a script and a director was to find a star to play Rob Roy. Up to this point, Alan and I had decided that there were only three actors in the world who could play Rob Roy with any authenticity. They were Liam Neeson, Mel Gibson and Daniel Day-Lewis. Gibson was already doing his Scottish hero; Day-Lewis had already done it in a sense, as Hawkeye in The Last of the Mohicans; which made it easy to go straight to Neeson, who was the only actor approached for the part.' Fortunately, Caton-Jones was already friendly with Neeson – they are drinking buddies in Los Angeles – and he got a script to the actor and encouraged him to read it.

Around the same time, Caton-Jones was invited by John Calley at United Artists to talk about the new James Bond film, Goldeneye. Calley wanted to know if he was interested in directing this, but as Caton-Jones was passing on the project, he said Calley should read a screenplay that he happened to have with him. By this stage Neeson was attached in principle to the project, although he'd found the first 25 pages of the script was too idiomatic for him, and he hadn't understood the Scottishness of it. 'It was a little incomprehensible,' Caton-Jones pointed out later, who by this point had started to work more closely with Sharp on the script.

Sharp shortly afterwards wrote a draft with considerably less dialect, which Neeson read and liked. Neeson was up for a Best Actor Oscar nomination for his role in Schindler's List, and was being inundated with material. Caton-Jones managed to convince him that Rob Roy should be his next film.

Broughan later had a feeling that if Neeson couldn't have been persuaded to do the film, it might never be made at that time or indeed at all. 'If we'd had to wait another year then elements would have fallen away, but somehow all the key elements came together – the director, the star, and the studio – in the same place at the same time. I think we were very lucky, and that Michael did wonderful things in pulling John Calley and Liam on board. Without that the film would have been struggling.'

Calley had read the screenplay overnight, and the following day he said that United Artists wanted to make the film. 'Nothing that happened thereafter was to the contrary of that statement. When this news caught up with Richard and me back home, we were both elated and terrified. I didn't want to open the champagne until I was absolutely sure that the film was definite.'

## The budget

During late 1993, a British-based subsidiary of a larger international company (which Broughan would prefer not to name), had become seriously interested in the film. It was prepared to put up a budget of about $15 million. 'It's a moot point as to whether we could have made the film at that level. I think that it was so star-dependent because a costly Scottish period film set on quite a grand scale was bound to need a name to carry it. By this stage Liam's name was well up there. And I think that Rob Roy would have been unfinancable at any level without a name of that calibre. It was a big film – not on the epic level of Braveheart – and it was difficult to see it as a low-budget film.

'Who else was going to play Rob Roy outside Gibson, Day-Lewis or Neeson? Those stars guarantee a certain amount of interest and audience potential. We never thought that an American actor could play the role, it had to be someone of Celtic or British heritage.'

Then the power of the agencies began to play its role. 'Agencies can be a mixed blessing, but it was certainly very convenient in the case of Rob Roy that Liam and Michael were with CAA, and others on the film ended up from CAA. But I don't think the agency set out to package it as such, because it happened more quickly than that. On the other hand, it wasn't inconvenient that people we needed to get the film made were with the same agency. That is what happened. The power wielded was enormously to the film's benefit.'

When Caton-Jones had become committed to the project, he had asked for, and got, the role of executive producer on the film. 'Having brought Liam on board, and having bridged the project with a studio, that made complete sense. Michael is a director, and the project very much became his film, and he cast the film according to his own mind. We very much let him get on with it, and didn't interfere much. I was delighted with his choices, including people like Brian Cox, who Alan and I had talked about being in the film a long time back.'

The film went into production in the Highlands of Scotland on 25 July 1994. It ended up being a very average Hollywood studio cost, coming in at around $30 million. 'You have to remember that that figure includes a lot of contemporary, smaller-scale domestic films, so when United Artists saw the rushes they were very happy that the studio was getting a film at an average cost but with above-average production values. It was a big film for the going rate.'

Within that overall cost was a basic development cost of around £100,000 before United Artists came on board. That included Sharp's fees, and the overall development of the package. Caton-Jones and Sharp had worked together on the script, and made the narrative a little clearer. All the actors interviewed afterwards paid homage to the screenplay, saying how much they had liked the script and been attracted to the film through its exceptional quality.

## Observations on marketing

'Having seen Braveheart now, which I liked enormously, I should say that they are very different films. They are linked by both being located in Scotland, although in very different periods and with very different kinds of approaches. And ironically, Rob Roy got a lot of political kudos by not relocating to Ireland!'

But nevertheless, there was an awareness that there were two potentially similar films gearing up for the summer of 1995, putting considerable pressure on the shoot and, in particular, on the edit in early 1995. Test screenings were proposed and then abandoned by the studio. The film had to be released as soon as possible, so their results were simply going to get in the way. UIP found that an older audience was attracted to the film. The film was very well covered in the American market, on TV, the press and magazines. It came out in April in the US and in June in the UK.

The film played in 25 major US cities during its first weekend, which was an unusual 'wide platform release' schedule, and then opened the following week on 1,500 screens. The studio was pleased with the opening figures, 'relieved that the film hadn't bombed' as Broughan put it. 'But while they really liked and supported the film, it was still seen as a European film. For a European art movie it did pretty well in America,' Broughan joked. 'It was always an intelligent film, and we hadn't compromised either in the script or in the direction. I like to see it as a film which doesn't seek the lowest common denominator as a success indicator.' *Variety* reviewed the film very negatively, but other consumer critics tended to warm to it. Scottish audiences responded well to the film, which is unusual given the tendency very often to hammer their own success stories.

Rob Roy reached Number 2 in the American Box Office in its first week of release, and it stayed at Number 1 in the International Box Office for three weeks. This was in spite of the fact that it performed weakly in France, which surprised Broughan. The UK was strong – it had taken £4 million ($6 million) by early August 1995; Germany was solid, while Japan was very poor, a fact that Broughan suggested was due to that market's reticence to embrace British period films.

Rob Roy ultimately performed solidly in North America rather than at a spectacular level, taking $32 million there. The film has reached around $65 million around the world, and subsequently performed well on video.

## Peter Broughan's future work

Peter Broughan is now working on a range of projects in development under his own company, Bronco Films. One is a dark, period thriller being written by Alan Sharp about the death of Christopher Marlowe. The other is a rock star comedy.

# TALES OF A HARD CITY

## Case Study No. 4

*Producers:* Alex Usborne and Jacques Bidou.
*Director:* Kim Flitcroft.
*Language:* English.
*Format:* Documentary – 80 minutes.
Shot in 16mm film/Beta SP and High 8.
A Picture Palace North/JBA Production/La Sept/ARTE Film, made in association with Channel 4, Yorkshire TV, the CNC and Eurimages.

### Outline

**Tales of a Hard City is the 'story of four showbiz dreamers in the old steel city of Sheffield', in the North of England. It is a documentary film shot over an eight-month period in Sheffield during 1993, following a three-year development period. Alex Usborne, an EAVE graduate from the 1990/91 course, and his production partner, Jacques Bidou, gave an interview presentation at EAVE in Vienna in November 1994. This case study is based on that session and two further interviews with Usborne.**

### Alex Usborne's background

Alex Usborne comes from Sheffield, a city in the North of England which he feels passionately motivated to tell stories about. After studying at Sussex University (1979–82), Usborne came up to London and spent time at the National Film and Television School as a producer, without formally being attached to the School. He produced a film called See You At Wembley, Frankie Walsh, which went on to win a Best Foreign Student Oscar, and also produced a range of pop promos and other short film projects. It was there that he met directors Kim Flitcroft and Sandra Goldbacher. The three of them went on to collaborate on two short films – Johnny Fantastic, and Brendan's Boys – both about boxers from Sheffield, backed by Channel 4. Johnny Fantastic is a 15-minute film about a young black boxer, Johnny Nelson; and Brendan's Boys is a 30-minute documentary about three Sheffield boxers. The two documentary films won prizes at Bilbao and Turin Film Festivals, and Palermo and Bilbao Film Festivals respectively.

Both stories were firmly rooted in Usborne's interest in Sheffield's changing urban landscape. 'Around the late 1980s, most of the steel industry was closing down in and around Sheffield. The psycho-geography of the place was changing, and we wanted to look at these economic developments and illuminate them through the stories of people who somehow depicted this state,' Usborne explained.

## The ideas and influences behind Tales of a Hard City

Following these two short films, the three young film-makers agreed that it would be good to pursue the idea of making a longer film about the city.

The main creative driving force behind the project was Usborne, who was also personally inspired by the work of a Sheffield-based writer, Geoffrey Beattie, who: 'writes lovely anthropological stories of low-life, about thieves, hustlers, dreamers, villains and night clubs. His work pointed out to me that the best stories were right there under my nose. I got to know him, to follow him around, and began to get into his world.'

Usborne gradually started to compile a range of material, which he gave a working title, Tales of the City, after the writer Armistead Maupin. 'I liked Maupin's narrative, especially the way he structures his stories, and I simply nicked and adapted his title for my project. I was constantly writing and re-writing my own stories, and trying to weave them together.'

Usborne was also working with a photographer, Bill Stephenson, who documented most of Usborne's research and talks with local characters. Gradually, the producer had a lot of stories and visual images, and it was clear that something was developing. He placed a strong emphasis on 'mooching around, going from gyms to bars, just picking up the feel of the City'. That was the best way to research the place for stories he wanted to tell about Sheffield, and it's an approach he still uses to this day.

## The early development phase

As Usborne's research gradually started to build, the producer applied for a £2,000 ($3,000) loan from the Sheffield Media Development Fund, a regional source of money for locally-based media projects. A panel of experts awarded the loan in late 1991, giving Usborne some more time and support to develop his stories further.

'This meant I could do some more hanging around, more photographs, more writing, and it did begin to get me somewhere. But the real problem I had at this stage was the sheer volume of all this material. I wasn't sure how to structure it, and I wasn't sure exactly what I was aiming for. Was it a one-hour film; or three 30-minute films, or two 45-minute films? The number of suggestions I got at this stage were incredible. People told me they wanted twelve 10-minute films; three 40-minute films . . . all sorts of combinations. I couldn't do anything, because I couldn't sit down and structure a proposal properly.'

At this stage, Usborne had teamed up with Malcolm Craddock's Picture Palace, launching a company called Picture Palace North. This helped cover his overheads and give him enough support to concentrate on developing a range of projects.

## The EAVE year and meeting Jacques Bidou

In 1990 Usborne applied and was accepted on to the EAVE producer training course that was to run throughout 1990/91. Initially he signed on as an observer, meaning a producer without a specific project on the course. At the first session, he showed Tales of a Hard City to Jacques Bidou, his group leader and an experienced French producer with a company, JBA, who found it interesting. Usborne then showed the Johnny Fantastic film to his group, which he felt showed where both he, and the project, were coming from.

Bidou and Usborne agreed to meet at the MIP TV market in April 1992, where Bidou outlined the way an EAVE observer could strategically move across to having a project on the course.

Usborne presented a lively pitch for the project to EAVE, and his group gave him backing to bring Tales into their sessions from that point onwards.

By the time the second EAVE session took place, Bidou had made it clear that it would be unethical for him to become involved officially in the project at this stage while still teaching at EAVE. However, he told Usborne: 'To be a European producer for this kind of documentary, you will have to travel and go to look for the money in France and Germany, and to use a network of friends to open doors. What you must avoid is to take on two or three official "co-producers". It's up to you to go everywhere yourself.'

Meanwhile, Usborne had decided to remove himself from a complicated horror feature film, Love's Executioner, which was not going well in development. After talking over the two main options with Bidou – to make the documentary or stick with the horror film – Usborne came firmly down on the side of Tales of a Hard City.

## DOCUMENTARY development support

Usborne clearly needed further development funding to keep Tales moving forwards. He applied to DOCUMENTARY, the MEDIA programme's strand for development support of documentary films. His first application was rejected, but Usborne reapplied, and was accepted in March 1992. 'I would advise anyone else applying to MEDIA funds that it is always worth having another go if your project gets turned down,' said Usborne. The ECU10,000 ($12,700) loan was 75 per cent payable on signature of the contract, and 25 per cent on the delivery of the developed script, production plan and accounts/budgets. The overall loan was re-payable, interest-free, within six months of the first day of principal photography.

The money was mostly put towards an 80-page dossier on the project, with a strong emphasis on excellent quality photographs, which Usborne felt were crucial to telling the story.

## Building the budget

Shortly after the DOCUMENTARY loan and additional dossier work had been completed, Usborne was introduced by Bidou to Thierry Garrell at the French broadcaster, La Sept. The broadcaster has a relationship with ARTE, the French/German arts channel, something that later was to help Garrell commit to the project. At the same MIP-TV market, a meeting was arranged for Usborne, Flitcroft, Goldbacher, Bidou and Garrell. 'We had dinner in Cannes, and I had already sent him the photographs and dossier,' Usborne explained, while Bidou acted as a go-between. At the end of the meeting, Thierry committed £57,000 (FFr500,000) to the project. Garrell wanted a feature-length documentary, which allowed Usborne to focus his stories, now knowing what format was to be used.

The next step for Usborne was to solicit support from the UK. Fortunately, Bidou knew Alan Fountain, the commissioning editor for independent film and video at Channel 4. Usborne wrote to Fountain, and received a fairly negative initial response, suggesting that the project 'wasn't really for him, but to come in and talk anyway,' mainly on the back of Bidou's personal encouragement.

'So I got in the door, and I used the photographs, and I just sat there saying this is Bamb, Bamb, Bamb!' Usborne explained. Usborne is a very energetic and enthusiastic pitcher of projects, which clearly impressed Fountain. After a short meeting, Fountain shook his hand and committed £50,000 (FFr460,000) in return for two screenings over a five-year period. 'You have to remember that Jacques had got me in the door. If I had just sent the proposal to Channel 4 blind, it would have been a direct no.'

At this point Usborne took a fairly unusual step. He approached a regional independent television company, Yorkshire Television, with a view to pre-selling the film for a regional screening. Yorkshire TV committed £30,000 (FFr250,000) in return for three screenings over a five-year period. The ITV company ended up having the UK premier to the film, while Channel 4's screening was not until mid 1995. This did lead to negotiations between Usborne and the two television broadcasters, but the matter was successfully solved.

By early 1993, Usborne had a total of around £140,000 ($210,500). 'Frankly, I thought that it wasn't enough to do the film that we wanted to make, but I took the attitude that if we didn't get any more then I was going to go ahead anyway,' Usborne explained. He phoned Bidou, explained the situation to him and asked for some advice. In April 1993, the UK had finally joined Eurimages, the Council of Europe's co-production fund. For a documentary, two members of Eurimages are required for an application to be considered. Usborne suggested to Bidou that it would be a strong possibility to apply for Eurimages finance, and could he help him with the application?

By this stage, Usborne had completed his EAVE course, leaving Bidou technically and ethically free to come on board as a co-producing partner. Two elements were required by Usborne to get closer to his £200,000 ($300,000) budget target. One was Eurimages; the other was financial support from the Centre National de la Ciné-matographie (CNC), the central subsidy body in France. La Sept's Garrell had also been keen to see Bidou become a more official part of the production, and Bidou's partnership was necessary if the CNC money was to be tapped. About £20,000 (FFr200,000) was raised through the automatic TV system, which advances finance towards future projects on the back of previous television work. By this time, Bidou had access to around FFr2 million via his former productions, including one movie for television and eight documentaries over six years. The budget had to be juggled so that JBA Production's expenses were above 30 per cent of the overall costs of the project.

Applying to Eurimages requires a considerable amount of work. 'It's a week of moving pieces of paper about,' Usborne confirmed. However, Bidou added that the real key is to make sure that your national Eurimages representative is fully aware of your project.

He subsequently had a one-hour conversation with France's representative; while Usborne saw Janet Walker, the UK representative and also, by chance, a Channel 4 executive. The Eurimages application was successful, and was the first majority UK production to receive financing since the UK had become a member that spring. The amount added to the budget was around £14,000 from the UK and £14,000 from France, a total of £28,000 (FFr250,000).

The total budget raised from sources outside the two producers by April 1993 amount-ed to nearly £192,000. This was still slightly short of Usborne's target of £200,000; and considerably shorter than the ideal budget of £250,000. 'We were always a little under-cut by the budget,' Usborne explained, adding that a percentage of his production fee was deferred to help make up some of the short-fall, but that sales of the film after pro-duction was completed were needed to make the film break even.

A French breakdown of the budget compiled on 25 October 1994 looked like this:

### Tales of a Hard City – budget

| French Section | French francs |
|---|---|
| JBA Production (producer) | 170,000 |
| La Sept/Arte (co-producer) | 200,000 |
| La Sept/Arte( TV pre-sale) | 300,000 |
| COSIP(CNC) (automatic) | 200,000 |
| Eurimages (subvention) | 125,000 |
| **Total French participation (50%)** | **995,000** |
| (JBA's French contribution 17%) | |

| English Section | French francs |
|---|---|
| Picture Palace (co-producer | 163,424 |
| Channel 4 (TV pre-sale) | 457,270 |
| Yorkshire TV (TV pre-sale) | 249,420 |
| Eurimages (subvention) | 125,000 |
| **Total UK participation (50%)** | **995,114** |
| (Picture Palace's contribution 16%) | |

**TOTAL**                                                    **1,990,114**

## The casting

Finding exactly the right 'real' personalities to focus the film on was a time-consuming process. 'From the start we were looking for a kind of story which would tell the economic state of the city. Kim takes a lot of time choosing the characters that he wants to work with, and they normally have something of a "performer" in them. Things happen to them' Usborne said. Although a number of interesting stories were shot during the main five months, ultimately the film narrowed down to four key characters and their stories.

- Glen is a car thief and karaoke king – but with a real talent for singing.

- Sarah is the dirty dancer who was thrown into a Greek prison for three days. She returned to Britain a national celebrity for one day, and was spotted by . . .

- Wayne, a rising media mogul and owner of a bar and nightclub, who fancies himself as a showbusiness promoter.

- Paul is an ex-boxer trying to make it as an actor. He survives through a series of minor sponsorship deals. He also has to handle his image consultant. He was also designed as a sub-plot for the other three main characters, who drove the narrative.

## Managing the production

'We had given ourselves five months to shoot the film, and the production team was in Sheffield full time' Usborne explained. 'After that five months, we kept going back, and during those later shoots we really started bringing the stuff home. Those were the days when we shot five or six minutes of film a day. The later the shooting, the more precise we were able to be in shooting specific scenes and almost slotting them into the film. We knew we needed certain scenes by then, whereas at the start of the five months we were just flailing about.'

One key piece of advice from Bidou and Garrell was constantly to review the material shot. Almost twice a day, Usborne and Flitcroft would sit down with the stories and look through the shape of the material together, trying to predict where something might happen and trying to stay ahead of the story. 'The film is absolutely a documentary, and there is no intervention from the film-maker whatsoever,' Usborne explained. However, certain of the characters – notably Wayne – were very aware of the camera and what it could do. 'Nevertheless, the film was going to be about exploitation, image, about making money and about the media. All those things were central, and when you go in to make a documentary, there's obviously a grey area where the film can change and alter people's lives,' Usborne stressed. 'Documentary film-making can impose you, the film-maker, on someone else's life'.

Funding the daily production proved extremely difficult. 'The one thing I really learnt on this film is the importance of cash-flow. Trying to keep the money together was a real struggle,' Usborne explained. Cash difficulties affected a number of elements, including the film being used to shoot Tales. Initially, the film was to be shot on 16mm. That proved too expensive, so it was changed to Betacam, plus some Super 8, then coming back to 16mm for certain shoots at night. A total of five camera operators were used during the shooting, with three from the Newcastle school of documentary, which helped in keeping a uniformity of style to the overall look and feel of the film. A total of about 70 hours of footage was shot during the eight-month period.

## The editing process

By September 1993, a one-day major discussion was held following a 'work in progress' screening attended by the commissioning editors and Bidou. Usborne suspected that this kind of screening 'can be a real nightmare, but in this case it worked very well because of a common sense of purpose. Editing the film was an enormous job, because we had shot hours and hours of footage, and there were many different stories in there.' However, some slight differences of opinion were held by Channel 4 and Yorkshire – something Bidou put down to the sheer volume of material they had to consider.

One of the editing problems was created by the fact that Usborne was creatively very close to the film. 'Alex had lived day and night in Sheffield, and was completely involved in the situation,' Bidou explained. 'There was a really strong relationship between Kim and Alex, but not so much on a director/producer basis, because Sheffield is Alex's town, whereas Kim comes from London. There was a moment where Alex's and Kim's vision were not the same, so we decided to take the film to France and put a French editor on it.' Bidou was particularly keen to make sure the editing process didn't go against the material, explaining that 'we were making a film, not a project to pitch for slots.'

Further discussions and subsequent screenings were held, while a top fiction editor, Yann Dedet, was brought in on the editing. Flitcroft and Usborne went over to meet Dedet in Paris on the suggestion of Bidou and Garrell, and the French editor liked the film.

The editing process also raised the question of the relationship between reality and fiction. Bidou pointed out that the subjects took a long time to shoot, making the handling of the editing difficult. 'For example, the sponsorship sequence with Paul looks like fiction, but the sequence took four months to capture. The moment when Paul asks to test drive a car is not organized or set up, but we had to edit the film as if they were stories.' Usborne and Bidou explained this dilemma to the editor, stressing that while of course an element of fictional storytelling was needed in the main part of the film, 'the reality needed to return by the end'.

Dedet managed to work on the film without taking over entire creative control, making the most of the material and adding fine touches, Usborne explained. The film ended up at 80 minutes long. For the additional editing period, a further £10,000 ($15,000) was raised via La Sept and Channel 4.

## The Marseille world premiere

The film was not fully mixed by the time Usborne and Flitcroft took it to the Marseille International Documentary Film Festival in June 1994. Flitcroft had also experimented with the grading of the film, bringing all the colours down. 'I hated it,' Usborne recalls. 'It looked and sounded terrible.'

Tales proceeded to win the Grand Prix.

Although elated about winning the £6,000 prize, Usborne and Flitcroft agreed to reinvest the money in a better grade and sound-track. Usborne also raised a small sum of money from DOCUMENTARY towards the design and production of some promotional posters and other marketing material.

During summer 1994, Usborne arranged for three screenings in Soho, London. He invited Miramax Films, who said they liked the film very much, but that they didn't distribute documentaries – especially documentaries that they saw as made for television.

Looking back, Usborne feels the theatrical screening of the film during the summer of 1994 to Miramax and others was a mistake. 'I wouldn't show a theatrical work on video again, but I was so fired up by the win at Marseille that I was pretty unstoppable! On reflection, I would hang on until the whole film was completed properly.' There was also the question of the strong accents, which are often off-putting to a North American distributor, making them consider sub-titles.

Usborne decided to change his tactics following these screenings, in an attempt to reposition Tales as more of a film and less of a documentary. 'If the film was going to play, I would have to create a buzz about it. So I showed in places outside of England – like the Galway Film Festival that July, and Edinburgh that August. I tried to get it into Venice and Toronto, but Venice didn't come through and Toronto couldn't fit us in. I didn't want to show it in London, and held back until November during the London Film Festival.'

Partly due to this strategy, and more importantly on the back of the film itself, Tales went down very well at London. However, critics tended to be divided about the film. Earlier that summer at Edinburgh, The *Guardian*'s Derek Malcolm had argued with Usborne about Tales, while *The Times* had run a positive review the next day, describing the film as 'fresh, cheering and often very funny'. 'I learnt that you have to try to get the film to critics who like it, and keep it away from those that don't, whenever possible,' Usborne explained.

## International sales

There are very few sales companies that specialize in selling documentaries around the world. They include ITEL (the sales arm for Anglia Television in the UK), Channel 4 and Jane Balfour Films. Usborne already had two contacts at Jane Balfour, and had known Balfour herself for some time.

Usborne was aware of the difficulties he faced in selling the film, but decided it was worth going with Jane Balfour to see what could be done. 'Documentary is such an unsexy word. It spells death for a film unless you can somehow attach a spin to the pitch, and make people feel it might play to a wider audience,' Usborne said. He went on to explain that the slots for documentaries on television are less frequent than they used to be, and that many potential buyers were only interested in a cut of 60 minutes. Also, the prices tend to be very low for a documentary: for example, a sale to a Swiss television company was worth just £3,000 ($4,500).

However, after the London Film Festival screening, Mick Southworth, a UK specialist distributor from the Feature Film Company, showed some interest in helping Usborne distribute the film. Southworth offered to put up between £3,000 and £8,000 towards a cinema and home-video release, while Usborne secured the support of a small art theatre in central London, the ICA. This was particularly good for Usborne, as it allowed him to pay for an optical print – a requirement for his cinema screen at the ICA theatre – and also gave him a modest advertising budget.

The UK release was set to run from 5 to 16 April, a tricky period as the second week was running into the Easter holiday. Matters were not helped when the ICA bulletin stated incorrectly that the film wasn't being shown on Monday and Tuesday of those weeks.

'It's about attention to detail, and it meant that all the listings magazines had printed it up wrongly. Nevertheless, the audience increased throughout the run, with a 70 per cent full house by the end. Mondays and Tuesdays were terrible, but overall it averaged about 34 to 40 people per day.'

What Usborne was aiming for was to whip up support and word-of-mouth via strong press notices. Given the budget available, he did extremely well. Tales succeeded in attracting about nine strong notices in contrast to two negative reviews on its release.

*Time Out* placed the film at No. 8 in its Critics' Choice, describing the film as a 'Witty, peceptive portrait of Sheffield's backstreet dreamers'. *New Musical Express* said it was 'almost certainly the funniest British film you'll see this year'; while *The Times* trumpeted the film as 'a hilarious documentary portrait of four Sheffield hopefuls'.

Usborne realized that the film had moved from being a worthy documentary to a comedy. While this was not the intention of the film-makers, he felt that with more marketing material and backing, he could have used that comedy pitch to help it break out with a couple of weeks at a larger cinema. 'However, the Feature Film Company didn't have the resources to accomplish this wider aim. I always hoped that it could grow out of something very small, and that good word-of-mouth was the only way to make that happen. But once again, documentary is a word you have to circumnavigate.'

A cinema screening was held in the home town of Sheffield, to which Usborne invited the cast and crew. 'It was a hoot,' Usborne recalled. 'The audience was laughing and cheering. It was fantastic, and then as the end of the film came, I thought I'd better take control. I got the cast to stand up and asked the crowd for a hand for them. Everyone was whooping . . .' Then some questions were asked, including how much of the film was true. Two members of the cast both responded with a spontaneous 'Yes, it was absolutely true'. This was an important moment for the film-makers, watching their subjects meet the audience, and stand by the authenticity of the film. The film went on to play for four days at a Sheffield theatre, but its regional screening was before any national press coverage had been achieved, hardly helping its marketing at that stage.

## The television screenings

Yorkshire TV had the first screening in the UK, in August 1994. The screening was a great success, trebling the normal audience and maintaining that level throughout the programme. 'You have to take your hat off to Yorkshire,' Usborne said. 'Yorkshire put their money in and got the first proper screening. It was right for the region, the local people, and I'm a small local producer who they are working with on more projects.'

The French television screening on ARTE, the French-German channel, on 3 December 1994, was very well covered by the French press. The journalists took the film extremely seriously, and wrote a lot of copy about the film, taking an interest in its cultural and social aspects. Channel 4 screened the film on 22 June 1995, during its documentary strand, True Stories. The slot is a high-profile one for a documentary film, and this screening was, over and above the others, the key screening for Flitcroft and Usborne.

Another unexpected plus was a prize announced in March 1995 – the INDIES AWARDS – for best regional independent film. Tales was in fine company with films such as Neil Jordan's The Crying Game. Tales was also selected for a screening at INPUT in April 1995, which boosted the film's sales considerably, clinching deals with TV Ontario, Swedish and Danish television stations.

## The EAVE network

Working through the year-long EAVE course put Usborne in touch with a group of young film-makers, who tend to stay in touch after the sessions are completed. 'During that first year or so I would phone up just for a chat. Then, as years passed by, I'd get in contact when I needed very specific information: "I have a project I want to do here, can you help me?" kind of thing. But where EAVE really works is at the markets and festivals. You can be at these events, not knowing anyone, when suddenly you're saved when you bump into an EAVE graduate from the same year.' Usborne also stresses that the market works by using up-to-the-minute information. 'Somebody comes out of a meeting, and says to you: "I've just pitched my thriller, but they don't want thrillers, they want comedies. And you have a comedy right there to offer them!" This approach works, 'because the network works fast and well if you share things.'

The openness of the EAVE sessions and its overall approach breeds a likewise generous sharing of information beyond the course. 'Don't hide things from each other,' Usborne advises, 'the openness works in everyone's favour.'

## Usborne's future projects

Usborne has committed himself to working in Sheffield for a two-year period, seeing how many of his projects can work. He shot a short documentary about Heavy Metal Girls in Sheffield during Summer 1995. The film is directed by Michael Clifford and is titled A Band Called Treacle. He is also developing a documentary, Shake Some Action, about 'love and crime' on Sheffield's Parkhill Estate, to be directed by Flitcroft. He recently produced (with David Muir) a short film, The Granton Star Cause, adapted by Irvine Welsh from the author's short stories, The Acid House Trilogy. The film was directed by Paul McGuigan and was screened at Edinburgh in 1996.

When asked about the possibility of moving across to produce feature films, Usborne stressed his main affection and commitment is towards producing television programmes. 'I love what I am doing, I love television. I do want to make feature films, but they have got to be a kind of hobby. I want to run a business successfully, and the bread and butter is in television, both on a domestic and European level.'

# THE NAME OF THE ROSE

## Case Study No. 5:
## The relationship between
## producer and director

*Producers:* Bernd Eichinger, Jean-Jacques Annaud.
*Director and co-screenwriter:* Jean-Jacques Annaud.
A West German/Italian/French co-production.
The principal members of the cast include Sean Connery, Christian Slater, Helmut Qualtinger and Elya Baskin.

### Outline

**The Name of the Rose is a $30 million European film, based on the novel by Italian author Umberto Eco. The film was one of the most complex European productions ever made, and also became one of the most successful. Here, Bernd Eichinger and Jean-Jacques Annaud talk to a European Film Academy Master School in December 1993 about the making of the film.**

### The origins of the film

The story of the making of The Name of the Rose – a screenplay adaptation of the highly complex novel written by Umberto Eco – is almost as overwrought as the book itself. French director Jean-Jacques Annaud became aware of the novel while promoting his film Quest For Fire in the Caribbean around 1982. He read an article in *Le Monde* about the novel, which caught his attention because the subject matter was very close to his studies, which had included medieval history. Through a friend, Annaud managed to get hold of a translation of the book, and after 60 pages of reading, he was already sure that he wanted to make a film from the story.

'I immediately flew to Rome, because I knew that the rights were owned by RAI television, so I went to see the president of production. I asked him who the director was for The Rose, and they said they didn't know. I said: "It's me."'

Annaud ended up initially working with a French producer who was clearly more interested in his directing skills than producing The Name of the Rose. Despite this, Annaud had to comply with the deal, and started to work on the initial screenplay version of the book.

Meanwhile, German producer and distributor Bernd Eichinger had read the novel in German, and was keen to acquire the theatrical rights. He was too late, but nevertheless enquired through Annaud about where the project stood. (Eichinger and Annaud knew each other from Quest For Fire, which Eichinger's company, Neue Constantin, had distributed in Germany.) Although clear that the film was likely to be a French production, Eichinger left the door open, saying that if Annaud ran in to problems later, to come back to him.

'I sensed that this project would be very large and complex to shoot because it was a sophisticated and entirely European subject matter, involving murder and comedy derived from Aristotle. There were many elements that were not obviously commercial, including the monastery setting in the fourteenth century; and yet it was clearly a very expensive movie, so you had to think about the American market. I thought that Jean-Jacques would come back. Fortunately for me, but sadly for that person, his French producer was shot.'

## Adapting the novel

Annaud worked on nine initial screenplay drafts, but found the novel very difficult to adapt. The 560 pages of complex material did not lend itself obviously to a movie-going audience. 'I hated my first scripts, because there was no emotion. It was too complex, and it was too long,' recalled Annaud. 'By script nine I knew I almost had the movie because I felt the major emotions, but there were still a number of scenes that had no muscle. If you start shooting a scene that doesn't read well, then it doesn't edit well. You can try to cut it, but that often doesn't work because you need the information. People might not have seen the difference between screenplay number nine and eleven, because the story, order and characters are still the same. But the rhythm's different.'

He also faced an ironic problem: when the book rights had originally been bought 'for peanuts', he had been certain that it would remain a largely unknown novel. But the book became increasingly famous, even though many buyers were not actually reading the novel from start to finish. 'It was the most unread best-seller ever,' joked Annaud, saying that Eco, a friend, agreed that many people never got through the complete book.

So Annaud was already facing numerous problems before his producer was shot in a car park. The project was taken over by another French producer, who was uneasy about the screenplay and the high budget, set at $35 million. 'Everybody looked at me, and said I could make it for $12 million. I said "No".'

A team was already scouting for locations, which were proving impossible to find; while Annaud's life was gradually grinding to a halt. 'We're talking about two years of my life – not being paid, unable to pay taxes, or go to restaurants any more. Then one day my producer sent the script to Bernd in Germany.' Eichinger came back with three options: to distribute the movie for a serious advance; to set the project up as a fully-fledged co-production but involving German talent; or lastly, for Eichinger and his company Neue Constantin to produce the entire film.

## Developing the screenplay

Annaud moved to Munich for 18 months. He remembers this time as one of the best experiences in his life. 'This was because I was working with people who wanted to make the same film, and they weren't afraid of this monster movie. So I went in to see Bernd with the tenth screenplay, and he said "You know what? This screenplay isn't all that good". I agreed, and we went on to do seven more versions, working with two writers', including Andrew Birkin, who later directed The Cement Garden.

The main problem was length, which by script number ten was an epic three-and-a-half hours long. 'We needed to make it a two-hour movie,' said Annaud. 'Nobody can stand a three-and-a-half-hour movie. Only the director thinks it's good enough to be that long, but most people don't. And it's very difficult to compress a story.'

By script eleven, Annaud started working on a storyboard for the film. Up to screen-play number nine, the script was in French. From nine to the final seventeenth script draft, he and his fellow writers worked in English. Annaud stressed that while getting the script right is absolutely critical, the hard part is about thinking in images rather than worrying about dialogue: 'European screenplays have too much dialogue, and this is a reason why European writers say they can't write in the English language. I don't think that's a problem. If the story is carried by images then you need to write with the right ones. Dialogue is important to an extent, but not as much as music, for example.'

While Annaud was busy with the script, Eichinger was finding it very hard to raise finance for the production. Fortunately, the story lent itself to a true European co-production – with monks from all over Europe coming together in one monastery – and offering strong roles for British, French and Italian actors. 'Bernd had many moments when he must have thought I was crazy, when the only thing to do was to build this monastery. We knew we couldn't compromise on quality, but at times he had to calm me down and make me realize the reality of the amount of money you can raise on the market.'

Eichinger stressed that although the raising of the finance was hard, the really long struggle was getting the screenplay right. 'My respect for Jean-Jacques was growing. If you have a director who is writing the screenplay himself, then he gets tired and doesn't want to hear anything for a while. And he'd already done nine drafts before we'd met.' To help the script get into shape, Eichinger hired two more writers, but it was still a year before it was ready to be sent out. Even at that point, Eichinger was nervous that it had gone out too early, pointing out that distributors only read a script once and then have to bite. They never read anything twice.

'What you need is a "Yes" from actors and distributors from around the world,' he said, adding that this is virtually impossible without a strong, fully completed script. What the production got was some verbal commitment, but most of these only translated into deals after the script was ready. While the script was being worked on night and day, the monastery was being built on a hill near Rome, taking half a year and costing more than $3 million alone. As Annaud pointed out, 'It's very unusual for producers to have the balls to invest so much money upfront, trusting that the screenplay will be right in 6 to 8 months' time. At the same time as writing, I was supervising the construction of this huge set.'

Eichinger managed to clinch a deal with Twentieth Century–Fox for North American theatrical and TV rights, along with worldwide video rights. The rest of the budget came from pre-sales around the world and an equity investment by Neue Constantin. This may sound straightforward enough, but Annaud pointed out that the US deal was very hard for Eichinger to pull off. 'The phonecalls always said "No". Instead of being depressed, we still had a good time together even though I knew he hurt inside. In Europe, a lot of people are frightened by the money, but it's the freedom to make a movie you really want. Lack of money takes away this freedom. If you can tame the money and convince people who have the money to invest in your picture, then you have the chance to make your dream come true.'

## The computer crash

Writing the script day and night on an Olivetti computer was tricky, because they didn't have a computer print-out. One night, co-writer Andrew Birkin hit a wrong button, lost the script, swore blindly; and in a desperate effort to recover the pages, pulled the plug out. He plugged it in again, but the script was gone. Someone tried to open up the machine to see if the document could be retrieved, but it was gone.

Annaud and Birkin went downstairs to tell Eichinger about the fifteenth or so draft that didn't exist any longer. They had plane tickets to Los Angeles, meetings planned and no script or even recent versions to offer. 'You're just joking, guys,' laughed Eichinger. Birkin nearly passed out. Guilty, tired and depressed, Annaud and Birkin found comfort in a local nightclub. When they returned, they found a note and a big bunch of flowers and fruits from Eichinger, commiserating and encouraging them to start again. 'They did a great job, because they started right away on the new script, and it was finished in just two weeks,' said Eichinger, adding that they were printing all the time. At no point from then on was the movie allowed to be carried on a computer. They used scissors and glue, and they 'carried the movie in a box'.

But the script was more than just lines on paper. Annaud has always storyboarded his films. 'My films are already in my head, and if they're not, then I'm not ready to shoot. Some say this means I can't possibly be inspired on the set. It's not artistic. But this mythology of the inspired director on set is all wrong. If it's all on paper, then my 250 people working for me know what the day is going to be about. It takes more time, but I feel that the film I have completed is the one I saw before shooting. Architects don't build skyscrapers without a drawing.'

## Casting the lead

After the new screenplay was complete, Annaud and Eichinger went to Los Angeles where some studios looked at the script. There was much discussion about a lead actor, and one early idea was to approach Sean Connery. 'You have to understand, everyone thought we were completely nuts,' said Eichinger. 'Including Umberto Eco' added Annaud. 'He said we were mad, and that we'd have to break Connery to do the part. Fortunately, Sean wanted to have his image changed after James Bond. Part of the problem was that the lead part didn't offer much range – only his hands and face were visible – so the personality had to be very strong.'

Mike Ovitz, the former super-agent at CAA, rang Annaud to canvas him about Connery, but the director wasn't convinced until Connery came to Munich to read the lines. 'I remember running down to the office ecstatic, because he was so right. Sean was reading the lines with the same melody that I had had in mind for three years.'

Annaud suggested that directing a star is not easy on occasion, and Connery was no exception. 'The first day we worked together I ran into trouble with him, because he didn't want to wear sandals in the snow,' said Annaud. He recalls the following exchange:

'What are those socks you're wearing?' Annaud asked Connery.

'Your costume lady gave them to me,' Connery replied.

'Renaissance monks don't wear socks.'

'Yes, but this one does.'

'No. This monk is about poverty and he wants to suffer.'

'Fucking monks, they're fucking stupid!' roared Connery.

To resolve the footwear conflict, Annaud instructed a longer cloak, because on the long shots Connery was going to use moonboots to keep his feet warm. On other occasions he'd wear sandals, but was in danger of catching a cold, which meant he'd lose his voice, and the production and Annaud would be in trouble. Much later in Munich when the film was being edited, Annaud instructed the foley artist to get the right sounds of the sandals – 'goatskin on granite' – and their echoes in the church. But when he checked it, the sound came out as a 'pathetic "squeak, squeak!"'. The foley artist had recreated the production track, hence copying Connery's moonboots.

Eichinger added that when making a big film with a big star, some directors are inhibited by the star's contract and status. 'The director needs to be confident that his or her own talent will be sufficient to convince the actor to perform in the right way. Great actors are great personalities, and you want to put that talent in the movie. It's terrible to see a director fail to get anything from a star because they handle him or her like a puppet.'

Annaud stressed that part of his job is to make each actor believe that he is the right person to make this film. 'You cannot write this into a contract, you need to do this every day. Sure, there are always new problems, like an actor doesn't want to do a certain scene, but you have to fight for what you want. You make a movie not through thick contracts, but with passion and understanding, and the ability to adapt to different situations.'

## Production time

Setting up production for The Name of the Rose was very complex. Both Eichinger and Annaud wanted to create a convincing fourteenth-century feel to the set. They decided to ask Italian craftspeople to build all the props, including tables, spoons and chairs. All the manuscripts were handmade, with original colour treatment. When the production started shooting in October 1985 for 75 days (already drastically cut to save money), more than 20 trucks had transferred the props used initially for interiors shot at a different monastery in Germany.

'The crew was so international that we had a soccer competition,' laughed Annaud. 'It was very positive to see that people in the film industry do all speak the same language. A grip from Poland knows exactly how to put the camera on a dolly. In France we always say we're absolutely the best. When I was working in England, they are absolutely convinced they're the best. But you can go to Austria, or Italy and they are also excellent.

'When you put everyone together it's important to avoid the crew dividing into linguistic clans. The unit should be fighting for the same movie. Movies are global, and should talk to the world. If our crews are not global, how do we talk to this planet?'

The production had a break from 23 December 1985 to 6 January 1986, during which the entire crew and set moved from Germany to Rome. 'It was a wise decision to invest in building the set, because it was very important that the crew could go back home at night. We weren't paying lots of hotel bills,' Eichinger explained.

For Annaud, the schedule was gruelling. The winter shoot left him with very short days, from 10am to around 4pm at the latest. He was doing 15 set-ups a day, compared to his normal nine or ten. Due to time, he cut out all dolly moves, and shot the film on Steadicam. 'It gives a consistent style and helps with the lighting, especially if you have candlelight, which is difficult because of all the angles. Sean Connery had to carry a lantern which had a light in it, but the camera had to see just the candle. It was a very exciting but excruciatingly tough shoot. I couldn't have done it without the enthusiasm of the crew.'

## Sharing the vision

Annaud decided to invest in his story-telling, rather than giving time-consuming attention to fancy camera work. 'If you tell your story well, you are 95 per cent there. I decided to tell the story I was passionate about, and in order to do that well, I wanted authenticity. That was the emotion I got from the novel – the feeling of being in that century, within the damp walls of that monastery.' Eichinger described the approach as an attempt to give the audience a time-trip – 'to make them believe that they really are travelling in time, and experiencing not just modern people dressed in costume, but what life was like in the fourteenth century.'

The key point is that Annaud and Eichinger shared this vision of the film, and the need to create a dream world that their audience would willingly embrace. 'I have never found that my producers are my enemies,' explained Annaud. 'They are fighting for me, so I have to fight with them. Bernd was the ideal partner because he's a real fighter.'

Eichinger was aware that the film could have been shot for $12 million, but that the quality both film-makers wanted would have been lost. 'For $12 million you wouldn't be able to make the film truly international and attract audiences around the world. We needed to get the maximum quality for the minimum amount of money – in this case $30 million – but be sure we'd reach the audience. Jean-Jacques says we could easily have spent $40 million, but that would have been a mistake, just as it would also have been wrong to have only spent $20 million. To find the right amount needs experience, and to discuss exactly what's needed to make the movie work.'

Directors can sometimes waste a lot of money through indecision. Saving money on extras can look cheap, and knowing that a script is more than an hour too long but still going ahead with it can be disastrous, warned Eichinger. 'Of course, you can shoot it, and cut it in the editing room, but you're cutting away $10 million. The other way to do it is to sit down for six weeks and trim the screenplay to the point where you really can shoot the script.'

## Post-production

Principal photography was wrapped in the middle of March 1986. The Name of the Rose entered post-production initially in Munich and was completed in America. The soundtrack was 100 per cent looped, and was produced on a Munich soundstage. Annaud always creates his sound after the shooting is completed. 'I know a lot of people hate this system, but I feel I have more freedom when I shoot the image first, and then recreate my sound later. It also frees me from the problems of language. I used actors of all nationalities, and I could loop them with other people. What it means is the German version is as good as the English. We spent a lot of time on it, and later won many awards for the film's soundtrack.'

Not only did the looping help speed up the shoot and free up locations, it also gave Annaud more freedom when it came to choosing his cast. 'There was a remarkable Austrian actor who didn't speak English, but I knew I could get a good visual quality from him and his acting was very special. He was looped in English and Italian, and it worked.'

Eichinger was very supportive on post-production, providing a unit of 40 people for seven months. 'Not only did Bernd understand things, but he pushed me on all the post-production elements,' said Annaud. 'One day he said he didn't like an ending, and asked to retouch it. I said fine; he did it, and I didn't like it. So he said we should change it back. If you trust your producing partner, then there is no clash of egos. The ego has to be the movie, not what who says what.'

Eichinger felt that while there may be reasons to argue about points, it should always be an objective discussion: 'Is this clear enough for the audience to understand? Are we listening to other people's reactions? Are we seeing it differently to them because the movie is in our heads by this stage? The editing process is almost an extra opportunity to rewrite, because you have the chance to shorten, speed up, make longer . . . and put the emphasis on certain moments. It's very wise for the producer and director to talk during this process.'

## Final cut

'I would never insist as a producer on a final cut,' confirmed Eichinger. 'But the whole debate over final cut is really absolute bullshit. If there is an understanding between a producer and a director about a project, then you go with arguments after hundreds of hours of talk. If you don't share a vision, then the best thing to do is not to do the movie together. It's not about proving points, but you fight over things as long as they make sense. If a director is adamant about keeping an editing point, then I'd never insist on something else. On the other hand, it's very important that a director understands that once you work with a producer, you should respect their opinions and take them seriously.'

Annaud argued that this issue of control highlights the extremes between the European and American approach: 'In Europe we say it's the director alone, in America they say it's the producer alone. The truth doesn't lie on one side or the other, but in a harmonious mixture and understanding between the two. Most of the artistically and commercially successful movies ever made have been undertaken by a producer and director who understand each other, and have fought for the making of the movie for the same reason.

'Directors must never take the wrong producer, because the project will go nowhere. The extreme is in America, where there are ten producers all fighting over the same movie. Only the people who've created the movie know what it's going to be like – the writer, the producer and the director. If they fight each other, they'll never get anywhere. It will be a disaster,' Annaud said.

## The release

The Name of the Rose opened on 14 September 1986 in North America, but the film attracted very mixed reviews. 'We were very disappointed,' said Eichinger. 'It was the film's first territory, and it was a very cold shower for us.' A month later the film opened in Germany, and took off: it attracted six million German admissions – taking around $45 million – and at that time broke many records. The French release attracted seven million admissions, and five million in Italy. Its European performance was a huge success, and the total gross at the box office topped $120 million, despite the poor US performance. When it opened in the Far East it became a cult movie, and is still running in Japanese arthouses today.

The Name of the Rose is now held up as a fine example of a successful 'European movie' that succeeded in crossing borders. The film recouped its large budget through a strong commercial performance across Europe, rather than depending on a strong American performance.

# BREAKING THE WAVES

## Case Study No. 6:
## Financing focus

*Producers:* Vibeke Windelov and Peter Aalbaek Jensen.
*Director and screenwriter:* Lars von Trier.
*Language:* English.
*International Sales:* World Sales, Christa Saredi.
*Production:* Zentropa Entertainments Aps, in collaboration with Trust
Film Svenska AB (Sweden), Liberator Productions Sarl (France), Argus
Film Produktie (The Netherlands), Northern Lights A/S (Norway).
*In co-production with:* La Sept Cinema, Swedish Television Drama, Media
Investment Club, Nordic Film & TV Fund.
Supported by the Danish Film Institute, the Swedish Film Institute, the
Norwegian Film Institute, the Dutch Film Fund, the Dutch COBO Fund,
Finnish Film Foundation, Eurimages, European Script Fund, Scale
Strategics.
*In association with:* Canal Plus (France), DR TV, Icelandic Film Corpora-
tion, October Films, Philippe Bober, TV 1000, Villealfa Filmproductions
OY, YLE TV1, ZDF.
*Cast:* Emily Watson, Stellan Skarsgard, Katrin Cartlidge, Jean-Marc Barr
and Udo Kier.
*Director of Photography:* Robby Mueller.
*Completion:* Premiere, 13 May 1996 at the Cannes Film Festival.


### Outline

In the early 1970s a naive young girl, Bess, living in a small community on
the north-west coast of Scotland, falls in love with Jan, an oil-rig worker
and man-of-the-world. Despite local opposition, they marry. Shortly
after their wedding, he returns to his job. Bess misses him badly, sure
that their love is made in heaven, especially as she is convinced that she
can mentally communicate with God. When an accident renders Jan
paralysed he is worried that Bess will cut herself off from a normal life.
Realizing that he will be bedridden indefinitely, he convinces Bess that
she will aid his recovery by taking a lover and relating to him their sexu-
al acts. 'God gives everyone something to be good at . . .'

## Development background

The screenplay's development was supported by the Danish Film Institute and the European Script Fund, and took more than three years to go into full production. According to producer Peter Aalbaek Jensen, who has previously produced a number of Lars von Trier's projects, including most recently The Kingdom, it took about three years to complete the screenplay and finally to decide where to shoot it – the Outer Hebrides.

Four screenplay drafts were produced. Lars von Trier wrote the first and the last draft himself. In between, he worked with two co-writers, Peter Asmussen and David Pirie, who produced the second and third drafts. Even though the final screenplay draft hardly includes any of the specific changes that were introduced by the two additional writers, the collaboration and their work indirectly brought von Trier further in his preparation of the script.

'I think that Lars was very much afraid of spending too much time on the project. If you are the writer and the director, and you spend four years on the writing, you can easily be faced with the fact that you are sick and tired of the movie before you have even started directing it. That's partly why Lars would do these very quick re-writes and then leave the project alone while we tried to raise the money. In a way, he's limiting his writing drafts to the number demanded by the [subsidy] financiers, and no more than that,' Aalbaek Jensen explained.

## The budget preparation

Aalbaek Jensen's initial budget projections in 1992/93 were for a film that would cost around $6 million. However, it was not until producer Vibeke Windelov became involved in the project that a proper budget was made, which helped to give a realistic idea of the production costs. The first budget turned out to be close to the $7.5 million that the final budget came in at. However, at that time it did not seem to be realistic that such a sum could be raised.

At this stage, von Trier was still writing the second draft of the script. He stated that according to the second draft, the film crew would not have to go to Scotland for the shoot, because it was his intention to shoot the relevant scenes as back-projection, which would bring the costs down extensively. Had there been no shooting in Scotland, a budget estimate of around $6 million would have been realistic. On this basis, a budget of $6 million was initially introduced to the Scandinavian funders.

However, once von Trier finally presented the second draft of the script, he no longer intended to work with back-projection and it was clear that the shooting would have to be done on location in Scotland; hence the budget went back to around $7.5 million. Although this was a considerable sum of money for a Scandinavian project, Aalbaek Jensen stressed that the budget was kept to a minimum.

## Raising money from Scandinavia

The first key block of finance came from the Danish Film Institute. Jorgen Ljundalh, one of the Institute's three main film consultants, liked the project and was keen to support von Trier's work. The Institute initially agreed to support the film with around $700,000, but Windelov and Aalbaek Jensen ultimately managed to raise a total of $2.5 million from the Institute.

The next step was to try the main Scandinavian territories. At first Aalbaek Jensen contacted Swedish producer Lars Jonsson, who agreed to co-produce the film. (Their subsequent collaboration in connection with Breaking the Waves has led to a fruitful partnership on several prior and future film projects.) Jonsson brought in the Swedish Film Institute, the public Swedish TV broadcaster and a Swedish pay-TV channel.

Aalbaek Jensen then approached Northern Lights, a Norwegian producer, in an effort to tap the Norwegian Film Institute. With the three Scandinavian territories co-producing the film, an application to the pan-Nordic fund, the Nordic Film and TV Fund was successfully completed. Later, co-producers in Finland and Iceland were brought into the picture.

In February 1994, Aalbaek Jensen and Windelov still needed to get all the Scandinavian funds to make a final commitment on the budget of the film. They decided to bring them all together at the Gottenburg Film Festival in Sweden, a major Scandinavian festival held every February. 'We got them all in a very big room that was very hot, with no daylight anywhere. We locked the door, and told them: "Nobody is leaving until we have the final money on the table."'

There exists a certain amount of competition between the funds, which helped force the issue. Also, once someone in Scandinavia has made a verbal commitment, then their word invariably remains good. 'It's true and this is important,' Aalbaek Jensen pointed out. 'We don't need to have all these letters and lawyers' contracts. Whenever someone has to sign a piece of paper like that, they become scared.' Hence it was an excellent policy to assemble all the subsidy heads so that they would make a verbal commitment in front of each other.

The meeting had taken place before the second draft of the screenplay had been completed. The lead producers promised the film institutes that by giving their commitment to Breaking the Waves, the film would be made even with a reduced budget. If it was to prove impossible to raise $6 million, then von Trier would have to make the film at around just $5 million.

Once the commitment was made in February 1994, the producers put the funders to the test. A small part of the film crew went to the Outer Hebrides in Scotland for four weeks in May to June of that year to shoot the panoramas of the film. (The panoramas are the chapter pictures in the film, which have been digitally elaborated after being shot.) At the time of the initial shooting, there had still been no definite decisions concerning the cast for the film. 'After having the commitment from the Scandinavian funds, I wanted to make absolutely sure that the project became a reality,' Aalbaek Jensen explained. 'Despite the cash-flow problems these early shoot days cost us, the shoot really helped to make the project real. And we'd spent so much money on these four weeks, that it was now very hard for any investor to pull out.'

### Raising money from Europe

Further money was raised from Eurimages, the pan-European co-production fund run by the Council of Europe in Strasbourg. Originally, when the application was made the film seemed to be a purely Scandinavian co-production. Eurimages, however, decided to support the project on the consideration that Denmark, Sweden and Norway are small film-producing territories. (Later it accepted that the introduction of two European principal co-producing partners, France and Germany, required a rather different co-production set-up to the one Eurimages had initially backed.)

The producers began to look for possible co-production partners elsewhere in order to complete the financing of the film. 'Then we went south, to Germany and France, because these are traditionally the best places to raise money for Lars' films.' These places were logical to turn towards, as von Trier's previous feature, Europa, and series, The Kingdom, were co-produced with both Germany and France, and because the director's work was already recognized and appreciated by audiences in those territories. In fact, however, both territories proved resistant towards the script. 'We approached everybody, and they all initially said no. It was only when the film was already in production that we finally managed to get Germany and France into the film.

'We also tried the UK, and we talked to British Screen, Channel 4, the BBC and various producers, along with the Scottish Production Fund. Simon Perry at British Screen wanted to participate [through the European Co-Production Fund], but because it's effectively an equity stake that he'd have taken, it was very hard work. There would probably be nothing left for the producers given his regulations. It's too tough a position for us. As the film was shot in Scotland, in English, with a majority of the cast from England, it seemed evident to have a co-production partner from the UK. However, they were reluctant about the script and we were unable to raise any money for the project.'

Finally, it was decided to turn the film into a Scandinavian–French co-production. La Sept Cinéma/ARTE became interested in the project after a successful collaboration on von Trier's series, The Kingdom, that won a host of prizes and was sold all around the world during 1994 and 1995. The money from ARTE was both in the form of a pre-sale and a co-production commitment, but they eventually agreed to recoup their investment on the French producer's part, which made their investment more reasonable than any UK offer.

In order to be recognized as a French co-production a certain part of the budget of the film needed to be spent in France. According to Windelov's estimations, co-producing with France actually raised the budget by around $150,000. In France, cheap solutions don't exist, and the travel and accommodation expenses involved with French co-productions are extensive.

As von Trier wanted to work the panoramas of the film with a digital technique which had not previously been used in Denmark, it was intended at the time to have this work carried out in collaboration with a French company. MEDIA I's Media Investment Club agreed to support the film due to the new technical processes demanded by the panoramas. Considering the importance of the French participation in the post-production work they accepted that their contribution would be divided equally between the Danish and the French co-producers, who would both be responsible for the repayment levels set by the Club.

Initially the producers were negotiating with the Dutch distributor of The Kingdom for distribution of Breaking the Waves in The Netherlands. However, they turned out to be interested in co-producing the film and managed to raise money from the Dutch Film Fund, as well as from Dutch television and a Dutch TV fund for co-productions, the COBO Fund. This came together after the start of principal photography and at a very convenient moment, as the producers had just had to turn down an agreement with a French distributor of the film.

## Distributors

Approaches to distributors had been made, but most of them regarded von Trier's work as fitting into a creative, arthouse market, rather than providing a commercial pre-buy opportunity. This situation later changed, however, following the enormous success of The Kingdom.

German, Italian and US distributors of The Kingdom turned out to be interested in pre-buying the film and the French producer was able to pre-sell the film to Canal Plus. It was, however, only possible to receive definitive commitments to these pre-sales after completion of principal photography, and, apart from ZDF, the money from such pre-sales is paid only on delivery of the film.

Hence Aalbaek Jensen remained reluctant to attract private investment in the film, either through a distributor or a sales company's advance. 'Sales companies demand a hell of a high percentage for taking on a film, so I wanted to avoid them if I could help it.' It was only by the end of post-production, shortly before the Première at Cannes, that an agreement was made with a sales agent, who would pay a minimum guarantee up front, which helped the cash-flow until the receipts of all the monies from the final instalments and pre-sales and distributors were paid. Furthermore, it became indispensable to work with a sales agent, as the film was selected to participate in the official competition at the 1996 Cannes Film Festival.

### Breaking the Waves: the financiers*

Danish Film Institute
Danmarks Radio/TV
Swedish Film Institute
Sveriges Television
Norwegian Film Institute
Nordic Film and TV Fund
Dutch Film Fund
VPRO/Cobo Fund
Eurimages
Media Investment Club
La Sept Cinéma/ARTE
Canal Plus
Lucky Red
TV1000
Villealfa
ZDF
October Films
Zentropa Entertainments Aps
Trust Film SvAB
Liberator Production sarl
Argus Film Produktie
Northern Lights AB

* The producers asked that the specific financial contributions remain private. Also as raising the finance for Breaking the Waves had been going on for several years, some of the companies that were involved at a previous stage had actually participated in the financing of the film without being considered as co-producers in the final project. A 'finder's fee' or limited distribution rights was granted to those partners as compensation and appreciation of the work that they had done.

### Financing the financing

One of the main problems facing the film's producers was how to get enough of the film's budget discounted into cash to pay for the production. The national public funders helped the film by paying most of their share of the budget up front. However, in addition, a local Danish bank lent the production $450,000, and the French co-producers discounted ARTE and Canal Plus' agreements. In February 1996 Christa Saredi was appointed as the sales representative for the film, and a minimum guarantee was paid up front.

## The lead element

For some time during 1994, the British actress Helena Bonham Carter was attached to the project, and was set to play the lead role, Bess. According to the producers, Zentropa 'got a message from Helena's agent that she had accepted the part. We then asked if it was okay for us to confirm this [to potential investors], and they said yes. We did that, and then she wanted to pull out. We said okay. That's okay.' The reasons for the actress's withdrawal were not made clear. However, her departure meant that the film's pre-sales potential was considerably lower in the international market. The North American pre-sale was initially based on Bonham Carter playing the lead, and was re-negotiated after her departure.

Bonham Carter was replaced by Emily Watson, who was not known to the wider cinema-going public at that stage. 'She came in for a casting session, and Lars saw her very much like the main character of the film. Already at the casting session her performance turned out to be outstanding and deeply moving.' Everybody connected to the film was happy with the new casting and following from the response at Cannes – from critics, the wider press and the public – the decision was inspired.

Breaking the Waves finally went into principal photography on 7 August 1995, and had wrapped by October 19 after an 11-week shoot. The film played in Official Competition at the 1996 Cannes Film Festival, where von Trier was awarded the Grand Prix.

# GUILTRIP

## Case Study No. 7:
## Financing focus

*Producer:* Ed Guiney.
*Director and screenwriter:* Gerry Stembridge.
*Language:* English.
*International Sales:* INTRA Films, Rome.
*Production company:* A Temple Films production, in association with the Irish Film Board, Fandango/Smile Films, Euskal Media, MC4, Eurimages and La SEPT.

### Outline

**Guiltrip is a low budget, $1.2 million feature film, developed over a period of two years. The contemporary story explores the relationship between a young married couple. Dublin-based producer Ed Guiney explains how the film was financed.**

### Ed Guiney's background

Shortly after graduating from Trinity College, Dublin, Guiney started to work for Strongbow Productions, where he developed and produced television programmes. From 1989 to 1991 he was head of development at Windmill Lane Production, and in July 1991 he set up his own production company, Temple Films. In addition to short films and TV series, Guiney has produced Ailsa, directed by Paddy Breathnach and the winner of San Sebastian's Best First-time Director award in September 1994. The financial award was to later have a considerable impact on Guiltrip's own financing package.

### The idea stage

Temple Films had been running for about eighteen months when Guiney and his partner, Stephen Bradley (a writer, director and co-producer) decided that they wanted to develop a slate of feature projects with new Irish talent. Guiney had worked with Gerry Stembridge on documentaries and also knew his theatre and TV work, so it seemed natural to approach him with a view to writing and directing a feature.

They first met up with Stembridge in April 1993, and discussed the notion of a contemporary Irish film to be made on a low budget. 'Low' in this case was definitely below

Ir£1 million ($1.6 million). 'We talked about the kind of thing we wanted – an oblique look at small-Irish-town life. We also discussed the notion of writing lead parts for the generation of Irish actors that are in their late twenties and early thirties; who have done solid theatre, and television work, and just bit parts in films,' Guiney explained.

At a further meeting two days later, Stembridge pitched the idea of Guiltrip to Guiney and Bradley, and presented them with a brief, two-page story outline. Temple commissioned him on this basis and he began to write a first draft.

## Development finance

In 1992, Guiney had been involved in a successful joint application with Samson Films to the European Script Fund for the company scheme, Incentive Funding. This meant that they knew they had raised at least a third of Guiltrip's development budget, which was calculated to be around Ir£25,000 ($37,200). In terms of the remaining balance, they had various ideas: UK broadcasters, British Screen, RTE and Temple's own (albeit limited) funds. Also, at the end of March 1993, there had been an announcement that the Film Board would be re-established, but the timing on this was still not completely clear.

The first draft was delivered in May 1993. 'This came to us incredibly fast, and we were extremely happy with it. I immediately sent it off to RTE, Channel 4, BBC and British Screen, asking them to become involved in the development. I was very confident that one of them would do so,' Guiney said.

In addition, by late May 1993, the make-up of the new Irish Film Board was announced. The support body for new films was open to submissions, so Guiney promptly sent the script to the chairwoman, Lelia Doolan, in a bid for development finance.

## Early financing models

Guiney was considering two possible finance plans at this point.

Plan A: 'I knew that the most we could raise for a new director and an unknown cast was around Ir£1 million. If I could interest a British source of finance, I felt that we might achieve this figure. They could come up with 50 to 60 per cent of the budget, and I felt if a UK source of finance were committed, then RTE, Section 35 and the new Film Board could make up the balance. This appeared to me to be the cleanest route.'

Plan B: 'If we couldn't interest a British source of finance, we would have to re-think the financing. This would mean raising the budget by pre-selling rights in different territories, and through co-production finance. This was the kind of model we had used for Ailsa. Under this plan I thought we could raise around Ir£500,000 ($800,000) relatively quickly.'

Although this was still at the early stages, Guiney believes in testing the waters, rather than fixing on a firm budget figure: 'In general I believe you raise as much as you can, and make the film for what the market is willing to pay rather than budget at a fixed level and then be restricted to raising that precise amount.'

During the summer and autumn of 1993 the rejection letters from the UK dribbled in. People said they admired the writing but they were not convinced about the project. As Guiney put it: 'Its darkness seemed to put them off and none of them saw what we thought was the humour of the piece. Guiltrip didn't fit into British preconceptions of the sort of story expected from Northern Ireland. It's different from the rural dramas and IRA films that have been coming out of here lately. We did get one piece of good news however. In August 1993 we were awarded a development loan by the Film Board. At least we had a development budget.'

In the autumn of 1993 Temple went into production on Ailsa, with the result that Guiney became consumed by the film until the New Year. Stembridge was also busy with various projects over this period. In early 1994 Temple held a week-long workshop for a number of actors in advance of Guiltrip's second draft. Following this read-through, Stembridge completed a second draft by the middle of February. The read-through helped the writer and producers work out the pace of the story, and which scenes worked, which didn't, and how the second draft could improve the screenplay.

### Production finance

Rod Stoneman, chief executive of the Irish Film Board, attended some of the actors' workshops, and was very enthusiastic about the project. At the end of January 1994, Guiney made an application for production finance to the Board. In terms of the film's shooting schedule, he expected Guiltrip to go into production in the autumn of that year. 'This was an important decision, because not only had we to plan for this date in terms of the production and our own time, but Gerry also had to make himself free. Obviously it was very important to him to make the film, but he was also being asked to get involved in other theatre and television projects that autumn. I also believe that setting a date really sharpens the mind and focuses energies in terms of pulling everything together.

'At this point it was very clear that I would have to revert to Plan B of our financing plan, involving pre-sales in Europe and co-production monies and a budget of around Ir£500,000 ($800,000). I was optimistic at this point the Film Board would invest in the film, and we were also planning on raising Section 35 tax-shelter money. Our ongoing discussions with RTE, however, resulted in the domestic broadcaster rejecting the project because they felt it was too controversial for their audience. I thought I still might be able to change their minds but I wasn't counting on RTE. I thought that we had about half of our budget and I really needed at least one foreign pre-sale to make sense of the whole thing.'

In early February 1994 Guiney sent the second draft screenplay to a number of financiers, including the American independents and mini-Majors (even though he did not hold out great hopes that they would become involved). He also sent it to German broadcaster ZDF, WDR (which had invested in Ailsa), the British Film Institute, and various production companies Guiney knew around Europe.

Guiney stresses that the chances for Guiltrip to attract a co-producing partner were slim, partly because it was a limited budget but also because it was so completely Irish in character. His main focus was on pre-sales to the French and German public broadcasters, and he didn't send the script to sales agents or any distributors outside the US because the combination of first-time director and an unknown cast would have made it impossible for them to get involved. He sent the script in February 1994 to the Americans and European broadcasters on the basis that people would have read it by Cannes, where he could meet with them if they showed any interest.

Guiney had been keeping in close contact with the Irish Film Board since his submission for production support. Following various discussions, Temple decided it would withdraw the project for production finance as it was at too early a stage in terms of other sources of finance. Guiney, however, points out that 'this decision came back to haunt us all.'

## SCRIPT's Incentive Funding Gathering in March 1994

The other very important event in the financing of the project occurred at the Incentive Funding Gathering in March 1994, held in Kildare. SCRIPT had invited all of the recipients of Incentive Funding for a weekend to meet and discuss co-production possibilities. Among these people were some of the most successful producers in Europe, and Guiney was hopeful of finding someone there who could help his project.

One of the people staying in his hotel was an Italian producer, Domenico Procacci, explained Guiney. 'I didn't think there was any way he'd be interested in the project because it had absolutely no obvious Italian dimension, but I spoke to him about it along with several other producers. He was interested (as were a few others) and took the script away with him. After the Gathering, he took a few days of holiday on the west coast of Ireland, and called me when he came back through Dublin. He liked the script and wanted to talk. Domenico was unusual because he was interested in financing low-budget English-language films and had enjoyed great success with an Australian film called Bad Boy Bubby, which had won the Critics' Prize at Venice in 1993. The market in Italy was in a very bad way, and he wanted to start to operate on the international market. We spoke about a basic deal and agreed to keep in touch and talk again at Cannes.'

## Guiltrip's Cannes 1994

By the time Cannes took place in May 1994, Guiney had had some feedback on the scripts he had sent out in February and from those he had given it to at the Gathering. Most of the Americans admired it very much but would not or could not get involved because Guiltrip had a new director, no stars and an inexperienced producer.

WDR and ZDF both liked it but ZDF's department was already committed that year, neither could WDR commit funds that year. If Guiltrip was going into production in 1995, WDR suggested that Guiney should come back and talk to them. Other European producers liked it very much but found it difficult to see how they could involve themselves because it was so Irish in terms of location, cast and crew. Guiney did however talk with a French producer (who was a friend of his), Lise Lemeunier. She had just left Pandora, and agreed to represent the project in France – in other words try and secure a pre-sale from French television or introduce it to a French producer who might help raise the finance.

Guiney also talked further with Procacci, who introduced him to an Italian sales agent, Paola Corvino of Intra Films. She had handled some of his previous films, and had sold Bad Boy Bubby very well in numerous territories. She liked the project a lot and the discussion led to the idea of her representing the international rights. Domenico reiterated that he was interested in the project and said he would give Guiney a definite answer after Cannes.


## Post-Cannes juggling

After Cannes, Guiney was facing a situation where he thought that about 60 to 80 per cent of a Ir£500,000 ($800,000) budget was raised, assuming the Fandango deal from Procacci came through. He decided to re-apply to the Irish Film Board for the 31 May deadline.

At the end of June he attended the Strategics film marketing course in Luxembourg, taking the project with him. There were various experts in distribution, publicity, sales and marketing at the event, and he was very happy with their reaction to the package.

Meanwhile, Guiney's French contact had introduced the project to MC4, a production company with close ties to La SEPT/ARTE, the French/German arts channel, who were interested in getting involved. Guiney and Stembridge went to Paris to meet their executives, and to discuss the casting and production. They were interested, but the head of La SEPT Cinema wanted to see a new draft before submitting it to his board.

During the Galway Film Fleadh in July 1994, Guiney also met Fabien Liron from the French sales/production company, Pandora, who asked to see the script. He sent it to him and thought nothing further of it.

Also that summer, Guiney travelled to Rome and met with Procacci once more. 'He confirmed that he would do the film and we negotiated a deal. I didn't realize it at the time, but at that point Domenico agreed to become co-producer without actually knowing where his share of the film's money was coming from.'

By late July 1994, Temple began casting the film with a view to a production start in November. Following Guiney's meetings with the Italians and French, he thought that things were looking good. RTE had passed but he was sure of the Film Board and RTE. It was at this point that 'disaster struck!'.

## The Irish Film Board problem

At the Board's meeting at the end of July, a decision was taken to defer the decision for a production loan on Guiltrip. The board said that it had some reservations about the script and that it was also worried about the scale of the production and the financing. They said they would reconsider it in mid-September after receiving a new draft.

'This was a blow to us,' Guiney explained. 'I felt that we had delivered good foreign investment and that the absence of a commitment from the Board meant that it was very difficult for us to plan a November shoot. We felt very hard done by, and over the weeks following the decision, I had several heated conversations and meetings with executives from the Board. During these discussions it became clear that the Board were supportive of the project overall but were unhappy with the draft as it stood at present. We decided to do a new draft taking their comments on board, and soldier on with our planned shooting date. I thought that if we got a positive decision on 19 September, we could go into pre-production a week later with a view to shooting in early November. It would be difficult but I thought we could do it.'

Casting for the film continued during August, while a new draft was completed by Stembridge. Guiney also firmed up the Italian deal, continued talking to the French and began to talk to Section 35 investors. It was also at this point that he realized that the project had the makings of a Eurimages application. Guiltrip had fulfilled the basic criteria of three European member co-producers, and although the financing wasn't quite there yet he felt that Temple should apply for the end-of-September round at which point the film would know where it stood with the Film Board and La SEPT/ARTE.

In early September Guiney re-submitted an application to the Film Board. At this point Pandora (who had finally read the project after the July Film Fleadh) came back to Guiney out of the blue. The French company loved the script and wanted to talk further. After two days of rushed faxes and phone calls, however, they decided to pass. In the end, Pandora could not justify investing in such a small film with unknown talent.

## The postponement syndrome

As the days passed by it became clearer and clearer that Guiltrip would be very lucky to make a November start date. David Collins (Temple's SCRIPT Incentive Funding partner) had agreed to help Guiney with the Section 35 deal, joining Stephen Bradley as an executive producer on the film, but it was impossible to make any real headway on the deal in the absence of clear numbers on the rest of their financing.

On 19 September the Irish Film Board decided to make a substantial production loan, having received a new script. 'Despite this good news other things weren't looking so good: La SEPT had postponed a decision until January 1995. Following a highly detailed application to Eurimages around 20 September, we knew we wouldn't hear from the pan-European body until after our production start date. The Eurimages Board met around 20 November, and even though they had given us special permission to start shooting in advance of this, there was no guarantee that our application would be successful.

'I remember well sitting down to take stock of the situation. We had a clear choice: either rush headlong into production on a budget of Ir£500,000, financed by the Board, Fandango, a Section 35 deal which was far from solid, and heavy deferrals; or postpone until the New Year with the prospect of a larger budget if La SEPT and Eurimages came through. Myself, David and Stephen were also in talks with ACCBANK (an Irish bank involved in film-related tax financing) about a deal which could have net us more than the going rate on the Section 35 scheme, but again this was going to take some time. Very reluctantly and with a good deal of soul searching and regret I decided to postpone until the New Year. In hindsight it was the only decision we could have made.'

## The Berlin Rendezvous

Guiney also attended the MEDIA-backed EuroAim Rendezvous finance and co-production meeting in Berlin at the end of September. One significant thing happened during the Rendezvous meeting, although Guiney did not realize it at the time. Guiney and Paddy Breathnach won the ECU300,000 ($370,000) Euskal Media Prize at San Sebastian for Ailsa. The money has rules attached to it, meaning that it was to be invested in their next production together, or split on a 50/50 basis. 'At this point Paddy and I thought we might get another film together for 1995, which could benefit from the prize, so I didn't think of it for Guiltrip,' Guiney recalled.

At the end of September, Guiney was looking at a budget of Ir£750,000 ($1.2 million) of which about 60 per cent was coming from Ireland, and the balance being met by the Italian and French producers and Eurimages (if the application was successful).

Guiney, Bradley and Collins continued to work on the Section 35 deal which was shaping up well. Then in late November they had some good news from Eurimages: 'By the skin of our teeth and with some frantic overnight faxing, Eurimages had agreed to invest FFr1 million (Ir£120,000) in the production of the film. It was also at this time that I decided to go with Paola Corvino as the sales agent for Guiltrip. She loved the script and the cast and I had met her on numerous occasions and really trusted her. I also wanted to go into the film with a sales agent on board and despite other offers (also without any money advanced), I felt she was the one to go with.'

## Pre-production delays

In early December La SEPT was unable to make a decision until January and Guiney began to get seriously worried. He knew that the film needed to go into pre-production very early in the New Year. They had committed all their money for 1994 and didn't know their budget yet for 1995. Furthermore, a new Head of Business was due to start after Christmas, and they wanted to involve him in the decision.

'This made things very difficult and tense with our French partners,' Guiney explained. 'I began seriously to think of a Plan B which would not involve the French and that plan involved using my share of the Euskal Prize. Paddy and I hadn't come up with a project together despite having talked about a few things, and I delicately mentioned to him that I might want to use my share of the prize for Guiltrip.'

At the beginning of 1995 Guiney set a production start date of 27 March, and the producers began to crew up the film. Guiney also faxed James Flynn (the Board's finance officer) a document outlining the film's options and asking him to advance Temple a small amount of money to keep them going as they moved from development to pre-production. At this point Temple's cash flow was in serious trouble and the producers were spending money on the film even though it had not officially started pre-production. As Guiney saw it, there were three possible ways to proceed: firstly, an Irish/Italian/French co-production with Eurimages, which he expected to total Ir£800,000 ($1.28 million); secondly, an Irish/Italian/Spanish co-production, again with Eurimages which would total Ir£720,000 ($1.152 million); and finally an Irish/Italian deal with deferrals which would total Ir£500,000 ($800,000). The problem here was that without a workable third country the film would lose Eurimages.

In mid January 1995, a month before formally entering pre-production, Temple was faced with several issues relating to the cash flow of the film:

- The Section 35 deal was proving difficult to close and Temple needed serious cash at the end of February to start pre-production. 'The problem was the absence of a firm financing structure in terms of the French/Spanish issue, and the absence of a completion bond which would ensure our investors that the film would be completed. Without these two things it would be difficult to close the deal. In addition, without a bond, the Italians would not pay us until we delivered the film at the end of the production.'

- Guiney was not sure that the French deal would come through. And even if he could replace the French with Euskal Media's prize money (which, incidentally, was not confirmed for Guiltrip) he also knew that without a bond, the Spanish would not pay for the film until the end of production.

La SEPT was forced to postpone until the middle of March. Guiney was concerned: 'At that point I was worried about the French investment, and I thought it was the right time to replace them with Euskal Media, and implement my Plan B. I checked this with Eurimages and they said it would have to go back to the Board as an Irish/Italian/Spanish deal but they felt this would be possible. In a panic I flew to San Sebastian and had a meeting with Euskal Media, effectively the Basque Region's Film Board, via an interpreter, and established that they could and would invest in the film. I then flew on to Rome and discussed the replacement of the French and the cash flow of the Italian money with Domenico.'

Back in Dublin at the beginning of February the film was gathering momentum. Temple was contracting cast and key crew members, who were passing up other offers of work in order to be available for Guiltrip. Guiney also knew that if the film slipped at all it would experience serious crewing problems as upcoming local productions, Ballykea and Moll Flanders, would soak up available crew in April. Guiltrip had to start production at the end of March if it was to start at all.

The new La SEPT decision was not going to be made until 28 February, which coincided with the film's new pre-production start date. As far as Guiney was concerned, this was much too late to wait, particularly if the French postponed once again. What was finally agreed was that Temple would keep the French as full partners until 28 February. If at that point they were unable to deliver, they would agree to withdraw, allowing Euskal Media to join as the Spanish partner.

Guiney was still working with two possible finance plans at this point, and he would not know which one would materialize until the day the film started pre-production. 'This made life very difficult in terms of contracting the film's other investors – we almost had to have two sets of draft contracts, one based on the French involvement and one based on the Spanish. We also finalized our budget at just over Ir£800,000 ($1.28 million) and decided we would have to get a completion guarantor to bond the film.'

This complicated structure also highlighted what became Guiltrip's single biggest headache: cash flow. The film was almost fully financed under either scheme but the way the payments from Section 35 investors, Fandango and Euskal Media (or La SEPT) were scheduled meant that the film would not have enough money to get through pre-production, never mind production. As Guiney explained: 'We had the money but we couldn't get our hands on it until after the shoot. I thought about borrowing against the Fandango and Euskal Media contracts but no bank anywhere in the world would regard these as good risks. Fandango are an Italian production company who were putting up the money themselves and I had no way of proving or for that matter even knowing whether they would in fact come up with the money. The prize from Euskal Media was there but the contract had yet to be negotiated and signed, and we still didn't know about La SEPT. In the absence of a guarantee that this money would eventually come through, ACCBANK would not release their investor funds via the Section 35 deal.'

This all became clearer and more starkly worrying to Guiney in the week before pre-production was due to start. 'Once we were in pre-production our costs would be on average Ir£50,000 ($80,000) per week. All our crew and cast were contracted, the main location and equipment deals were done and we were ready to go. I just didn't know how to get my hands on the money to pay for it all.

'All the way through the weeks before pre-production I had been keeping the Film Board up to date on our progress and we eventually hit upon a structure [with the Board] the Friday before pre-production began. Once this deal was in place we were able to draw down funds and close our Section 35 deal.' The film went successfully into production.

# ANTONIA'S LINE (ANTONIA)

## Case Study No. 8:
## Sales focus

*Producer:* Hans de Weers.
*Co-producer:* Judy Counihan.
*Director and screenwriter:* Marleen Gorris.
*Language:* Dutch.
*International sales:* The Sales Company, London.
*Co-producers:* Prime Time, Belgium; Bard Entertainments, UK in association with the Dutch Film Fund and the European Co-production Fund.

### Outline

**Antonia's Line (known as Antonia in The Netherlands) is a £1.835 million ($2.845 million) film made in the Dutch language. The story is centred around Antonia, an old woman in her 80s who looks back on the time just after the Second World War when she returned to her village for good. Antonia is a distinctly independent woman, and the film focuses on the cycle of birth, life and death and her surrounding family of mostly female relations.**

**The film's sales representative, Carole Myer explains how the film was marketed to international distributors.**

### The background

Carole Myer has always admired Marleen Gorris's work, which includes her debut, A Question of Silence (1982), Broken Mirrors (1984) and more recently, The Last Island. Myer had been keen to represent The Last Island's sales, but despite chasing the production company, the film went to another agent. So her appetite was whetted when Antonia's Line was presented to her, albeit in the form of an English-language screenplay.

The screenplay had been forwarded by Judy Counihan, the UK co-producer on the film, and Myer really liked it. In addition to reading the screenplay, she also watched The Last Island, the only films of Gorris's she hadn't seen.

A meeting was held at the Cannes Film Festival in May 1994 between Gorris, Simon Perry (representing the European Co-Production Fund and a Sales Company investor), Counihan and Hans de Weers, the lead Dutch producer.

'The plan at that stage was to make the film twice: once in English and once in Dutch, and Julie Christie was supposed to play the lead,' Myer recalled. However, neither Perry nor Myer were keen on the dual-language approach, with Myer explaining that 'it is really hard to make a good film once, let alone twice! We used to do this at Channel 4 when I was first started as a sales agent, and guess what? The films didn't work in English and they didn't work in French either.'

During the meeting, Myer asked why the film wasn't just being made in Dutch, to which the producers explained that they were very keen for the film to reach the international market-place. 'Now my experience is that what helps a foreign-language film reach the international market-place is by having a good movie, not by changing tack and making it in English.'

The result of Myer's and Perry's advice was somewhat ironic. 'By the time I had finished talking the producers out of making the film in English – and then pointing out that Julie Christie's Dutch wasn't exactly up to scratch – I had also managed to talk out the UK element of the movie, thus endangering my handling of the sales – the thing I had been aiming for in the first place.'

What happened next was an unusual piece of flexibility on the part of public funders. Perry made a deal with Ryclef Rienstra, managing director of the Dutch Film Fund, that the European Co-Production Fund would still support the Dutch production of the film, in return for the Dutch Film Fund supporting a later English-language project that was to be predominantly British-funded. Antonia's Line was saved.

## The Cannes dilemma

In early spring 1995, Antonia's Line was completed and was screened to investors, including staff from the Sales Company and British Screen. 'We were all very excited,' Myer recalled. 'The whole audience, including Simon, was in tears. It went down just wonderfully. And yet I couldn't get the film into any section in Cannes.' This was a serious blow for the film and for Myer's chances of being able to gain the attention of the international distributors. Cannes' different sections help the profile of a film, and distributors and journalists tend to be drawn to those in the main sections. None of these sections, including the official competition, Director's Fortnight and Un Certain Regard, was interested in Antonia's Line, and Gorris had made too many films to qualify for the Critics' Week brief (which concentrates on first and second features). Part of the problem was the film itself, which is an emotionally warm, crowd-pleasing story that despite its size, has a definite populist edge to it.

'This is a well-known and well-trodden path for me,' Myer explained. 'You cannot take a foreign-language movie and simply screen it in the market. A new Dutch movie might attract five people at a market screening, because you are up against hundreds and hundreds of films, all of which are having a fortune spent on them.' Myer needed to come up with a ploy to win the film some attention at Cannes.

## The big idea

'By accident, I thought about the fact that women who had seen the film really loved it. I talked to Alison (Thompson) at the Sales Company, and asked if anyone had ever tried an all-women screening at Cannes. We couldn't remember anyone doing so, and if they had it must have been a very long time ago, so it wouldn't have mattered. The idea came to me partly via a friend of mine who used to organize all-women dinners in the 1980s. So I tried it on Marleen, who replied: "Very 1980s!"'

'It may be for you and me, but I don't think these women remember a time when it was new having just women to an event,' Myer replied.

Finding women buyers in the international territories, however, was less easy. 'Trying to make a list of women buyers to invite to a screening was truly depressing. There are entire countries who have no women in these positions, including Spain, Italy and Germany for example.'

Myer invited a mixture of female buying representatives and wives of distributors and senior executives, who she knew would report back to their partners how good the film was, if she selected the right ones. 'Men still have an antagonism to this kind of thing, otherwise the idea would never have worked, and I wouldn't have got the press coverage that the ploy inspired.'

## Execution of the idea

For the plan to work, the door policy at the market screening had to be very tight. Literally no man could get in to the cinema. At one point the entire plan nearly backfired, when a Dutch male journalist came to the door to make trouble. This presented a real problem, as both Gorris and Myer knew him personally, and he was going to be important to the coverage of the film in its home territory. Gorris, whom Myer had taken the additional step of inviting to the market screening, was growing anxious about the fuss the journalist was creating. Myer took him to one side and explained the marketing ploy, and asked him not to destroy the chance for a Dutch movie to do well. He relaxed, and later wrote favourably about the film and the marketing tactics.

Meanwhile, more than 200 women had turned up for the screening, a phenomenal figure for a small foreign-language film screening in the market-place. Television cameras were there filming all the women going into the cinema. None of the male producers of the film could go into the screening, leaving Counihan as the only producing representative able to see the film. Some men had even joked with Myer that they would turn up in drag.

## The post-screening impact

In an attempt to capitalize on the 'event' aspect of the film, and stimulate word of mouth around the market, Antonia's Line's publicist, Ginger Corbett, had hired a restaurant on the other side of the street from the cinema. A lunch was held in the garden restaurant, and the women were queueing up along the street, all talking to each other about the film, while many of them were still in tears. The shared experience and the opportunity to talk about it straight after the film was important, Myer added, saying that the word-of-mouth continued more widely than a straight screening might have encouraged.

Two further screenings of the film were held, which were open to men and women. Both were packed out. The first sales deals for the film were with North America, Australia and New Zealand, rather than foreign-language territories. 'It proved a much harder task to convince European buyers and sell into Europe. The film obviously struck a chord with the American buyers.' The buyer from Sony Classics said to Myer that it was the kind of film that he would want his daughters to go and see.

Other key international sales were very slow, and then during the Toronto Film Festival in September, Antonia's Line won the audience prize – the People's Choice Award – which was impressive, given that 300 films screen at Toronto. As a result of the Toronto triumph, Myer managed to sell the film to Italy. At MIFED in November 1995, Myer sold the film to South America and a couple of other territories, but it was still slow progress.

Meanwhile, the film had not been sold to the UK by the end of 1995. Myer suggested that despite the Cannes tactic, some of the obvious buyers still had not seen the film. Rather than push for a deal, she decided to wait until after the Oscar nominations, as she and the producers were confident that Antonia's Line was in line to receive a best foreign-language nod. With this in mind, the film opened in North America on 2 February.

Myer referred to The Crying Game's experience, which picked up so well in North America following an Oscar campaign in 1993, and subsequently played well in European territories which had held the film back. 'I told everyone to hold back. The Israeli distributors were all set to go before Christmas 1995, but they put their campaign on hold until after the nominations.'

Antonia (as it is known in The Netherlands) opened in September 1995 on the back of the Dutch Film Festival in Utrecht. 'I think they were disappointed by the result,' Myer commented. 'It's always difficult when you go with the domestic territory first, and the Dutch obviously haven't learnt this rule. I personally always go everywhere first with a British movie before coming back to the UK, because you have to take it somewhere else to make its reputation. Otherwise only the Americans and the French think that whatever they make is the best. Everybody else suffers from a deep insecurity.'

Antonia still managed to perform moderately well for PolyGram's Meteor Film in The Netherlands, placing fourth in the domestic top ten chart and grossing $272,294.

In March 1996 Antonia's Line won the Oscar for Best Foreign-Language Film.

# CIRCLE OF FRIENDS

## Case Study No. 9:
## US marketing focus

*Director:* Pat O'Connor.
*Screenplay:* Andrew Davies, based on the novel by Maeve Binchy.
*Producers:* Frank Price, Arlene Sellers, Alex Winitsky.
*Executive producers:* Terence Clegg, for the Irish Film Board: Rod Stoneman.
*Language:* English.
*Cast:* Chris O'Donnell, Minnie Driver, Geraldine O'Rawe, Alan Cumming, Saffron Burrows and Colin Firth.
A Price Entertainment/Lantana production, in association with Savoy Pictures. With assistance from the Irish Film Board/Good Girls Productions.

### Outline

**A rites-of-passage story of three Irish girlfriends growing up in the early 1950s. Bennie (Minnie Driver) falls in love with the college rugby hero, Jack (Chris O'Donnell). All seems fine, until Nan (Saffron Burrows) falls pregnant from her affair with a local Protestant landlord, Simon (Colin Firth).**

### The international approach

'There is nothing innocent about the single-mindedness with which this film is directed at the international market,' wrote Ben Thompson when reviewing Circle of Friends for *Sight & Sound* (May 1995). For once, a *Sight & Sound* review got it right, but so too did the producers of Circle of Friends. The film is unashamedly targeted at the widest possible audience, something it has succeeded in achieving when judged by its international box-office take.

The talent behind the film offers considerable experience and mainstream potential to a feature film project. Maeve Binchy, author of the book on which the film is adapted, is a best-selling mainstream author, whose books have sold well around the world, and particularly in the UK, Ireland and North America. Andrew Davies, who adapted the book, is best known for his BBC adaptations of classics and contemporary political sagas, but has also written *B. Monkey*, a biting and satirical contemporary novel currently being made into a film by Scala Productions. Director Pat O'Connor's debut film, Cal (1984) attracted considerable critical acclaim, but his career faltered some-what following US productions, Stars and Bars (1988) and The January Man (1989).

The cast for the film was led by Chris O'Donnell, whose recent previous outings included Scent of a Woman – playing opposite Oscar-winner Al Pacino – and The Three Musketeers. Although at that point he was seen as considerably less than a 'bankable star', O'Donnell was precisely the kind of up-and-coming actor who gives investors modest confidence and promises distributors a name to help pin the marketing on. He was surrounded by young American actresses – all of whom had to perfect Irish accents – and Colin Firth, who plays the uptight Protestant.

### The North American release

Circle of Friends was released by Savoy Pictures (which had already secured the North American rights pre-production), on 15 March 1995. The film opened on four screens in its first week; rising quickly to nearly 190 by its second week. At its widest, it was on just over 900 cinema screens, a considerable number for an Ir£5.8 million ($9 million) independent picture.

Research screenings were held prior to the release of the film, with forms filled that helped gauge the reaction of the audiences. This information was used to work out where the advertising should be targeted. In the case of Circle of Friends, women responded particularly favourably. In addition, a company was hired by Savoy to handle group sales of tickets, and a special campaign was designed to try to draw in the Irish-American community. Regular advertising on television and in newspapers was prepared and booked by Savoy.

### A platform approach

According to TC Rice's heavily-researched report, North American Distribution of Irish & Low Budget European Films,[1] the strategy for the release of Circle of Friends was to plat-form it in specific cinemas in Los Angeles and New York, and then open it wider to cinemas in those regions. Over a period of a few weeks, the same tactic was used for other regions. A platform release is a term that applies to a film that is only played on a very limited number of screens in its first week, and then is played much wider with the hope that word-of-mouth on the film will have created awareness and personal rec-ommendation of the movie. For more extreme or tricky subject matters, those films will normally open wide more slowly, giving them a chance to build up critical support and for audiences to keep building positive word-of-mouth. Steve Rothenberg, senior vice-president and general sales manager at Savoy, told Rice that the marketing budget for the North American release of the film was 'north of $10 million'.

In the case of Circle of Friends, the film went wider quickly, as the story and style of the film were not particularly contentious. Savoy went for a 'spend high, distribute wide, collect fast' policy. Most importantly, the idea behind opening wider quickly was to capitalize on good critical reviews, and benefit from strong word-of-mouth.

The film's timing was deliberately planned to coincide with Maeve Binchy's most recent book, which reached and stayed on the US best-sellers list throughout the release of the film. In addition, a publicity tour was launched which billed Minnie Driver as that year's 'new discovery'. Driver's performance had attracted high critical praise, and was certainly worth focusing attention on.

## The fall-off

The high advertising budget and the excellent review coverage led to strong audiences in the film's opening week. By the fourth week at the box office, however, the film had stopped growing, and took $3.73 million from 788 screens in a three-day weekend gross. Savoy took the film up to 891 screens the following week, when it took $2.72 million. By the sixth week, it had opened out to 902 screens, but took $1.84 million at the box office. As Rice points out in his report, 'the expenditure of "north of $10 million" indicates only that money spent can buy a gross but not necessarily a profit. Gross at the box office is a relative thing and is rarely considered in terms of dollars spent for dollars earned. At $23 million [US final estimated gross], Circle earned $2.3 for every dollar spent.'

## The UK impact

Certainly the film's North American success helped the UK and Irish releases considerably. North American coverage and the perception of an established success boosted the film's UK opening in early May 1995, some seven weeks after the American opening. Released by Rank Film Distributors, the film played on 156 screens for a £600,738 take after seven days. Its subsequent three-day gross was £301,409, placing the film at number three in the Screen International UK Top 15 for 19–21 May 1995. After seven weeks of playing, the film had grossed £2.27 million, and was still playing on 105 screens. By week ten, the film was trailing off, playing on 53 screens, and had grossed £2.51 million ($3.9 million) by 16 July 1995.

## Note

1  T. C. Rice, *North American Distribution of Irish & Low Budget European Films*, report prepared for the Irish Film Board, 1995.

# THE FLOWER OF MY SECRET

## Case Study No. 10:
## Marketing focus

*Writer and director:* Pedro Almodovar.
*Executive producer:* Agustin Almodovar.
*Language:* Spanish.
*International Sales:* CIBY Sales, London.
*Cast:* Marisa Paredes, Juan Echanove, Imanol Arias, Carmen Elias and
Rossy de Palma.
An El Deseo S.A./CIBY 2000 co-production.

### Outline

**Leo is a romantic novelist, who is fantastically successful at writing sentimental trash under a pseudonym. But she is depressed. Her soldier husband, Paco, has left for Brussels after a breakdown in their relationship. After deciding to commit 'artistic' suicide by criticizing her own work under a different pseudonym, she suddenly finds out that Paco is returning from Brussels for just one day.**

**The Flower of My Secret is the third Pedro Almodovar international film sales agent Wendy Palmer has handled. Here she explains how his films are marketed.**

### Background on Almodovar's market

Producer Agustin Almodovar (Pedro's brother) has stressed in previous interviews that he never encourages the domestic pre-selling of his brother's films to Spanish broadcasters unless he has to. CiBy Sales handles all other broadcasting pre-sales around the world.

After The Law of Desire (1987), El Deseo found it considerably easier to raise budgets for the director's films. As a result, Agustin always tried to keep back the domestic broadcasting rights on each Almodovar film in an effort to retain independence.

Almodovar's back-catalogue of earlier films only found wider distribution post-Law and Women On the Verge of a Nervous Breakdown (1988). Women won more than 50 domestic and international awards, and took nearly $9 million at the Spanish box office, and more than $20 million around the world. The film allowed Almodovar to break completely from a domestic market, and win an international following, albeit mostly on the arthouse circuit.

## The market-place for an Almodovar film

When working with CiBy 2000, the green light for Almodovar's films is given by Jean-Francois Fonlupt, who takes the final decisions on all CiBy's film productions from the Paris office. A screenplay will normally have been prepared in English (translated from the Spanish original), which Palmer will have read. Palmer will have done sales estimates on the film, based on the project, but mostly dictated by the business Almodovar's previous films have attracted.

From Palmer's point of view, over the last six or seven years since Women On the Verge, 'Pedro Almodovar' is the key selling point of his films: 'When you're selling an Almodovar movie, the star of the movie is Pedro, and that's what people want to buy.' On a general level, the main market for Amodovar's films is obviously Spain, followed by Latin territories, including Italy and South America. France is a strong territory, although English-speaking territories are less easy to predict. Germany presents the strongest resistance, followed by Scandinavia, while North America has been 'a bit tough due to the results of High Heels and Kika,' Palmer said, adding that she was not convinced that the heavy marketing emphasis on sex helped either of the two films.

The Flower of My Secret was budgeted at around $7 million, slightly higher compared to Almodovar's previous films such as High Heels, Tie Me Up, Tie Me Down, and Kika, which were around $5.5 million. High Heels, which Palmer sold while working at Manifesto Film Sales, was the best performer at pre-sales, while the last two films have subsequently not performed so well. This led to a slight decline in the prices Palmer could ask from distributors, although there is a host of loyal Almodovar distributors across the world that are first ports of call for Palmer.

## The North American deal

The English-language version of the Flower screenplay was sent to internatonal buyers by Palmer. In North America, Sony Classics liked the screenplay very much, but wanted to wait to see how the film worked before buying it. 'If another US distributor had come up with a suitable price beforehand, we would have done a deal, but everybody wanted to see where Pedro was going,' Palmer explained. 'Sometimes it can be much better in difficult markets to wait – both for the distributor and the seller – because if the distributor doesn't like the film you are facing a serious problem. It's ultimately much better that a distributor sees the movie and you do a deal, knowing that they are right behind the film.' On the other hand, the North American market has become very hard for foreign-language films over the past three years. As Palmer stresses: 'It's very very rare to pre-sell a foreign-language film into the US today.'

Germany was also sold on completion, while PolyGram/Electric Pictures picked up the UK rights. About 50 per cent of the world was pre-sold, which essentially covered most risk for CiBy, and as Palmer pointed out, 'It wasn't as if we really had a financial need to pre-sell the film in every territory.'

## Marketing materials

One of the key areas that is given high priority is the still photography on set. 'It's interesting the way Almodovar deals with this, because he has the classic everyday stills photographer, but he also does these special set-ups, and it's those that you end up mostly seeing in the marketing material,' Palmer said. 'Many of his films have a lot of dialogue, and are rarely shot outside. The everyday sets are not hugely photogenic.' Also, unlike his previous films, the colour on Flower has been stripped down, and has far less distinctive contrast than in previous films.

On most films, CiBy Sales go through all the stills which normally total at least 2000 shots. A set of stills is then selected, which is sent out to distributors. In the case of El Deseo, Pedro Almodovar makes his own selection of between 50 and 100. 'We care deeply about the photographs, and it's one area of a film where we have more control. Athough Almodovar's films are very much produced and marketed by El Deseo, they have got used to us being useful when it comes to selection of photographs for the marketing. On Karma Sutra, we had a first lot of photos that were completely out of focus, so we sent another photographer out there, but by contrast we're happy with the way El Deseo handle this side of the marketing.'

CiBy Sales is normally jointly involved in choosing the photographer, although this depends on the film and the way the producer and director feel about the sales company's involvement. The photographer is then carefully briefed before going on set. One recent film that Palmer was handling sales on focused on two females, and yet the photographer never took one photograph of the two women together. As Palmer stresses, the photographs are the first key visual image that most people will see of the film, and form the basis of all the subsequent marketing material, including the poster, press packs and trade photographs.

## The dubbing question

Almodovar personally supervises the dubbing of his films in the territories where it is dubbed (including German-speaking territories). However, Palmer has mixed feelings about the value of trying to broaden Almodovar's audiences by dubbing in territories that traditionally sub-title their foreign-language films. She applauds the current experimentations by Guild, Miramax and Unifrance to try supporting European films in the UK and the US, but points out that there is a danger that Almodovar's loyal audience might be alienated. 'They simply don't want to see a dubbed movie. Whether you could break his films out to a wider audience by dubbing is debatable. Actually, Almodovar's work is pretty mainstream. It's an intelligent, sophisticated bill, but it's not inaccessible. Then there's the problem with the way the Spanish speak. You know, they talk at a million miles an hour!'

# Appendix I

Box office performances of the case study films (at 31 August 1996).

| Title | International | US | World |
|---|---|---|---|
| Trainspotting | $30.5m* | $9.5m* | $40m* |
| Name of the Rose | $116m | $7.2m | $124m |
| Farinelli | $3.3m** | $1.6m | $4.9m** |
| Rob Roy | $27m | $32m | $59m |
| Antonia's Line | $4.1m*** | $4.8m | $9m* |
| The Flower of My Secret | $13.6m | $1m | $14.6m |
| Circle of Friends | $4.1 | $23.4m | $35m** |

(Guiltrip, Tales of a Hard City and Breaking the Waves are not included due to difficulties of tracking figures, and the respective timing of their releases)

   * Still on release

  ** Estimate

\*** Antonia's Line opened in the UK, 20 September.

(*Source:* Ralf Ludemann, Screen International)

# Appendix 2

Key territory-by-territory statistics (data is for 1995)

| Austria | | Denmark | |
|---|---|---|---|
| Population | 7.8m | Population | 5.2m |
| No. of households | 3.0m | No. of households | 2.4m |
| No. of cinema screens | 391 | No. of cinema screens | 309 |
| No. of TV households | 3.09m | No. of TV households | 2.32m |
| Video penetration | 58.1% | Video penetration | 63.4% |
| Cable penetration | 33.5% | Cable penetration | 57.4% |
| Satellite penetration | 30.5% | Satellite penetration | 11.0% |

| Belgium | | Finland | |
|---|---|---|---|
| Population | 10m | Population | 5.0m |
| No. of households | 3.9m | No. of households | 2.6m |
| No. of cinema screens | 409 | No. of cinema screens | 326 |
| No. of TV households | 3.81m | No. of TV households | 2.00m |
| Video penetration | 61.0% | Video penetration | 68.9% |
| Cable penetration | 92.2% | Cable penetration | 43.5% |
| Satellite penetration | 00.3% | Satellite penetration | 1.0% |

| Czech Republic | | France | |
|---|---|---|---|
| Population | 10.3m | Population | 57.2m |
| No. of households | 3.8m | No. of households | 22.6m |
| No. of cinema screens | 1,845 | No. of cinema screens | 4,414 |
| No. of TV households | 3.95m | No. of TV households | 22.03m |
| Video penetration | 9.1% | Video penetration | 66.4% |
| Cable penetration | 15.3% | Cable penetration | 5.6% |
| Satellite penetration | 1.5% | Satellite penetration | 3.4% |

## Germany

| | |
|---|---|
| Population | 80.3m |
| No. of households | 35.9m |
| No. of cinema screens | 3,763 |
| No. of TV households | 36.09m |
| Video penetration | 64.6% |
| Cable penetration | 41.2% |
| Satellite penetration | 18.3% |

## Greece

| | |
|---|---|
| Population | 10.2m |
| No. of households | 3.7m |
| No. of cinema screens | 280 |
| No. of TV households | 3.56m |
| Video penetration | 32.6% |
| Cable penetration | -- |
| Satellite penetration | 1.3% |

## Hungary

| | |
|---|---|
| Population | 10.5m |
| No. of households | 3.8m |
| No. of cinema screens | 595 |
| No. of TV households | 3.87m |
| Video penetration | 34.9% |
| Cable penetration | 25.5% |
| Satellite penetration | 4.3% |

## Iceland

| | |
|---|---|
| Population | 300,000 |
| No. of households | -- |
| No. of cinema screens | 24 |
| No. of TV households | 92,800 |
| Video penetration | 58.5% |
| Cable penetration | 31.1% |

## Ireland

| | |
|---|---|
| Population | 5.5m |
| No. of households | 1.2m |
| No. of cinema screens | 194 |
| No. of TV households | 1.11m |
| Video penetration | 62.8% |
| Cable penetration | 42.3% |
| Satellite penetration | 3.2% |

## Italy

| | |
|---|---|
| Population | 57.8m |
| No. of households | 21.8m |
| No. of cinema screens | 3,800 |
| No. of TV households | 21.18m |
| Video penetration | 47.7% |
| Cable penetration | -- |
| Satellite penetration | 0.4% |

## Luxembourg

| | |
|---|---|
| Population | 400,000 |
| No. of households | 131,000 |
| No. of cinema screens | 17 |
| No. of TV households | 136,700 |
| Video penetration | 56.4% |
| Cable penetration | 93.4% |

## The Netherlands

| | |
|---|---|
| Population | 15.2m |
| No. of households | 6.1m |
| No. of cinema screens | 423 |
| No. of TV households | 6.31.m |
| Video penetration | 61.8% |
| Cable penetration | 93.5% |
| Satellite penetration | 3.4% |

## Norway

| | |
|---|---|
| Population | 4.5m |
| No. of households | 1.8m |
| No. of cinema screens | 394 |
| No. of TV households | 1.77m |
| Video penetration | 57.5% |
| Cable penetration | 39.0% |
| Satellite penetration | 16.9% |

**Poland**

| | |
|---|---|
| Population | 38.4m |
| No. of households | 13.3m |
| No. of cinema screens | 773 |
| No. of TV households | 10.88m |
| Video penetration | 27.9% |
| Cable penetration | 16.6% |
| Satellite penetration | 3.4% |

**Portugal**

| | |
|---|---|
| Population | 9.9m |
| No. of households | 3.5m |
| No. of cinema screens | 249 |
| No. of TV households | 3.44m |
| Video penetration | 37.5% |
| Cable penetration | 0.2% |
| Satellite penetration | 2.5% |

**Russian Federation**

| | |
|---|---|
| Population | 148.7m |
| No. of households | 52.8m |
| No. of cinema screens | 1,468 |
| No. of TV households | 49.13m |
| Video penetration | 13.5% |
| Cable penetration | 9.7% |

**Slovak Republic**

| | |
|---|---|
| Population | 5.3m |
| No. of households | 1.7m |
| No. of cinema screens | 433 |
| No. of TV households | 1.47m |
| Video penetration | 30.1% |
| Cable penetration | 13.7% |
| Satellite penetration | 2.7% |

**Spain**

| | |
|---|---|
| Population | 39.1m |
| No. of households | 14.8m |
| No. of cinema screens | 1,930 |
| No. of TV households | 12.09m |
| Video penetration | 55.5% |
| Cable penetration | 6.2% |
| Satellite penetration | 4.2% |

**Sweden**

| | |
|---|---|
| Population | 8.6m |
| No. of households | 3.6m |
| No. of cinema screens | 1,177 |
| No. of TV households | 3.39m |
| Video penetration | 71.5% |
| Cable penetration | 55.5% |
| Satellite penetration | 9.7% |

**Switzerland**

| | |
|---|---|
| Population | 6.8m |
| No. of households | 2.9m |
| No. of cinema screens | 483 |
| No. of TV households | 2.85m |
| Video penetration | 64.5% |
| Cable penetration | 78.6% |
| Satellite penetration | 2.2% |

**United Kingdom**

| | |
|---|---|
| Population | 57.7m |
| No. of households | 23.4m |
| No. of cinema screens | 1,969 |
| No. of TV households | 22.75 |
| Video penetration | 74.5% |
| Cable penetration | 4.1% |
| Satellite penetration | 14.7% |

(*Source: Screen International*, with thanks to Oscar Moore, editor-in-chief and editor of the Euroguide, 1996.)

# Bibliography

Martyn Auty & Nick Roddick (Editors), *British Cinema Now,* British Film Institute, London 1985.

John Boorman, *Money into Light*, Faber & Faber, London 1985.

Martin Dale, *Europa, Europa: Developing the European Film Industry*, Media Business School/Academie Carat, France 1992.

John Durie (Editor), Annika Pham and Neil Watson, (Authors), *The Film Marketing Handbook: A Practical Guide to Marketing Strategies for Independent Films*, Media Business School, London 1993.

Jake Eberts & Terry Ilott, *My Indecision Is Final: The Rise and Fall of Goldcrest Films*, Faber & Faber, London 1990.

Angus Finney, *A Dose of Reality: The State of European Cinema*, European Film Academy/*Screen International*, Berlin/London 1993.

Angus Finney, *Developing Feature Films in Europe: A Practical Guide*, Media Business School and Routledge, London 1996.

Angus Finney, *The Egos Have Landed: The Rise and Fall of Palace Pictures*, William Heinemann, London 1996.

Julian Friedmann, *How to Make Money Scriptwriting*, Boxtree, London 1995.

Neal Gabler, *An Empire of their Own: How the Jews Invented Hollywood*, Doubleday, New York 1988.

Hans Gunther Pflaum and Hans Helmut Prinzler, *Cinema in the Federal Republic of Germany*, Inter Nationes, Bonn 1993.

John Hill, Martin McLoone and Paul Hainsworth (Editors), *Border Crossing: Film in Ireland, Britain and Europe*, Institute of Irish Studies/British Film Institute, London 1994.

Ephraim Katz, The Film Encyclopedia (Second edition), HarperCollins, New York 1994.

Art Linson, *A Pound of Flesh: Perilous Tales of How to Produce Movies in Hollywood*, Grove Press, New York 1993.

David Mamet, *On Directing Film*, Faber & Faber, London 1991.

John Pym (Editor), *The Time Out Film Guide,* Penguin Books, London 1995.

Eric Rentschler (Editor), *West German Film-makers On Film: Visions and Voices*, Holmes & Meier, New York/London 1988.

Jason E. Squire, *The Movie Business Book*, Prentice-Hall Inc., New Jersey 1983.

Nick Thomas (Editor), *The British Film Institute Film and Television Handbook*, 1996, BFI, London 1996.

Andrew Yule, *David Puttnam: The Story So Far*, Sphere Books, London 1989.

# Index